THE LIMITS OF LANGUAGE

THE LIMITS
OF LANGUAGE

STEPHEN DAVID ROSS

FORDHAM UNIVERSITY PRESS
New York
1994

Library of Congress Cataloging-in-Publcation Data

Ross, Stephen David
　The limits of language / by Stephen David Ross
　　p.　cm.
　Includes bibliographical references and index
　ISBN 0-8232-1518-0 (cloth) : $32.00
　　1. Language and languages—Philosophy.　I. Title.
P106.R66　1994　　　　　　　　　　　　　93-17970
401—dc20　　　　　　　　　　　　　　　　　　CIP

PUBLICATION OF THIS BOOK

WAS AIDED BY A GRANT FROM

THE HENRY AND IDA WISSMANN FUND

CONTENTS

ACKNOWLEDGMENTS

Material from chapter 6 was previously published as "Foucault's Radical Politics," *Praxis International*, 5, No. 2 (July 1985), and "Belonging to a Philosophic Discourse," *Philosophy and Rhetoric*, 19, No. 3 (1986), 166–77.

INTRODUCTION

THIS IS A CENTURY of language. It has seen linguistics develop into a science[1] and philosophy take a "linguistic turn."[2] It will have witnessed the disappearance of half the world's languages, with no children today who speak them, and can expect most of the rest to disappear in another century. Language has been said to express the essence of humanity, or of reason, even to surpass both humanity and rationality.[3] That these functions, separately and together, threaten to overwhelm more proximate questions of language, especially what, under particular circumstances, would be best to say and why, is the least of the difficulties, engendered by such extravagant views. Yet this extravagance is not without plausibility or significance, and language transcends whatever limits we set for it. This phenomenon is the burden of the ensuing discussion.

Four general questions express the focus of our attention on language as a prevailing characteristic of human experience:

1. What is language? Is it an identifiable subject matter (beyond the rudimentary sense that we are located within it)?

2. What is its relation to the world we speak of or write about, that is, to what we may address through language?

3. What is its role in human life and experience, especially in relation to the characteristic traits of human being?

4. Are there determining characteristic traits of language and of human being, or does language place every "we" and "us," every "natural creature" and "thing," in jeopardy?

These questions shape the ensuing discussion, though we may find that the answers elude us. But whether or not we can answer such questions about language may be the issue that concerns us, and, more important, if we conclude we cannot do so, just why we cannot, whether this inability reflects an important truth about language, or even about humanity or nature.

If there can be a science of language along with other human sciences, if human being is something that can be known as well as lived through, then each of these questions may be supposed to have a definite answer.[4] And there have always been philosophers who believed that we can provide a definitive if not exhaustive account of the nature of language and its role in human experience. An important question, raised by Saussure, is whether, if there is to be a science of language, language must be sharply, if not precisely, delimited, a unique object of thought, or whether language is to be understood instead as complexly situated among an inexhaustible multiplicity of sciences and subject matters, situations and contexts.

We will explore why language cannot be delimited as a proper object of thought, any more than can human being. In neither case should we conclude that no science of language or of human being is possible. That conclusion depends on a restricted view of science. Language is not an object, neither an artifact nor a tool, nor is it unique in its important characteristics within human experience and nature. We are surrounded by many other forms of representation and meaning; we are surrounded by many forms of culture and humanity. Here Heidegger's claim that language is the house of being, and Gadamer's and Wittgenstein's related claim that we always find ourselves within language, embody profound insights.[5] So does the related claim, in Levinas, Lyotard, and Irigaray, that language whispers of a Forgotten, an Unsaid, in whose silence ethical responsibility is born. As a consequence, as Irigaray also says, the deepest questions of humanity and the world fall where language meets sexual difference, questions of inexhaustibility and heterogeneity.[6]

These claims reflect many of the issues to be discussed below, including that of the nature of language. We have characterized this issue as the question of whether language is a proper object of thought, an instrument or thing that can be precisely delimited. But it may be more felicitous to pose the question in terms of the uniqueness of language: whether language is capable of delimitation to the extent that it may be understood as a separable subject matter, based on principles unique to it, or whether it is to be understood in terms of other generic traits of human life and experience: thought, reason, culture, and environing natural events. The question is one of limits, of the limits of language, nature, humanity, and culture, and of the limits of limits. Our response, along with that of many contemporary philosophers, though from a somewhat different perspective, is that language cannot be properly delimited, that it bears too intimate a relation with human being on the one hand, pervading all our characteristic activities, and with being and nature on the other, with plenitude, excess, and inexhaustibility. Two important themes of our discussion may be marked here, that of propriety, where the proper always entails what is improper, heterogeneous, and excludes it; and that of nature, whose inexhaustibility permeates the inexhaustibility of language.

The views developed here differ with other contemporary views of language in concluding that language is not unique in its indeterminateness and inexhaustibility, that it is no different in these respects from other pervasive characteristics of human being or from any natural being except in the intimacy of our relationship with it, which it shares with other conditions: thought, reason, emotion, power, and desire, to name a few, including nature and being. As Gadamer says, we cannot hold language up for scrutiny without being immersed within it, employing it and being influenced by it while we interrogate it, unlike an object like a clamshell or a hammer, which we may regard so to speak from without. Nor can we hold nature up for scrutiny without being immersed within it, though most views of the physical sciences suggest we do. Yet it does not follow that hammers and shells are more determinate simply because we are not immersed within them in quite the ways we are immersed within language. We never entirely master any tool or instrument, any object, in or out of our experience, for each is inexhaustible, takes on unknown and unanticipatable properties, exceeds any specified powers.

The entanglement of human life within language is profound: we are always within language in far-reaching ways. Yet we can take no external perspective on human culture or experience, on visibility or our bodily selves, not even on the earth and nature, which we are inescapably located within. Language is inexhaustible in the ways that pertain to every being, but also in the ways that pertain uniquely to human being. Such inexhaustibility is not incompatible with a science of language nor with a science of culture and experience. This inexhaustibility does, however, strongly indicate some important characteristics of a science of language—in particular, that such a science, to be viable, must open itself to the wider relations of language in experience, as language is open to wider relations throughout humanity.

Put another way: that there are limits to science does not mean that there is something other than and superior to science that transcends its narrowness, that science is narrow or constricting in a unique and intelligible sense, but rather that if it is distinctive as a way of understanding our surroundings, including language, then it must possess limits and must interrogate those limits. Limitation here is not narrowness but determinateness, and is one face of inexhaustibility.

The other face of inexhaustibility is indeterminateness, essential to the capacity of language to be creative and to the novel and transformative aspects of nature and experience. This self-canceling complementarity of determinateness and indeterminateness, equivalent with supplementarity, excess, is pervasive, and is the source of the aporias that compose every form of human thought, including science, the recurrent epistemic tensions that are the manifestation of inexhaustibility in thought. Inexhaustibility here expresses the double excessiveness of complementarity and supplementarity, of belonging together. Indeterminateness and determinateness each exceed the other as its complement, always present together, and each exceed the other as its supplement, aporetically broaching its limits. A viable science of language must find a way to include within itself, explicitly, the aporetic contrasts that inhabit language, its excesses and heterogeneities. An effective understanding of heterogeneity must find a way to include within itself the specificities of the structure of language and nature.

The phenomenon that defines many contemporary approaches to language and being is the immersion of human life and experience within the lived world, an immersion so thorough and pervasive that we cannot regard language, with technology and representation, as separable objects that may be manipulated and known. This phenomenon of locatedness, this fact of always being within and among, has been recognized profoundly by many twentieth-century philosophers, Husserl and Wittgenstein among them. We think and act always from within a form of life, and there is no authority for our understanding of such forms that is not itself such a form. Language, then, may be judged by what it does, as an instrument, but the canons of reason, the purposes that language fulfills, are not separable from representation and culture, as if something wholly other were the standard against which language could be measured. If humanity is not simply the measure, as Protagoras claims it is, neither is there a measure independent of humanity and its most characteristic forms of life. Location in a form of life does not give a measure but expresses excess, supplementarity. Locality is a pervasive ontological condition, equivalent with inexhaustibility, but it pertains emphatically

within human experience, to language and other forms of representation.

The nature and phenomenon of language have always fascinated
those who have thought about human being and reason; nevertheless, our own century, at least in the West, has taken an important
turn away from nature and toward language as the proper object
of philosophical speculation and analysis. This move to language
is one of the prominent forms of post-Kantian critical philosophy,
the affirmation that no unmediated relation to the world is possible
or intelligible. Language is both the medium of thought (including
philosophy) and an essential intermediary in whatever we may say
about the world. In this respect, there are many skeptical or
idealistic strains within the linguistic turn, a repudiation of natural
philosophy. There are also important ethical and political implications for creatures said to be without language, animals and
plants. The proper appears again as a principle of exclusion.

These strains are offset by a striking movement toward the
transcendence of the limits of language, the other face of our
location in language. For language and understanding have developed together, and if we cannot understand the advance of science
as altogether governed by its objects, unmediated by cultural and
linguistic forms, we cannot assume that language and culture are
the only determinants there may be of our forms of knowledge,
unchanging and all-pervasive. What we would have found necessary to say about the world, for example, that it is both regular
enough to be brought under law and changeable enough to allow
us to live within it, we find necessary to say about language. It is
both regular and determinate and indefinitely (but not altogether)
malleable. Here we see the importance of a wider understanding
of the inexhaustibility of our surroundings as the basis of the
inexhaustibility of language.

Something must be said here about the concept of "Language."
For language does not exist in abstract form, but only embodied
in manifold languages, and even more important, in manifold
utterances. A striking phenomenon concerning language is the
diversity and plurality of languages, natural and artificial. One
question concerning language is whether it possesses sufficiently
determinate limits that it composes a specifiable object: language
as against thought and reason. Another form of the same question
is whether language composes a determinate object as against many
particular utterances, many *paroles*, many languages. Saussure's

claim that language is marked by particular characteristics above and beyond diverse utterances and natural systems of utterance is by no means obviously true. No one can deny that languages exist, are spoken and written. The question is whether *Language* also exists, in some generic or abstract form beyond the generality of a particular language. That this question is analogous to the question of the nature of *Being* above and beyond, though in relation to, many and diverse beings, is no accident, and is the focus of the metaphysical discussions below.

To our opening questions, then, we must respond with caution. We may say much about language, from within philosophy as well as poetry and a science of linguistics, but we will not give the essence of Language, for there are no such essences for inexhaustible things. This is not, however, to say that there are not determinate properties of languages and natural beings. To the contrary, again, inexhaustibility entails the togetherness of determinateness and indeterminateness. Similarly, we cannot characterize the relation between language and the world in a wholly definite way, not because there is no such relation, or because it is altogether indeterminate, but because there are too many, inexhaustibly many, such relations. And finally, we cannot expect to find a particular way in which our humanity is characterized by language, but manifold ways and diverse forms, making us inseparable from other creatures. This multiplicity is aporetic, because aporia is the manifestation of inexhaustibility in human experience.

More interesting from the point of view of any workable understanding of language are manifold questions concerning our relationship to linguistic utterances and our interpretations of that relationship, expressed particularly in how we understand the importance of language to being human. These restricted questions are the ones to be addressed specifically in this volume, one of three connected works that aim to define generic perspectives on the heterogeneity of languages and their relationship to heterogeneous humanity. In particular, then, we may consider the following questions:

a. To what extent should we regard language as governed by intrinsic rules whose norms we accept even where we cannot articulate them? To what extent is the concept of rules applicable to a natural and historical phenomenon such as language? To what extent may we be said to follow rules that we do not explicitly acknowledge?

b. To what extent is language similar to other natural or social phenomena in the ways it is to be understood, and how is it unique? Three considerations may be mentioned: (1) the reflexive capacity of language to include itself; (2) the necessity of using language to describe language; (3) the standpoint of native speakers within language, with their linguistic intuitions.

c. To what extent may we regard grammar as intrinsic to language and, if so, also intrinsic to thought and truth, to knowledge in some or all of its manifold forms, finally, to humanity in its lived contexts? In an extreme formulation, if a priori forms of thought are the expression of our intrinsic humanity and rationality, and grammar is one of these a priori forms, is grammar an intrinsic condition of human being?[7]

d. To what extent is there a primary function of language (propositional, literal, or semantic) in contrast with which other functions (poetic, rhetorical, persuasive, expressive) are to be understood as deviations? Language functions in a great variety of ways; there is also a great variety of languages. To what extent does the propositional core of linguistic utterances play a primary role; to what extent does emphasis on such a core, on the "literal" side of language, distort the everyday as well as the rich poetic nature of language? Here we must consider the social nature of both thought and language.[8]

e. To what extent is language less embodied in its words and sentences, phonemic and syntactic elements, and more a function of social intercourse given particular linguistic expression? This is a question of the locality of language. It is also a question of language's limits and heterogeneity.

f. To what extent is language both the mark of being human and its intrinsic characteristic?[9] The immediate issues here concern the uniqueness and nature of human being and its relation to language. The deeper issue, however, is why the question of the uniqueness of human being is so fundamental and important. What is there about the nature of language (or of human beings) that leads us to questions about uniqueness and dignity of human beings in every fundamental interrogation of the phenomenon of language? How does the nature of language bear upon the heterogeneous divisions of gender, race, and sexuality that tear at human history? The natural conclusion is that language is not a phenomenon, as it is neither an object nor an instrument.

g. To what extent is language a unique object with unique

properties? Are the specific properties of language—in particular, semantic, referential, instrumental, and intentional—unique to it, or do they belong to it in virtue of a wider domain of meaning, *semasis*,[10] signification, or representation? Is language perhaps best to be understood as one of the primary forms of thought, culture, and social interaction, one of the generic forms of humanity that are exemplified in but not unique to language? This is one of the most important ways in which language might compose no specific and definite object of study.

h. What are the consequences of the fact that we are always located within language, that there is no independent standpoint relative to which we may interrogate language? This is not a very different question from that of the locatedness of human beings in culture, society, political circumstances, prior forms of thought and rationality, and nature. In the case of language, the question touches on what Saussure calls the arbitrariness of the sign and on the effectiveness of language.

i. The political form of this question is how we are to understand the functions of political norms, in particular the possibility of political transformations, in the context of our always being already located in political circumstances that characterize our political forms of thought intrinsically. This is the question of the We that characterizes whatever we say and do: who is speaking or acting, and for whom? The parallel question in relation to language is how we are to understand the transformations necessary to bring language into new relations in our experience when we are always within language and think within language, so that norms of judgment and evaluation are always characterized by prior linguistic and conceptual developments. To what extent is language something generic, pertaining to something generically human, when "we" are always located in particular languages and cultures? To what extent is language, neither a phenomenon nor an object, open indefinitely to transformation?

j. How can an inexhaustible language be the object of a science, and what are language's inherent limitations? Here we must consider some related concerns. (1) Given the relation, discussed above, between language and humanity: if human being has intrinsic limits, are these limits of language? If human being stretches into nature, widens its purview to include any natural phenomenon, is language equally open and widening? (2) Heidegger claims that language is the house of being. Such a claim suggests that being is contained within language. Yet neither being nor language here has definite limits, and neither can be understood as a container or as contained. The question is how we are to understand the togetherness of language and being, especially how they may possess definite limits while transcending any limit. Closely related is how we are to understand and speak of the unsaid, forgotten, or silent from within language and representation. These compose some of the aporias that pertain to language.

k. To what extent can nature be characterized by or within language? To what extent can whatever can be known or thought be said? These are questions of the nature of limits generically in relation to language. The issue is of the ways in which reason is limited by language on the one hand and humanity on the other. Because language is so clearly human rather than anonymous, and because thought is so clearly characterized by language, the question then becomes that of the ways in which nature and truth are typically human.

l. To what extent can language and nature be understood only aporetically in virtue of their inexhaustibility? To what extent can a science of language, or any other science, include or manifest heterogeneity and aporia? To what extent are inexhaustibility and heterogeneity incompatible with science? The questions here concern the nature of any human understanding including science and of how radically self-critical a form of understanding may be.

Questions of language are inevitably questions of being and human being, nature and truth, knowledge and reference, but also questions of politics and social interaction. The limits of language are always in question, along with the limits of limits themselves. The ways in which we may represent and think of limits and their aporias, in terms of locality, inexhaustibility, and ergonality, the work that inexhaustible beings do, will compose the recurrent focus of subsequent discussions.[11]

NOTES

1. See Noam Chomsky, *Syntactic Structures* (The Hague: Mouton, 1957); *Aspects of the Theory of Syntax* (Cambridge: The MIT Press, 1965); *Cartesian Linguistics* (New York and London: Harper & Row, 1966); and so forth; B. F. Skinner, *Verbal Behavior* (New York: Appleton-Century-Crofts, 1957); Ferdinand de Saussure, *Course in General Linguistics*, trans. Wade Baskin (New York: Philosophical Library, 1959),

originally published as *Cours de linguistique générale* (Paris: Payot, 1916).

2. See Richard Rorty, *Philosophy and the Mirror of Nature* (Princeton: Princeton University Press, 1979), chaps. 4 and 6.

3. See note 5.

4. This is the burden of Saussure's argument in the introduction to his *Course in General Linguistics*.

5. "Language is by no means simply an instrument, a tool. For is in the nature of the tool that we master its use, which is to say that we take it in hand and lay it aside when it has done its service. That is not the same as when we take the words of a language, lying ready in the mouth, and with their use let them sink back into the general store of words over which we dispose. Such an analogy is false because we never find ourselves as consciousness over against the world and, as it were, grasp after a tool of understanding in a wordless condition. Rather in all our knowledge of ourselves and in all knowledge of the world, we are always already encompassed by the language that is our own. . . .

"We are always already biased in our thinking and knowing by our linguistic interpretation of the world. To grow into this linguistic interpretation means to grow up in the world. To this extent, language is the real mark of our finitude. . . .

"Hence language is the real medium of human being, if we only see it in the realm that it alone fills out, the realm of human being-together, the realm of common understanding, of ever-replenished common agreement—a realm as indispensable to human life as the air we breathe. As Aristotle said, man is truly the being who has language. For we should let everything human be spoken to us." (Hans-Georg Gadamer, "Man and Language," *Philosophical Hermeneutics*, trans. David E. Linge [Berkeley and Los Angeles: University of California Press, 1976], pp. 62, 64, 72). See also Martin Heidegger, *On the Way to Language*, trans. Peter D. Hertz (New York: Harper & Row, 1971); Hans-Georg Gadamer, *Truth and Method* (New York: Seabury, 1975); Ludwig Wittgenstein, *Philosophical Investigations*, trans. G. E. M. Anscombe (Oxford: Blackwell, 1963).

6. See Luce Irigaray, *This Sex Which Is Not One*, trans. Catherine Porter with Carolyn Burke (Ithaca, New York: Cornell University Press, 1985), esp. "The Power of Discourse and the Subordination of the Feminine," pp. 68–85; and Jean-François Lyotard, *The Differend: Phrases in Dispute*, trans. Georges Van Den Abbeele (Minneapolis: University of Minnesota Press, 1988).

7. See Edmund Husserl, *Formal and Transcendental Logic*, trans. Dorian Cairns (The Hague: Martinus Nijhoff, 1969); and the works by Chomsky cited above, note 1.

8. See Erving Goffman, *Forms of Talk* (Philadelphia: University of

Pennsylvania Press, 1981), and *The Presentation of Self in Everyday Life* (Allen Lane: Penguin, 1969); Lev S. Vygotsky, *Mind and Society* (Cambridge: Harvard University Press, 1978); George Herbert Mead, *Mind, Self and Society*, ed. Charles W. Morris (Chicago: The University of Chicago Press, 1934); Rom Harré, *Social Being* (Totowa, N.J.: Rowman and Littlefield, 1980).

9. Joseph Margolis argues that the primary defect of most theories of personhood, including behaviorism, is that they do not adequately reflect the capacity of persons to ascribe language to themselves and others *in language*. He argues that the reflexive properties of language on the one hand and of persons on the other are the primary indications of the uniqueness of persons. This is an interesting if not altogether persuasive argument concerning the uniqueness of human beings—assuming no other creatures that we know of are linguistic to the extent that we are. But the argument that language is a manifestation of human uniqueness is quite different from the argument that language is the cause or primary condition of that uniqueness. (*Persons and Minds* [Dordrecht, Holland: Reidel, 1978], esp. pp. 14, 97.)

10. The term I use to designate signification or meaning generically, the genus of which language is the species, is "semasis" with its associated forms, "semiate" and "semasic field." For a detailed discussion of semasis, including my reasons for avoiding both Peirce's term, "semiotics," and Saussure's notion of a linguistic "sign," see my *Inexhaustibility and Human Being: An Essay in Locality* (New York: Fordham University Press, 1989). See also *The Ring of Representation* (Albany: State University of New York Press, 1992), where I associate semasis with judgment and representation.

11. See chap. 2, note 6, and chap. 7. See also *Ring of Representation*.

THE LIMITS OF LANGUAGE

1
INITIAL CONSIDERATIONS

WE HAVE RAISED the question whether language is a phenomenon that can be known generally and holistically. In this chapter, we will consider some generic perspectives on language and semasis. In every case, we will be dealing at once with language distinguished from the phenomena and capacities with which it is naturally associated—reason, knowledge and truth, communication, and judgment—and the inseparability of any complex phenomenon like language from wider spheres of human activity and meaning, and from nature. These two tendencies permeate our efforts to understand human experience and characterize it pervasively, and their inseparability is one of the most important manifestations of inexhaustibility in relation to human experience in general and to language and meaning in particular.

ARBITRARINESS

I . . . cannot convince myself that there is any principle of correctness in names other than convention and agreement. Any name which you give, in my opinion, is the right one, and if you change that and give another, the new name is as correct as the old. . . . For there is no name given to anything by nature; all is convention and habit of the users.[1]

The bond between the signifier and the signified is arbitrary. Since I mean by sign the whole that results from the associating of the signifier with the signified, I can simply say: *the linguistic sign is arbitrary.* . . .

Unlike language, other human institutions—customs, laws, etc.—are all based in varying degrees on the natural relations of things; all have of necessity adapted the means employed to the ends pursued.[2]

What can be meant by claiming that names are conventional, that the linguistic sign is arbitrary? Socrates points out in *Cratylus* that we name things in all sorts of different ways and frequently change the names of persons and things. There is no natural connection between signifier and signified. But what is a "natural connection," and what is meant by noting its absence? Perhaps that no causal law determines the choice of signifier for a given signified object. Perhaps that no particular kind of resemblance is necessary to enable a semiate to function. Yet that there are degrees of choice in our names for things, lexically and grammatically, does not seem to support so strong a claim as that of arbitrariness.

The issue has been formulated traditionally as one of nature and convention. A plausible response is that it has been formulated poorly, since the choice is not simply between these exclusive alternatives. Where are the natural relations in language and human action? How do conventions function to modify genetic endowments? But there is a deeper response: to consider the possibility that the terms of discussion—in particular, the notions of what is natural as against conventional and arbitrary—are unintelligible.

If the relation between the linguistic signifier and signified is arbitrary, what relation would be natural? Three candidates appear to be plausible.

1. The most obvious is a cause-and-effect relation between signified and signifier: a perceived object causes in us an image, visual or sonorous, of a particular sign.[3] There is something to this view, since for a speaker of a particular language, immediate linguistic associations are normally awakened in any encounter with a novel object. Yet there are thousands of different languages with thousands of different words for the same objects. Moreover, causal relations do not as such entail semasis. It follows that causal relations do not hold between physical or natural objects alone and the signifiers they evoke, but only among natural objects and a system of signs in a cultural context. Yet this conclusion does not justify the claim of arbitrariness, but rather shows us the complexity of causal relations in human contexts. We can plausibly claim neither that there are no causal relations between signifiers and signifieds in the absence of cultural factors nor that such causal relations are entirely determining or necessary, since the cultural determinants must also be taken into account.

Suppose it were true that under certain perceptual conditions, presented with certain visual stimuli, we respond with learned verbal responses: certain words and sentences come to mind; we may utter them covertly to ourselves or aloud. Some observations are in order:

a. It would be remarkable as well as perverse if we did not respond to perceptual stimuli by both covert and overt causal responses, if, that is, we were not causally influenced by our perceptions to respond physically, linguistically, or conceptually. Similarly, it would be extraordinary if semasic connections were not frequently a function of causal relations between signifiers and signifieds. Not only is there no way to attach a name to its referent, or a verb to an action, except through causal responses, however contextually variable, but the pace of human interior and exterior life would be quite different without such causal responses. Causal connections are essential to associations in thought or language, and cannot be absent from any linguistic or epistemic situation.

b. To interpret the linguistic and conceptual responses of other people, we must be able to establish recurrent patterns of stimulus and response. That is, we must come to know how people typically respond to an event, physically or verbally, as well as how they may respond in atypical ways under particular circumstances. This requirement of pattern and recurrence is one of the features that contributes to the conception of language as governed by rules, though the latter concept may involve too strong a sense of norms beyond patterns. In any case, whether inhabited by rules or recurrent patterns, language could not function without sufficient causal regularity to produce dependable connections and recurrences.

c. The remaining question is whether we could have language, or thought, with causal connections alone, if causal relations became entirely supervening. This is certainly a question of arbitrariness in language, but has a much wider significance. The question is whether we could have language, thought, knowledge, or action if the only system of relations were causal. This appears to be a question of determinism versus freedom, but that formulation is somewhat misleading although the question of determinism may be involved. The relevant question is less one of whether human beings are capable of acting or thinking other than as determined by their causal relations than of understanding how norms function in relation to knowledge and practice.

The point is that language, thought, knowledge, and practice, indeed, everything that a human being does as a human being, other than as a "mere" organism or body, is subject to and interpretable under norms that do not coincide with, though they depend on, causal relations. This principle is closely related to the principle that there can be no truth without judgment and error. Every means for producing knowledge is susceptible to error, therefore every such means presupposes unceasing choices between erroneous and accurate perceptions and judgments. Error is everywhere. It is not necessary that knowledge be interpreted exclusively in propositional terms, but may include actions and images, attitudes and reactions, so long as there are in every case alternatives that are to be rejected. It is the notion of rejecting alternatives that must be emphasized. Alternatives can be rejected only if they are relevant; and it is the unremitting copresence of alternatives that is what is meant here by arbitrariness, alternatives that are adjudicated in lived human experience through custom and convention.

What is true about epistemic conditions is true as well about all forms of language and semasis as well as action. First, these are indeed forms of knowledge and judgment, and it is as judgments that we will discuss them. More important, however, each depends on a contrast involving alternatives and latitude. This is closely related to the contrast between determinateness and indeterminateness that we associate with inexhaustibility. Thinking is not a forced sequential display of images and words parading through one's interior theater, but images and elements composing a discourse, with logical, epistemic, and normative force. Actions are not movements, not because they are free, uncaused—they certainly are not—but to the extent that they function under interpretive norms that are intelligible only relative to contrasting alternatives. We think one thought rather than another; do one thing rather than another; say one thing rather than another.

The conclusion is that language involves causal connections and recurrent patterns, but also alternatives, variations in and departures from norms and patterns, choices and contrasts. One of the common ways of distinguishing higher and more complex forms of language in human beings from less sophisticated forms of animal communication is in terms of "symbols" that involve something other than causal connections, and "signs" that are simply causally-based signals. While this distinction poses severe difficulties, the principle underlying it is important, for signals cannot mean if they cannot err and inhabit no range of alternatives.

Do animals err? Birds signal danger when none exists or may overlook existing danger. Are they incapable of making the judgment that they have signaled too late or too soon? Animals err in all sorts of ways and display embarrassment. But that is not so much the point here, for they might not do so. The point is that we can interpret signaling that indicates danger or security, as signaling, only in terms of some degree of latitude and choice.

d. The question, then, is how we are to understand an interpretive system containing only causal relations. Billiard balls appear to be governed entirely by natural laws and inhabit exclusively causal relations. (We may neglect, for the moment, the by no means trivial point that it is we who strike the cue ball with our stick, setting the billiard balls in motion.) We do not want to say that billiard balls are free to reflect and speak: they are neither cognizing nor linguistic. Similarly, perhaps, we may suppose that rudimentary organisms function entirely under biochemical laws, that what they do is entirely a function of causal relations. Again, however, such organisms cannot be held to think or act, know, or speak. It is not causation as such that is incompatible with epistemic capacities, but a causation without contrasts and alternatives. We will later explore the possibility that nature's plenitude and inexhaustibility also require alternatives and contrasts. We are speaking again of the inseparability of determinateness and indeterminateness, limit and unlimit.

It might appear that we have no more here than Kant's point that we can consider ourselves to be knowing and experiencing subjects only under the guise of freedom, though that freedom can only be supposed and not demonstrated.[4] That is a misunderstanding. The issue is less one of freedom than of alternatives and contrasts. Knowledge and power are unintelligible except in terms of alternatives. Furthermore, not only must there be alternatives before us as linguistic and epistemic beings but we must ascribe alternatives to ourselves and others as such beings.[5] The word "alternatives" may be poorly chosen, since it suggests freedom from causal necessity: the point is that there is an inherent plurality in epistemic powers that is not expressed in a rudimentary conception of causal influences. If we adopt a more sophisticated view of causation, for example, one involving causal powers, we introduce a very different understanding of causal necessity and its relation to possibility.[6] Powers are potentialities: and potentialities are intelligible only when they coexist with alternatives.

e. The conclusion is that to the extent that the arbitrariness of language is to be understood in contrast with a notion of natural causal necessity, arbitrariness is not incompatible so much with causal relations altogether as with a view of causation in which contrasting alternatives are unintelligible and nonexistent. Rather, an epistemic theory, and arbitrariness in language marks its epistemic nature, must accommodate diverse alternatives, choices and mistakes. Two related conclusions are, then, that arbitrariness is not incompatible with causation but one of its complexities, an "indeterminateness together with causal determinateness"; and that such a pluralization of alternatives is not in any respect unique to language, but inherent in all epistemic powers as well as in any concept of a person, self, or social group—that is, throughout human life.

We will arrive in later discussions at a much stronger conclusion: that causation without alternatives, necessity without possibility, determinateness without indeterminateness, are all unintelligible, that our understanding of things entails the pervasive relevance of inexhaustible possibilities to every being, human and natural. Here it is sufficient to conclude that the arbitrariness and conventionality of linguistic signs is part of their causal and natural necessity, not opposed to it, that it is incoherent to suppose that possibilities and alternatives are somehow imported into events by human languages and epistemic powers.

2. The second candidate for natural necessity in contrast with the arbitrariness of language and thought is "onomatopoesis": a natural similarity between signifier and signified. Yet in *Cratylus*, Plato presents a detailed and principled criticism of such a resemblance amounting to a full-scale rejection of a correspondence theory of linguistic truth. The correspondence rejected is between any linguistic expression and any reality. The argument is that if names correspond to things, then so must the elements of names correspond to the elements of things, and so forth. But letters, phonemes, pieces of inscribed letters, and so forth, do not correspond to anything.[7] This argument has less to do with the origins of words than with the unintelligibility of any interpretation of correspondences involving complexes. It generalizes to any view that quantities and measures can be epistemic as they stand, rather than as interpreted or judged.

The question is not whether words correspond to things, but how they could. Saussure emphasizes that onomatopoetic words and phrases differ from language to language, that there is a profoundly interpretive element in our claim to similarity in sound or texture. Peirce calls signs "iconic" that depend on a natural relation, of similarity or function, to their objects, and it has frequently been held that iconic relations are both more natural and more authentic than are the arbitrary relations in symbols.[8] We may note Nelson Goodman's argument concerning visual representation, that there are no "normal" standards of similarity in representation, that there is no normal way of seeing, no normal bundle of light rays present to the eye as expressed in linear point perspective.[9]

Goodman's argument is not simply that we do not "see" things in particular ways, but that things "are not" in any particular ways, but in many. This is our fundamental response to the question of what a natural correspondence relation might be between signifiers and signifieds. What are signifieds, exactly, that we may expect iconic resemblances? What does resemblance mean at such a generic and systematic level?

Signifiers and signifieds, in any of their normal semasic forms, cannot be identical. The exotic case of found sculpture demonstrates this plainly: if a bicycle wheel is "simply" identical with a bicycle wheel, then it is not a work of sculpture. Differences are essential between it and whatever it may stand for or represent, in this case, semiotic, signifying, or semasic differences. Signs cannot be identical with their referents. It follows that what Saussure calls "arbitrariness" is explicit acknowledgment of the differences between signifier and signified that are essential to semasis, signification, and truth. Put another way, and this is the inherent difficulty for any correspondence theory of truth, anything less than perfect correspondence and identity requires construal and interpretation; total and perfect correspondence is a non-epistemic identity.

The argument is that difference is as essential to knowledge and truth as resemblance, that resemblance and difference go hand in hand, that perfect identity cannot be epistemic. Any semasic relation, linguistic or not, is arbitrary, excessive, in the sense that it involves more than resemblance, involves differences in certain respects as well as concurrences in other respects. But the point may be expanded in a metaphysical direction, since not only epistemic but ontological relations require differences as well as similarities. Anything but total and undifferentiated monism, allowing no meaning whatever, involves contrasts as well as resemblances. Alternatively, resemblance and repetition always involve differences. However paradoxically, arbitrariness and contingency are conditions of being. They compose heterogeneity. Perfect necessity is equivalent with perfect lack of differentiation, which is neither intelligible nor ascribable to anything. Again, heterogeneity is a generic trait of nature, neither unique to language nor intelligible in relation to language alone.

3. We may momentarily retreat from the force of this ontological disclosure to consider our third and remaining candidate for linguistic natural necessity, the candidate central to the Platonic discussion. For Socrates' argument concerning the conventionality of names depends neither on causal relations nor similarity, but on the capacity of names to be true, that is to function epistemically, as propositions. Now we may not be surprised that names are not propositions; far more important is whether propositions could be entirely natural—corresponding, we may say, exactly to the facts. Here we approach the long tradition of the quest for an ideal language, from Leibniz to Wittgenstein, that perfectly establishes a correspondence between language and reality.[10] We repeat that no one has succeeded in defining such a correspondence, and that such a correspondence is profoundly implausible. But the deeper point is that the notion of such a mirroring is incoherent. This is not so much a property of language as a property of reality and nature as well as truth. But it is the source of some of the most striking properties of language.

The claim here is that the notion of mirroring as an epistemic norm is unintelligible. There is no mirroring without difference; knowledge is not mirroring but conformation together with variation. In order for a sentence to function epistemically, it must be different from the proposition and fact it would express to the point that both interpretation and error are relevant and possible. The notion of an ideal language is epistemologically incoherent: an ideal language could not be epistemically relevant. The notion of an ideal translation is also incoherent.[11] Finally, knowledge is finite, and language, insofar as it functions epistemically, is finite. The manifest forms of such finiteness are the impossibility of perfect mirroring in knowledge, the conventional or arbitrary character of all signs, language, and knowledge, and the impossibility of an ideal language, not because we are finite, but in the nature of both language and things: there are no coherent norms of ideality, only proximate and qualified norms. The burden of much of our discussion is that finiteness entails heterogeneity and inexhaustibility.

The argument is that even in the propositional mode of linguistic semasis, perfection is unintelligible. We may add that language serves more functions than propositional ones. Whether or not all of these are epistemic is an open question, well worth examination. But the socially interactive, coercive, evocative, persuasive, affective, and ornamental functions of language are in competition in any utterances with their propositional functions. Linguistic resources are effectively finite and excessive at the same time, restricted yet inexhaustible, most obviously in poetry, and there is no ideal proportion of these diverse functions and qualities, only a tenuous truce and balance (as well as imbalance) of forces in particular applications. The consequence is that mirroring is not a propositional notion alone, that ideality in language is a complex function of manifold functions, not all of which can be assimilated to some higher ideal. Conventionality and arbitrariness in language are a consequence of the epistemic powers of human beings and their locations in language, but also a consequence of the inexhaustible richness of the functions of language.

SEMIOTICS

Peirce defines a sign, or "representamen," as "something which stands to somebody for something in some respect or capacity. It addresses somebody, that is, creates in the mind of that person an equivalent sign, or perhaps a more developed sign."[12] It is tempting to emphasize the "somebody" referred to and "the mind of that person," emphasizing the varying ways in which human beings—"persons"—interpret utterances. Yet one of the most important facts concerning language is that many of its features—syntactic and semantic, conceptual and phonological—are public, indifferent to individuals. Put another way, little purpose is served in referring to the ideas or concepts engendered "in the mind" by linguistic signs where we have no access to minds' interiors and the ideas and concepts are interchangeable among different individuals.

This is no small point, and bears heavily on inexhaustibility in language, experience, and being. We may assume, for sake of argument, that there are no minds without bodies and, similarly, no signs without minds. Nevertheless, it does not follow that signs always involve human individuals significantly. In conversation, the presence of individuals is normally important—individuals including both bodies and minds—but by no means in documents and narratives, or in the public spaces that utterances inhabit. Even in conversations, many features of what is said make no reference to the particular participants, but are anonymous and public features of language, conversation, or experience in general.

A dictionary gives us the meaning of a word, frequently many meanings. We may be sure that without speakers and writers, at particular times and places, such meanings would be unintelligible, in the double sense that the dictionary meanings are explications of what people say and mean and that the dictionary was written by individuals who said and meant what they wrote. But the meanings that the dictionary expresses belong to it indifferently with respect both to different readers and to different social contexts of utterance. We are distinguishing the ways in which speakers and listeners are relevant differentially to their utterances and interpretations.

We note, then, that Peirce largely ignores his reference to "somebody" in his definition of a sign, except where he emphasizes the "ultimate logical interpretant," based on habit.[13] Interpretants and signs could not function without interpreters, but different interpreters are not differentially implicated in every sign. Thus, Peirce elaborates his definition of a sign with no reference to individual interpreters: "A *Sign*, or *Representamen*, is a First which stands in such a genuine triadic relation to a Second, called its *Object*, as to be capable of determining a Third, called its *Interpretant*, to assume the same triadic relation to its Object in which it stands to the same Object."[14] We may certainly add here "to somebody" provided we understand that the somebody is in most cases "anybody," not a particular somebody at all. Meaning and signification may be individually variable, but in the respects that they are not so variable, individual particularities are not relevant. This is true even where we wish to hold that individuals vary in how they interpret every sign, how they understand every word. For they do understand some meanings in common.

Peirce was infatuated with triadic relations, and they recur throughout his theory. We may wonder whether the triadic relation of interpretation might be in fact a quadratic relation involving human individuals. The point is that meanings and semiotic relations are triadic even in documents and anonymously stable contexts that are not variable with individual human beings. In every case, the sign and its relation to its object require interpretation, another sign or interpretant. Two features of this relation as described by Peirce are worth noting.

One is that the interpretant is itself a sign: we interpret one semasic relation through another, and the sequence of interpretants is theoretically (but not practically) unending. This is an overt expression of inexhaustibility. Semasis works in an endless succession of signs and interpretants. Such a view has suggested to many readers that we inhabit a closed realm of signs and interpretants, not of things. Here it is essential to emphasize the second feature of Peirce's semiotic theory: his pragmatistic realism. In pragmatism, signs and objects are not distinguished as kinds of beings, but as relational and functional characteristics. This is clear in Peirce's view of truth and reality: "The opinion which is fated to be ultimately agreed to by all who investigate, is what we mean by the truth, and the object represented in this opinion is the real."[15] We may take issue with the optimism inherent in the consensus to which Peirce suggests that we will ultimately be led, but from within a pragmatistic position, truth and reality are defined by human activities.

May we not, however, agree collectively on what is in fact untrue? May we not suppose to be real what is only a human construction? The generic reply is that truth and untruth, reality and "mere construction" are not unsituated concepts, but belong to those human activities and are functional within those human contexts that define them. There is no unlocated truth that sets the standard against which all situated inquiries are to be measured. Peirce's pragmatism rests on the principle that inquiry is both self-critical and successful: at least, that no other epistemic activity, no way of "fixing belief," can be more so.[16] The same presumption of the effectiveness and authority of inquiry is found in Dewey: knowledge is the outcome of successful inquiry.[17] But the same respect for inquiry, if a different view of what knowledge is, can be found in Plato.[18]

Pragmatism depends on two fundamental assumptions, the second of which is frequently overlooked: (a) that both the meanings of signs, including concepts and words, and their truth are given by their functions in human experience, particularly in inquiry;

and (b) that we possess adequate epistemic capacities to interrogate our surroundings and ourselves, that we are both self-critical and successful in inquiry. To this largely epistemological reading, we may add the ontological principle that there is no reality other than that defined by successful inquiry, so that in pragmatism, there can be no sharp distinction between nature and experience, but rather, aporetically, nature is the object of experience while experience is situated within and among natural events. Further, we may generalize inquiry into what we will call "query" to include all forms of unending interrogation and self-criticism, taking for granted that such query is potentially capable of success, or at least, where it is unsuccessful, only other query can show us that and how.

The implications of this discussion in relation to Peirce's theory of signs are: (1) there is no sharp distinction between signs and objects, or signs and interpretants, but objects may be signs, where interpreted, and signs are objects, functioning in inquiry and experience in certain distinct ways; (2) the unending succession of interpretants and signs is not unique to human experience, but a manifestation of inexhaustibility in natural events and things as well as judgment; (3) language (along with other semasic systems) plays at least a double role in semasis, as both instrument and object of inquiry, sometimes virtually indistinguishably. Here a fundamentally instrumental view of meaning and language becomes, in virtue of its pragmatistic naturalism, effectively a rejection of a merely instrumental view of inquiry. This is why we may characterize the pragmatist position as "functional" or "ergonic" rather than "instrumental," though instruments manifest the same richnesses of function and being as do signs and interrogations. The unending succession of signs and interpretants is in Peirce, and all such pragmatistic views, a manifestation of the unending and inexhaustible nature of reality and experience. Pragmatism is less a theory of the practical consequences, utilitarian and instrumental, of utterances than a functional theory of the work that utterances perform, including not only what they do but the roles they serve in different contexts of human life and thought.

Two additional issues in Peirce's theory may be considered, one the relation of "standing for" explicit in his definition of a sign, the other the role in his theory of signs assigned to language. The former is problematic, for even if we interpret the object or representamen in some cases as itself a sign, semiotic relations are not always relations by proxy, a sign "standing for" something outside itself. Prepositions do not stand for any objects other than themselves; indexical signs, related by causation as clouds are related to rain, do not stand for their objects, but point to them. Some signs function within the universe of other signs, neither standing for objects or signs nor pointing to them, but filling out the system of utterances, prepositions and conjunctions, possibly adjectives and adverbs. A consequence of surplus of meaning, semasic inexhaustibility, is that if some signs stand for other objects and signs, then some other signs will not so stand for objects and signs, but will function semasically in other ways. This is a direct consequence of the indeterminateness inherent in semasic determinateness; that signs escape any particular functions or norms. Saussure captures the force of this insight in his view of differences, though his position is weakened by its own extremes of formulation.[19]

The role of language within a more general theory of signs is more interesting for us here. Peirce defines a triadic distinction among iconic, indexical, and symbolic signs—signs representing by configurational properties, by causal connections, and by custom and convention—interpreting language as largely symbolic and conventional. He sometimes suggests that there are different kinds of signs, some with purely configurational or iconic properties, others with entirely indexical properties, and some largely conventional and arbitrary signs, but he also emphasizes the complex intermixture of these different functions throughout language and semasis. The latter suggests that the triad defines not different kinds of signs but different ways of functioning semasically, that configuration, causal connection, and custom be interpreted as dimensions of semasis, not as kinds of signs. All signs have configurational properties, can function effectively only based on causal connections, and also depend on social conventions and traditions.

Peirce introduces a distinction that he claims applies to symbols or language uniquely, to signs created by custom and convention, a distinction between types and tokens. A word is inseparably a type and token, a universal of sorts exemplified in its inscriptions and utterances, but a universal that (a) can be created or destroyed, as a word may be brought into a language or vanish from it; (b) behaves in many respects like an individual; (c) is inseparable in any particular case from its instances or tokens. Several other

important features of this distinction are not worth dwelling on
here. More important in the present context is the question of
what the distinction tells us about language. Yet Peirce's argument
that linguistic signs are uniquely types and tokens is not persuasive, for we find types and tokens, or their equivalents, in all the
kinds of symbols that we must regard as repeatable and creatable.
As I have suggested elsewhere,[20] types express something fundamental about paradigms or models: that they may be invented or
created, that they are intentional and epistemic, and that they are
repeatedly applicable. Any paradigm is repeatedly exemplifiable in
its applications and intentionally created to serve epistemic purposes. Thus, symbols but also created forms and patterns in
painting and sculpture, recurrent cadences and modulations in
music, are paradigmatic, therefore tokens and types together. If
there are tokens and types in language, there are tokens and types
wherever there are intentionally created symbols that function
semasically and recurrently.[21]

We conclude this brief discussion of Peirce's semiotic theory by
pointing out that the attempt to locate language in a wider theory
of signs has the consequence that virtually none of the important
properties of language appears in this light to be unique to language. This may be a result of the generality of the approach, and
is the issue in question: how we are to understand language in
general as a unique semasic system. We have observed that signs in
general, in Peirce's theory, do not share the singular properties of
language, syntactic properties in particular, but are defined by
their capacity to be interpreted, while language does not possess
any uniquely defining properties within the world of signs, for
syntactic properties are clearly present in such semiotic spheres as
music and algebra. Thus, we virtually and aporetically cannot
avoid using language as a model or paradigm for semasis in general,
in which case it is too narrow a paradigm, at the same time that we
use our general understanding of semasis to characterize language,
in which case our theory of language becomes too general. We
have characterized this interplay of specificity and generality,
similarity and difference, as inexhaustibility. Both semasis and
language are inexhaustible, leading in different directions. Neither
can simply be embedded in the other or be regarded as a generalization of the other. This is the most important truth involved in
the general view of language developed here: language is simulta-

neously too generic to be an object of analysis and too specific to be located within a more general theory of signs or semasis.

REFERENCE

Goodman calls his general theory of symbols *Languages of Art*, suggesting that to regard other symbolic domains as languages is by no means abhorrent to him.[22] In the present context, we may consider his position to be similar to Peirce's in important ways, as an effort to define so general a theory of semasis, in this case, of symbolic reference, as to include language entirely within it.

Goodman develops a theory of reference as the cornerstone of a theory of symbols. He defines three types of reference: *representation*—where a symbol both denotes and refers to its referent; *exemplification*—where a symbol is denoted by its referent but refers to it; and *expression* or "metaphorical exemplification." The name "Julius Caesar" both denotes a historical individual and refers to him. Denotation is to be understood in the standard sense of being satisfied by instances. Thus, a symbol that represents a man or thing refers to him or it while the latter is an instance or application of the symbol. In exemplification—Goodman's major example is a swatch of cloth used as a sample—the swatch refers to the bolt of cloth but is an instance of it, denoted by it. Employing this set of distinctions—important for works of art, which exemplify and express more than they represent—Goodman defines a system of reference or symbols (possibly a language) as meeting specific conditions, articulative, syntactic, and semantic. Included here are relations among the elements of the symbolic system as well as relations within what Goodman calls its "compliance class." Art here meets the following conditions (Goodman calls them "symptoms of the aesthetic" in order to avoid questions of necessity and sufficiency):

(1) syntactic density, where the finest differences in certain respects constitute a difference between symbols—for example, an ungraduated mercury thermometer as contrasted with an electronic digital-read-out instrument; (2) semantic density, where symbols are provided for things distinguished by the finest differences in certain respects—for example, not only the ungraduated thermometer again but also ordinary English, though it is not syntactically dense; (3) relative repleteness, where comparatively many aspects of a symbol

are significant—for example, a single-line drawing of a mountain by Hokusai where every feature of shape, line, thickness, etc. counts, in contrast with perhaps the same line as a chart of daily stockmarket averages, where all that counts is the height of the line above the base; (4) exemplification, where a symbol, whether or not it denotes, symbolizes by serving as a sample of properties it literally or metaphorically possesses; and finally; (5) multiple and complex reference, where a symbol performs several integrated and interacting referential functions, some direct and some mediated through other symbols.[23]

These five "symptoms" or characteristics are distinguished from the characteristics of a notational system in which both the symbols and the referents are disjoint, defining a finite set of elements and a finite set of referents. Thus, what one might want to say of any natural language such as English is that its elementary symbols are syntactically disjoint—letters and phonemes, for example—and combined in specific and determinate ways, but it is semantically dense, sometimes replete, sometimes exemplificational, and filled with multiple and complex references. Some linguists would argue that natural linguistic utterances are always replete, simplified by context.

What does such a theory tell us about language? Very little, we may say, but not because it tells us little about symbols and reference. A way to make the relevant point is to ask what we know about the reasons for the properties we find a language (or any other particular symbol system) to possess. For example, why is a language syntactically disjoint, composed of finitely articulated elements? What is a disjoint system able to do that a dense one cannot? What are the limitations of different kinds of symbolic systems? We do not know, any more than we would know how to answer the question of why music has an adequate system of notation, but painting and sculpture do not, perhaps almost entirely due to historical and technological limitations. But the consequence, from Goodman's view, is that works of plastic art are "autographic" while works of music are "allographic": only the former are susceptible to forgery, the latter to plagiarism. This is by no means a minor difference, though Goodman may exaggerate its importance. The difficulty is that we would like a functional answer to the question of why a given art or language possesses the syntactic or semantic properties it does, and no such answer could be forthcoming in Goodman's analysis.

Suppose music were entirely improvisational, without notation. How would its expressive and cognitive powers be affected? If we could develop a notation for painting, for example, a grid defining articulate elements and their locations on a canvas, used by machines or draftsmen to make individual works from a model, would the referential and exemplificational properties of such works differ significantly from the properties possessed now by autographic works? Goodman argues persuasively that we cannot discriminate what in a painting counts or does not count, a consequence of both syntactic and semantic density. Yet he may not pay enough attention to the repleteness and density present in music, in relation to pitch, rhythm, tempo, and phrasing. The articulateness of musical pitches is less a feature of the music, especially on a string or woodwind instrument, which can vary pitch in subtle ways, and more a feature of notation and of the quirks of particular instruments, the pianoforte, for example. More important, natural languages possess the same kinds of richnesses and variations.

The richness and subtlety of linguistic expression in most languages is captured eloquently in arguments for the capabilities of American Sign Language: fluent signers utilize a remarkable range of subtle but recurrent and publicly interpretable variations to express aspect, tense and adverbial and adjectival qualifications. The deeper truth of language is not that it is an articulate notational system, with specific rules of combination and analysis, but that every language is profoundly structured, based on clearly defined elements and principles of combination, while at the same time it both tolerates and demands a remarkable range of publicly interpretable styles of variation that are utilized for and interpreted as increasing the range of expression and eloquence in the language. Foucault says something similar in *The Order of Things*, in relation to classical representation:

> What distinguishes language from all other signs and enables it to play a decisive role in representation is . . . that it analyses representation according to a necessarily successive order: the sounds, in fact, can be articulated only one by one; language cannot represent thought, instantly, in its totality; it is bound to arrange it, part by part, in a linear order.[24]

Whatever would be said in language must be said successively, dispersed linearly in time, with a certain grammar. Language's structure is inescapable, in tension with both the unity of the thoughts and objects that give rise to it and the inexhaustible multiplicity of its variations.

Structure in language is of enormous importance, but it is by no means clear that it is the essence of either language or thought. Here Goodman's more general view of syntactic properties, among the class of symbols as against their referents or compliance class, offers a welcome alternative to narrower emphases on the grammar of languages. Even so, however, his treatment of syntactic and semantic properties tends to suggest that they are relatively stable over a symbol system, not allowing for the remarkable range of variations in symbolic practice. (Yet this limitation is not intrinsic, for Goodman's is so thoroughly a functional theory that it might well accommodate individual variations, provided we could specify how different interpreters and symbolizers employ different syntactic and semantic relations.)

Goodman's theory shares with Peirce's some of the limitations of reference as a generic basis of meaning: not every word or phrase, not every letter, has a compliant. The letter "a" is a label or inscription (token) referring to a class of a's, but it succeeds in such reference only by being a sample of an "a." Now anything can be taken to be a sample of some of its properties, but this does not tell us anything of the properties that are essential to its symbolic functioning. Thus, prepositions like "to" and "from" are examples of prepositions (tokens of types; labels of classes), but that they are does not express their semasic function of connecting object-symbols vectorally. Although some semiates refer to specific objects, stand for them, others are intralinguistic, and do not so much refer to anything as play relational roles in connected semasic expressions. We have considered the relevant principle: if some semiates possess particular semasic properties, other semiates in the same system or relational context will possess quite different properties in relation to the first, an expression of the indeterminateness in every determination that pervades language and being.

Under any natural interpretation, some symbols refer, others do not, some symbols have compliance classes, others function intrasemasically and systematically and do not have compliants (though we may regard them as doing so by treating them in every case as tokens of some type). One of the most interesting of Goodman's points is that in syntactically and semantically dense systems, we cannot in any straightforward way specify what is being referred to or what is doing the referring, since the minutest variations and subtleties, which we may not be able to discriminate at a particular time, may be relevant. This is offered as a point about art, utilized in Goodman's analysis of forgery: the fact that we may not be able to distinguish an original from an excellent copy at a given time does not mean that we will never be able to do so, and our inability to do so is a challenge to refine our sensibilities and cognitive capacities so that we are able to make the distinctions. Yet the principles Goodman espouses in relation to an autographic art like painting apply to all arts and to all spoken language as well, even to written language. Music is a notational system, but subtle variations in pitch are utilized in performances involving string and woodwind instruments (though not the piano, for which such variations are technically impossible). Subtle variations in phrasing, pitch, attack, and tempo are intrinsic to every performance, and it is impossible to specify which are relevant or irrelevant. But similarly, in any ordinary language, tone of voice, gesture, subtleties of context, bodily posture, cadence of voice, and so forth, are part of any linguistic utterance, part of language we may say. Articulateness of syntactic resources is significant only in artificial contexts, and is entirely proximate and qualified in any natural context of linguistic utterance. Analogously, syntactic or grammatical rules are only relevant in qualified respects, never entirely constraining or determinate.

What we may conclude from the approach to language through a more general theory of meaning or signs is that the specificities of language tend to be absorbed into generic semasic categories to such an extent that we are no longer dealing with language proper (if there is a language "proper"), while at the same time language tends to take on the full range of semasic resources found both within and without language, throughout experience, again undermining its specificity. All of this suggests that we may have fundamental and intrinsic difficulties treating language as a distinctive object of discourse.

INDETERMINATENESS AND APORIA

In his general semiotic theory, Peirce distinguishes three kinds of signs: iconic, indexical, and symbolic, based on configuration, causation, and convention, respectively.[25] He suggests that his triad expresses different kinds of signs, thus that some signs are configurational, related for example by similarity to an original; others are related by causation. Yet he also suggests that signs are mixed: for example, no sign, of any kind, can function without configurational properties. Pushing somewhat further, we have wondered whether any sign can function without causal or conventional properties, therefore whether the triad expresses three functional dimensions of any sign. Goodman argues along similar lines that similarity always involves convention and decision, degrees of freedom or arbitrariness;[26] there are no criteria independent of human practices that determine either the kind or degree of similarity that would justify a claim to truth or establish a particular semiotic relation.

The notion of causation may be more problematic, not because it embodies a different range of properties within human experience, but because it expresses a different contrast: that of selection with mere (causal) impact. Utterance is always a mixture of compulsion and convention, determination and latitude, but some human events are either entirely governed by causal necessity, at rudimentary and (at least for now) uncontrollable levels of bodily functioning, or entirely functions of chance and fortune.

Causation thus has a divided nature: on the one hand, it embodies the mode of relation that contrasts most sharply with evaluation and knowledge—"mere" causation, governed by natural law. Here there is always a suppressed "merely" or "only" in relation to causation. On the other hand, signs, understandings, references, insights, norms, inspirations, and spiritual affinities would be unintelligible without causal connections.

Causation has this double nature, as does everything else. It is striking that signs and utterances may function semasically only in a causal context, although causation alone, at least in rudimentary terms, cannot support semasic relations. Causal relations are rudimentarily dyadic; semasis depends on interpretation, which, Peirce argues, involves triadic relations. The third term, generically, is convention or arbitrariness. No doubt we could not recognize a relation of similarity without causal connections, but similarity is not a causal relation. More accurately, every being is similar in some respects to any other: the determination of relevance and the discrimination of relevant similarities would be unintelligible without causal patterns but go far beyond them to signification and interpretation involving latitude and arbitrariness. Similarly, conventions, habits, and rules are unintelligible without both causation and latitude.

We are exploring the possibility that Peirce's triadic distinction in terms of semiotic functions is not into kinds, differentiated exclusively, but into co-relevant functions in every semasic relation, throughout language and signification. If causation is regularity and repetition, then it must be supplemented by variation and departure, latitude and convention, in order to be semasic. Signs differ from causation in being interpreted and interpretable; and whatever is interpreted may be interpreted in another way. The point has wider epistemological applicability: whatever we know or can say, mean, or intend must also be expressive in other ways, must fail in myriad ways unknown and unrealized. There are deep parallels among the unavoidability of error, the omnipresence of alternative modes of expression in language, the unceasing variation in interpretations of texts, and the irresistible imperfections of human foresight and planning.

However, we are not interpreting these parallels as the Western tradition has frequently interpreted them, as manifestations of imperfection and error to be overcome by strenuous methods and the pursuit of perfection. They are not to be overcome, not because we or the world are imperfect, but because overcoming would be self-destruction. Error is something to triumph over in knowledge, but not by methods that eliminate its possibility. Latitude, which permeates all semasis and truth, is the face of judgment in contrast with causation.

There is no ideal method or way of knowing, no ideal language or method of action, only effective and ineffective means of expression and utterance. We reject the argument that imperfection presupposes perfection, that error presupposes ideal accuracy, that indeterminateness in being presupposes an entirely determinate and self-sufficient being. Whatever we may mean, in an utterance, is permeated by inexhaustibly manifold indeterminatenesses: variations in how others interpret a given utterance and in the ambiguities and richnesses intended by its author but never entirely under the author's control. No utterance, no judgment, can be entirely within an individual's control, not only because no one can control the public life of an utterance, the reactions of others, but also because utterance and validation cannot be made identical, for no utterance is self-validating. Every expression is permeated by a plurality of indeterminatenesses, in its meanings and in its implications, in its relations to both past and future. Writing, speech, and thought all share in this aporia.

The indeterminateness in language and semasis has been called by many contemporary writers—Ricoeur and Derrida, for example—a "surplus of meaning."[27] This is a persuasive phrase, suggesting inexhaustible transcendence of any determinateness in meaning, an unending "more," relevant to the inexhaustibility and arbitrariness of language. We have also spoken of it as "excess," closely related to the forgotten, the silent, in language, and as inexhaustibility. It is manifested in Peirce's endless interpretants,[28] in Derrida's infinite play of language,[29] in Merleau-Ponty's invisible in the visible.[30] This surplus is one side of inexhaustibility, but only one of its sides. Two qualifications are called for. One is that inexhaustibility pertains to nature as well as meaning: there is therefore also a surplus of being, closely related to ontological difference in Heidegger and to what Levinas calls "otherwise" than being, except that for us the otherwise belongs to being.[31] It resembles Levinas' otherwise in another respect, that the surplus or excess recalls the Forgotten, where this oblivion echoes the call of injustice. As we will see, there is something profoundly ethical and political about the surplus of language and semasis, about inexhaustibility.

The second qualification is reaffirmation of the principle that surplus, excess, and inexhaustibility are not incompatible with determinateness and definiteness. Nor is aporia incompatible with understanding and truth, but necessary to them. Inexhaustibility is not indeterminateness, but an interplay of determinateness and indeterminateness. The surplus of meaning is not the incompleteness of all meaning and signification, suggesting that being altogether escapes such meaning, but an incompleteness inherent in nature's plenitude and inexhaustibility. This inexhaustibility arising from difference and heterogeneity leads to ethics. The inescapability of heterogeneity imposes ethical and political responsibilities on us to judge and to speak that are inherent in language.

If we understand the surplus, excess, and arbitrariness of meaning as inexhaustibility, then the surplus of meaning is the condition that every semiate is multiply located, possessing multiple significations and references, associations and implications, depending on context and situation. The surplus is not something that forever escapes, but rather eludes certain particular determinations to be determinate in others. We may introduce here two additional ideas. One is that of locality, where to be is to be located in many different locations, and to mean is to belong to many different cultural and historical locations. The second idea is that of functionality or ergonality, drawn from our discussion of pragmatism above, where meaning and identity are functions of locality. What something is or means is a function of its location, always many locations, expressing nature's excess. This excess is closely related to the unending openness of query and the aporias of truth, both ethical conditions at the heart of truth and judgment. They are at the heart as well, together with language, of the history of differences by gender and blood that give rise to ethics and politics.

Inexhaustibility does not point to something altogether beyond reason and truth. To the contrary, nothing is unsayable, in some form of language or utterance, not even unsayable in any particular form. In this sense, we do not follow Wittgenstein's suggestion in the *Tractatus* that "something" cannot be said.[32] There is nothing that cannot be said; but we add that nothing can be said completely in the sense that more can always be "said" in other forms of language and discourse, that "saying" is always "more." This inexhaustibility imposes a demand to say more, in this or another language, imposes a profound ethical responsibility upon us toward judgment.

Our conclusion is that language is inexhaustible, that whatever we might want to say or know can be said in language, but that there is a plurality, multifariousness, and aporia in language and being that entails that there is always more to be said, new discoveries to be made, and properties to emerge, but also errors to be disclosed and connections to be produced; that while language is itself inexhaustible, there are inexhaustibly manifold utterances expressible in other forms, and these are in certain important respects incommensurate with expressions in language; that this incommensurateness or heterogeneity imposes upon us profound ethical and political responsibilities.

Notes

1. Plato, *Cratylus* 384d. In *The Collected Dialogues of Plato*, edd. Edith Hamilton and Huntington Cairns. Bollingen Series 71. (Princeton: Princeton University Press, 1969), p. 422. All quotations from Plato are from this edition.

2. Saussure, *Course in General Linguistics*, pp. 67, 75.

3. Peirce calls this an indexical sign. Charles Sanders Peirce, "Logic as Semiotic: The Theory of Signs," in *Philosophical Writings of Peirce*, edd. Justus Buchler (New York: Dover, 1955), pp. 98–120; *Collected Papers of Charles Sanders Peirce*, edd. C. Hartshorne and P. Weiss, 6 vols. (Cambridge: Harvard University Press, 1931–1935), II 231–232.

4. Immanuel Kant, *Critique of Practical Reason*, in *Kant's Critique of Practical Reason and Other Works on the Theory of Ethics*, trans. T. K. Abbott (London: Longmans, Green, 1954).

5. Margolis makes this point effectively in *Persons and Minds*: human individuals both employ language and ascribe linguistic (and other epistemic) powers to themselves and other creatures. This he takes to be the informal criterion of personhood. See Introduction, note 9.

6. Rom Harré and Edward H. Madden, *Causal Powers* (Oxford: Blackwell, 1975).

7. Plato, *Cratylus* 422–428.

8. Peirce, "Logic as Semiotic."

9. Nelson Goodman, *Languages of Art: An Approach to a Theory of Symbols*. 2nd ed. (Indianapolis: Hackett, 1976), pp. 6–20.

10. This tradition represents the burden of Rorty's *Philosophy and the Mirror of Nature*.

11. See my "Translation and Similarity," in *Translation Spectrum*, ed. Marilyn Gaddis Rose (Albany: State University of New York Press, 1981), pp. 8–22.

12. Peirce, "Logic as Semiotic," p. 99.

13. Charles Sanders Peirce, "Pragmatism in Retrospect: A Last Formulation," in *Philosophical Writings of Peirce*, pp. 269–289; *Collected Papers*, V 11–13, 464–68, 470–90, 491–96.

14. Peirce, "Logic as Semiotic," pp. 99–100.

15. Charles Sanders Peirce, "How to Make Our Ideas Clear," in *Philosophic Writings of Peirce*, p. 38; *Collected Papers*, V 388–410.

16. Charles Sanders Peirce, "The Fixation of Belief," in *Philosophic Writings of Peirce*, pp. 5–22; *Collected Papers*, V 358–87.

17. John Dewey, *Logic: The Theory of Inquiry* (New York: Holt, 1938).

18. "[O]ne thing I am ready to fight for as long as I can, in word and act—that is, that we shall be better, braver, and more active men if we believe it right to look for what we don't know than if we believe there is no point in looking because what we don't know we can never discover" (Plato, *Meno* 86C).

19. Saussure, *Course in General Linguistics*, esp. Part II.

20. Stephen David Ross, "The Work of Art and its General Relations," *Journal of Aesthetics and Art Criticism*, 38, No. 4 (Summer 1980), 427–34.

21. See Joseph Margolis, "The Ontological Peculiarity of Works of Art," ibid., 36 (1977), 45–50; also *Persons and Minds*.

22. Goodman, *Languages of Art*.

23. Nelson Goodman, "When is Art?," in *Ways of Worldmaking* (Indianapolis: Hackett, 1978), pp. 57–70.

24. Michel Foucault, *The Order of Things: An Archaeology of the Human Sciences* (New York: Random House, 1973), p. 82.

25. Peirce, "Logic as Semiotic."

26. Goodman, *Languages of Art*, chap. 1.

27. Paul Ricoeur, *The Conflict of Interpretations: Essays in Hermeneutics*. (Evanston: Northwestern University Press, 1974).

28. Peirce, "Pragmatism in Retrospect," pp. 269–89; *Collected Papers*, v 11–13, 464–81, 470–90, 491–96; "Logic as Semiotic."

29. Jacques Derrida, *On Grammatology*, trans. Gayatri Spivak (Baltimore: The Johns Hopkins University Press, 1974).

30. Maurice Merleau-Ponty, *The Visible and the Invisible*, trans. Alphonso Linguis (Evanston: Northwestern University Press, 1968).

31. Emmanuel Levinas, *Otherwise Than Being or Beyond Essence*, trans. Alfonso Linguis (The Hague: Nijhoff, 1981).

32. Ludwig Wittgenstein, *Tractatus Logico-Philosophicus*, trans. D. F. Pears and B. F. McGuinness (London: Routledge & Kegan Paul, 1961), p. 151.

2

GENERAL PRINCIPLES

In his *Course in General Linguistics*, Saussure introduces a number of principles that have had profound influence on subsequent views of language. However, his structuralist view of language depends on and introduces a far greater number of important principles of language, semasis, and meaning than those he explicitly considers. In this chapter, we will examine several of these principles as well as some others to determine their range of plausibility and how they are interrelated. We will discuss most of the principles in greater detail in subsequent chapters. The purpose of this chapter is to establish the aporetic nature of language by examining the interrelations and incompatibilities of the principles that pertain to it generically.

Autonomy and Stability

We may derive two central principles from Saussure's view of language: (a) language comprises a distinct object of linguistic science—in Saussure's view, *langue*, to be distinguished from both *langage* and *parole*, that is, from the general phenomenon of speech and from any particular utterances or from speaking; (b) the "value" or signification of any sign is given by its differential contrasts within a system of signs—in Saussure's view, a "system of pure differences."[1] Principle (a) is the principle of autonomy. Saussure presupposes that without a unique subject matter or object, linguistics cannot claim to be a science. Principle (b) is the principle of difference. *Language* is distinguished from both speech and utterance as a system of differential contrasts.[2] Closely related to both principles are Saussure's view of the "arbitrariness" of the linguistic sign and his distinction between synchronic and diachronic views of language.[3] *Langue* is an ahistorical, structural system of arbitrary differential relations.

There are, in Saussure's approach to language, several principles that have come to characterize linguistic structuralism. Yet he also holds that "the concrete object of linguistic science is the social product deposited in the brain of each individual, i.e. language,"[4] attempting to mediate among the constraints demanded of linguistics as a science, the social milieux of language and human life, and physiology. This attempt to mediate features of language that do not, so far as we know, have common elements is an important characteristic of certain views of language, those that regard it as a unique object of analysis, and is not regarded with sympathy from the standpoint of other views for which language is unmistakably aporetic, excessive, and inexhaustible. The purpose of the present discussion is to examine the compatibilities and incompatibilities among the principles that have been claimed by important contemporary writers to characterize language intrinsically, thereby to evaluate the plausibility of the claim that it may constitute a well-defined, autonomous object. We may begin with the first of our list of principles with the questions it raises.

(a) *Autonomy.* Like many of the principles discussed below, this principle has a wider and a narrower purview. In every case, it raises the question of whether language, in a particular manifestation or interpretation, is a unique object or capacity distinct from other human capacities and achievements. Thus:

(a-i) Language itself (as distinct from speech, utterance, rationality, thought, knowledge, agency, purposiveness, etc.) is singular and unique in human life and the world, so different from other human capacities as to require specific human linguistic capabilities;

or,

(a-ii) Some part of language is unique—syntax or grammar, rich and subtle linguistic performances, fine distinctions that require careful training for their discrimination but that nevertheless are relatively stable in their public interpretations, a linguistic logic or rationality.

Such autonomy suggests a "linguistic organ" with which human beings are uniquely endowed that is not found in other creatures, including those with clear epistemic capacities like dogs and monkeys. This principle must be contrasted with what we may call a "principle of continuity" that holds that while some of the characteristics of linguistic production and interpretation are unique to language and perhaps human beings, they are to be understood as largely intelligible transformations of broadly conceived epistemic and practical capacities.

The most famous argument for the autonomy of language is Chomsky's, an important component of his innatist view of language competence. He argues that the acquisition of language by children cannot be explained by inductive models of reasoning and learning. In particular, children acquire effective linguistic competences—the ability to recognize well-formed utterances and to employ them—that cannot be explained in terms of a statistical-inductive model.[5] Several features of this argument are worth considering:

(1) Fundamental to Chomsky's argument is the distinction between linguistic competence and performance, closely related to Saussure's distinction between *langue* and *parole*. Two claims inherent in Chomsky's position are important. (i) A distinction between competence and performance, or the equivalent, is required by any conception of knowledge, and is required for linguistics to be a cognitive science. What we know may be divided into certain minimal conditions that constitute competence in the particular domain or skill, and more stringent conditions that constitute performance of that skill. (ii) Competence is a rule-bound, systematic capacity, while performances are heterogeneous and vary with circumstances and context. There is something stable over different contexts, and largely systematic, that is part of our understanding of language. Neither of these claims is plausible as stated here.

There is an important, if highly qualified, distinction between what we may call active and passive epistemic capacities. The distinction appears to echo what we have called surplus of meaning, but with largely opposite implications. We always (passively) know far more than we can be said to know or be thinking of, more than we can call upon, in any given situation. There is, furthermore, a range of knowledge that we rely upon but do not (possibly cannot) articulate, implicit or tacit knowledge.[6] Yet these distinctions, though important, are functional, not systematic. They do not imply a stable or general structure to either implicit or passive knowledge. The example frequently given, chess, is based on a small number of codified rules. One may know how to play chess (know the rules) without being able to play it well. If we set aside the explicit rules that define the game, and consider the sense of knowing chess that involves being able to play it well, then there are no rules, no specific criteria, for such a practice that are stable over different individuals and circumstances. And if we take a different sort of example, that of knowing how to paint, compose, write poetry, even how to write a moving appeal for financial support, there may be guidelines and procedures, but there is no competence that is sharply distinguishable from performance. Those who can do; those who don't probably cannot.

(2) Chomsky's argument against induction is based on a particular view of inductive empiricism. He argues that only an aggregative and incremental model of induction can be well defined and that no such model is compatible with the facts of language acquisition. The range of utterances surrounding a child is immense, and no child could acquire linguistic competence by induction from the heterogeneous mass surrounding him. Several points must be considered in response:

(i) Virtually everyone agrees that there are innate capacities; disputes concern their specificity and reference to language. There may be processing techniques that are not systematically grammatical that nevertheless facilitate language acquisition. Similarly, inductive inference need not be as austere as Chomsky and his followers postulate.[7]

(ii) Language competence is not acquired instantly, without mistakes, but only after several years of trial and error.

(iii) Caretaker languages and other simplified modes of speech have been found to be common among the ways adults speak to children, greatly simplifying their task in acquiring linguistic capacities.

It follows that the case for the autonomy of language or of any specific linguistic capacities cannot be based on particular features of exhibited linguistic behavior, but presupposes a great variety of other principles, including certain presumptions about the nature of science and scientific explanation.

We turn now to the principle of stability. While the meaning of utterances is frequently sensitive to context, and a given phrase or expression may mean one thing in one social situation and something quite different in another, meaning is not something that can be held to vary altogether from context to context, theory to theory. Recent writings on language have tended to emphasize the radically relative nature of meaning: for example, that the meaning of an expression or utterance is a function of context of utterance, the theory in which the utterance is embedded, or a system of language.[8] In the extreme, all such views violate the principle of stability of meaning, that:

(b) *Stability.* Even if context- and theory-dependent, meanings cannot be altogether relative.

This principle is not unique to language and meaning, but is far more general, for nothing can be "altogether relative" and still be anything at all. Yet it is important to emphasize the particular aspects of stability that are of importance to language. We will see that some version of the principle of stability is essential to any theory of meaning: meaning can be intelligible only if stable. However, no particular kind or degree of stability can be inferred from this principle. The requirements of the principle of stability for language are anything but clear, a consequence of the aporetic nature of linguistic semasis.

Relevant here is Wittgenstein's argument that no language can be entirely private.[9] This has evoked a great deal of controversy, but in certain forms it is probably unexceptionable. It is clear that an individual could invent a language or a code that no one else understood, that such a code could be unbreakable by any practicable means of decoding. In this sense of private language, there could well be such a language. Nor is it useful to stress the fact that such a code would be parasitic (in some sense) upon prior linguistic capacities of a publicly decipherable nature. No one who had no prior, public, semasic knowledge could invent such a private language. Children deprived of social and sensory stimulation during the language-formative years tend to have radically stunted linguistic capabilities.[10]

The issue involves what we may call "intrinsically" private meanings: meanings so internal to the experiences and subjectivities of individual human beings that they cannot be shared. Wittgenstein's point is that no meanings can be intelligible if they cannot be shared, at least in principle, or, inverting the claim, there cannot be internal, entirely unshareable, private experiences that can be said to be or have meanings, that can belong to language.

Even here, however, there are certainly experiences that have a private, inner side that no other person can share or have explained, at least in any significant detail. The relevant metaphysical principle is that a dimension of uniqueness and singularity pertains to every being, throughout nature and experience, and is shared by nothing else, that each thing in this sense is uniquely what it is, therefore that the uniqueness of private experience is not intrinsic to its subjectivity or awareness. Still, what is so singular and unique is, on Wittgenstein's argument, neither knowable nor meaningful, though it may indeed be whatever it is. Knowledge and meaning are public and shareable.[11] Dewey holds a related view, though without so strong a distinction between public and private.[12]

This is one version of the principle of stability of meaning. Meanings are stable over some public range of interpretations, social, historical, contextual. One construal of Wittgenstein's argument is that meanings are always inevitably public, that a language is always something shared. A more plausible position is that privateness and publicness are inseparable sides of every meaning (metaphysically, of every being[13]) and that a wholly private meaning or truth would be unintelligible (as would be a wholly public meaning, which would entail that meanings could not be assimilated idiosyncratically by different interpreters). This more relaxed interpretation of the public and stable side of semasis has the important consequence that meanings are inexhaustible in always having two sides, public and private, in complementary interplay. The movement of signs and semiates from public conceptual spaces into private or idiosyncratic experiences, engendering singular interpretations, only to return thereafter to public conceptual spaces, and conversely, is the fundamental movement of the life of mind.[14] We add to complementarity not the autonomy expressed here but supplementarity, heterogeneity and excess. Complementarity and supplementarity, like publicness and privateness, and determinateness and indeterminateness, are themselves complementarily and supplementarily related. The indeterminateness in determinateness is its supplement.

Another consequence, more important for our immediate purposes, is that while stability is essential to meaning and identity, no a priori assumptions about the nature of stability are persuasive. Here we may consider two extreme positions, effectively caricatures of established positions: (a) every meaning is singular and unique, reflecting the uniqueness of interpreting subjects and their singular contextual situatedness; (b) every meaning inhabits a stable public conceptual space, shared by other persons, as we may speak of the meaning of a word or sentence, a label or sign. The former expresses the unintelligible position that meanings are "altogether relative"; the latter leads to the notion of language as a rule-governed institution.[15]

A useful reference in relation to (b) is found in Hilary Putnam's longstanding argument against the radical relativism of (a) that we cannot plausibly claim that the meaning of concepts varies (altogether) with context, theory, or person. Putnam argues that although physics has changed greatly since Galileo, it is absurd to say that he would not have understood the *meaning* of the claim that mass is not a constant, independent of inertial frame of reference.[16] Our understanding of "mass" may have significantly changed, but only to the extent that we do understand its meaning. Too unqualified a radical relativism cannot be accepted because there can be no (public) language in which it can be expressed. It follows that meaning must be stable over some historical variations and social contexts, however transitorily. Nevertheless, that some version of a principle of stability is essential (and metaphysically, some version of a principle of identity) does not tell us anything about the characteristics or domains of application of the particular stabilities involved.

In the past few decades, the following conclusions have been claimed to be entailed by a principle of stability:

a. Meaning and language are public and communal.

b. In order that individual utterances may be interpreted stably by different audiences, some system of linguistic relations must be shared by all interpreters.

c. In every utterance situation, there is a stable, unvarying, synchronic system of linguistic relations on which interpretation publicly depends.

d. This system of relations is less a function of what language speaks of and refers to than a grammatical or syntactical system, at least a system of differences and contrasts.[17]

e. Such a syntactic capacity must be shared by all human beings who can be said to share any meanings in common, and therefore must be innate.

Each of these principles has a plausible and an implausible reading, yielding different interpretations of the stability required within language and semasis. We may consider the following alternative versions:

a. Every meaning, in language or other semasic spheres and activities, has both a public and a private side, a side shared and shareable throughout a community and over time and idiosyncratic variations engendered by individual and subgroup interpretations. These different sides cannot be entirely distinguished or separated, for even their separation has the two sides, and will manifest both a communal understanding and individual variations.

b. In order that different audiences, or speakers and audiences, may communicate, they must share semiates and semasic principles. It does not follow, however, that we can designate what they share in common generically, over any and all communicative situations. That is, there may be no communicative norms and ideals that are not themselves variable with context and situation.[18] The public and private sides of semasis are not distinguishable structurally or generically.

c. Every language and system of semasic relations may be interpreted both synchronically and diachronically. Everything that exists in time has a synchronic and a diachronic dimension. But these dimensions are not entirely separable or autonomous; just how autonomous they are must be determined in particular cases, and can be given no generic resolution. The stability necessary to semasic understanding need not be structural, synchronic, or systematic.

d. To understand any utterance or semiate, we must understand how it functions in a particular semasic context. Such an understanding presupposes both that the context has a public, stable side, and that the semiate functions differentially in relation to alternatives that might have been selected instead. Two principles are relevant here, one of differential contrasts, the other of choice. Yet neither presupposes either a systematic structure or synchronicity. Stability and contrast may be interpreted as features of and variable with context rather than as features hostile to contextuality. A consequence for syntax and grammar is that these are to be regarded not as invariant, systematic relations, but, in Peirce's sense, described above, as dimensions of semasic relations. Grammar, here, is not a system of rules or differences, but a dimension of stable semasic conditions. It follows that there is a logic of inquiry (or query), but not that there are universal principles of logic transcending all inquiries and epistemic contexts.

e. Something is certainly innate in human beings, possibly throughout human experience, if only after Humpty Dumpty's description: two eyes, a nose, and a mouth, one under the other. The question is just how specific the innate capacities relevant to language are: grammatical, lexical, or more generically, capacities to master communicative and epistemic tasks. One of the most remarkable implications of innatist theories is to limit human capacities severely, based on extreme assumptions of stability and universality, in ways incompatible with the very human epistemic and scientific achievements they are designed to explain.

The conclusion of this discussion is that language and, more generally, semasis presuppose stability and genetically-endowed capabilities but not the stronger forms of syntactic and genetic structure that have been proposed in the name of the principle of stability.

STRUCTURE

The principle of stability is closely related to the principle of structure, and the two share many characteristics, particularly their implausibility in stronger, more specific formulations. In general terms, the principle of structure is:

(c) *Structure.* Meaning implies structure.

To what structures does the principle refer? We have considered several different kinds of structure, ranging from Saussure's system of differential relations to Chomsky's recursive syntactical structures. We have seen that neither of these interpretations of structure in language follows routinely from the principle of structure. For this principle is plausible only under so general an interpretation as to support virtually no specific claims to structural principles. We have also observed Foucault's account of the unique characteristic of language, to be linear in form and successive in temporality, while what is meant may be unitary or heterogeneous.

We may compare the above formulation of the principle of structure with two older views of intelligibility: meaning implies generality; meaning implies form. The principle of structure appears to be no more than a contemporary interpretation of these traditional views of what it is to understand something, of what it is to be intelligible. Nothing may be regarded as intelligible in itself, only in terms of something general, formal, of which it is an example: natural laws, recurrent patterns, definite structures.

What we are concerned with here is not so much semasis,

meaning, or intelligibility, regarded as properties of the mind or human experience that we impose on things in order to understand them, as with whatever properties something must possess in order to be definite. Thus, there is a highly generic interpretation of the principle of structure (or form) that renders it both highly plausible and largely devoid of content: that in order for something to be understood, conceived, to have meaning for us, it must both be and be definite; and definiteness is a function of form (or structure).

What does it mean that something, whether individual or aggregate, class or universal, attribute or condition, state or process, is definite, determinate? We might claim that definiteness and determinateness are attributes of individuality, except that both universals and attributes are definite in some ways and indefinite in others. Definiteness or determinateness belongs to anything whatever, anything that can be, of any kind, any object of thought, but so equally does indeterminateness or indefiniteness. Nothing is perfectly clear, definite in all ways, settled, complete, for everything is open and variable in some ways. The conclusion is the belonging-together of determinateness and indeterminateness, the aporias of supplementarity and complementarity, as well as their joint applicability to anything whatever, any being and any object of thought. Definiteness and intelligibility are inseparable, but so are indeterminateness and intelligibility.

We may return to the principle of structure to observe that in any plausible formulation it is largely negligible while in any significant formulation it is quite implausible. What makes something meaningful on the one hand, determinate on the other? We are exploring the possibility that these conditions are not distinct: something has meaning because and insofar as it is determinate, but also insofar as it is indeterminate. If we identify determinateness with structure, then only structures open to variation and modification can be intelligible. The principle of structure is only part of the story.

There are weaker and stronger versions of the principle of structure. We have explored the possibility that it is plausible only in its most generic forms, that explanation, understanding, and knowledge (including description) depend on structure.[19] In this highly generic and largely negligible form, structure, of some sort, is the basis of any understanding we may achieve, of any meaning we are able to interpret. This sense is so general and vague that any forms, universal or more restricted in scope, formal or sub-stantive, idiosyncratic or public, may satisfy such a principle. The question is how we are to make plausible the specific structural principles of language and other cultural domains. Our immediate concern, therefore, is with the principles that have been taken to define structure in some versions of linguistic structuralism. Three particular concepts have frequently been taken to characterize the structures essential to language and thought: composition (and decomposition), generation, and mechanism.

That there are structures or forms essential to understanding, generic concepts or categories, constellations of features, does not entail a theory of elementary constituents. Yet Saussure's theory of differential contrasts presupposes routine analytical methods for producing the elements of the linguistic domain. Indeed, it is difficult to see how differential contrasts can be understood syn-chronically without the assumptions that there are elementary components that are combined differentially and systematically in complex forms, and that we are to understand these complex forms in terms of the interrelations of the different elements in conformity with the rules of their combination.

COMPOSITION

(d) *Composition.* We will consider the subject of rules in the next subchapter. We are concerned here with two formulations of a principle of composition:

(d-i) Elementary components can be discovered, routinely or by sophisticated procedures, and conjoined in complex forms to produce higher-level components of the domain of analysis;

(d-ii) Intelligibility demands the ability to analyze any domain of knowledge into complexes.

Composition in the sense we are considering here is given by the first of these two formulations: simple elements, at least, routine and straightforward elements, are composed into complexes; what is presupposed is the ability, through some methods of analysis, to display the elements of the system that in differential contrasts compose the relata of the system.

Yet we should not pass over the second formulation too quickly, for it manifests a more general view of structure and analysis. Analysis in (d-i) is an asymmetric form of decomposition, and presupposes an adequate account of the elements of the system. In the case of language, the assumption is plausible: every known language employs certain minimal phonological and morphological units. Unfortunately, it is far from plausible to hold that these units are the relevant ones for differential analysis, the ones whose contrasts produce the relevant syntactic and semantic relations. To the extent, for example, that utterances inhabit a public, social milieu in which they do work, the relevant contrasts are alternative purposes, social functions, and semantic ramifications, or, alternatively, conversation and narrative. The phonological and morphological elements, for example, vowels and consonants, are vehicles for social exchange and expression.

The argument is similar to that discussed above in connection with Goodman's theory of notation. Given a notational theory composed of elementary units and a semantic domain (what Goodman calls a compliance class), we have a system with syntactic and semantic features. But, as in the case of music, the relevant features of expressiveness, dynamic variation and modulation, cadence and rhythm, are not included within the semantic domain of the notation system, though they are certainly features of the object system, that is, music. Similarly, to the extent that speech is accompanied by expressive gestures and facial movements, by intonation and emphasis, the morphological and phonological elements may be largely irrelevant. It follows that in a rich cultural and human context, the units of analysis may not be the natural or productive elements of language.

Thus, the second alternative, (d-ii) above, cannot be ruled out as less appropriate to language than (d-i). The latter manifests what we may call a "mechanical" analogy: mechanisms of combination and aggregation. But if neither the elements of the system nor the principles of combination and aggregation are routine, straightforward, or mechanical, then structural and differential analysis tends to approach a negligible if generic level. Nothing can be understood without differential analysis, that is, analysis in terms of relations of similarity and difference. These similarities and differences are generic: they approach metaphysical generality. As a consequence, they have no intrinsic or unique applications to language and semasis; moreover, the principles of contrast and comparison are, unlike Saussure's syntagmatic and associative relations, equally generic and therefore varied. There are no particular relations that have primacy among similarities and differences in this kind of analysis. In the case of language, for example, not only linear and associative relations, but relations of reference, history, tradition, influence, truth and understanding, larger forms of discourse, and acquired internal processing techniques all provide differential contrasts. Any elements may be combined and sorted into aggregates and differential contrasts, but without given elements and given principles of combination, no mechanical system is engendered.

We have characterized the type of structural theory dependent on elementary constituents and principles of combination as a mechanical system. Two different meanings of mechanism are relevant in connection with language, both dependent on a notion of elementary constituents. In one case, closely related to the principle of generation discussed below, the elementary constituents are taken as given, and complexes are constructed out of combinations of the elements into which they are subsequently to be analyzed. Here we have a straightforward system of composition. In the other case, however, probably the one closest to the traditional sense of linguistic structuralism, the aggregates and complexes are what is given, and procedures are developed to manifest the elementary constituents in a routine way. Thus:

(e) *Mechanism.* A language is composed of elements related to its complexes by principles of composition or decomposition.

In both these cases, elementary constituents are presupposed as essential to a structural description, either by generation or by division. Yet as we have seen, most complex semasic domains, including language, are more holistic than mechanical, that is, they do not altogether admit of standard and repeatable analytic elements. We may observe that holism need not entail indivisibility, that is, need not be incompatible with analysis. We have examined two different interpretations of analysis, one mechanical, the other based on a more generic meaning of both structure and elements. Analysis in the latter case is one of the dimensions of episteme, understanding in terms of components, but the latter need not be simple, elementary, primary, or in any sense given (even under a routine method of analysis), nor need the principles of combination, any more than the principles of division, be routine or mechanical, given in advance. Rather, analysis is some form of division, complemented by combination and aggregation, but analysis and synthesis, division and combination, are in a more reciprocal than mechanical relation. Put another way, there is no understanding that does not divide, that does not present complexes in relation to their constituents, but the latter may themselves be complexes, and the former may be divided only contextually, in terms of the epistemic conditions and purposes at hand.

Much of the epistemological tradition has been mechanistic, both in early forms of empiricism based on associative principles, and in later forms of logical and structural analysis, including Saussure's. The differential contrasts that define *langue* presuppose a system of elements, words and other signs. The development of nonmechanical forms of structuralism, as in Roland Barthes and Lévi-Strauss, led to a very different understanding of both linguistic knowledge and of language and its structure. But what is even more at stake is the distinction between synchronic and diachronic principles that appears to lie at the heart of linguistic structuralism.

According to Saussure, *langue* is a system without history: a synchronic system of relations.

(f) *Synchronicity.* A language may be given a nontemporal description.

One alternative is that language is mediated by a social and public system of relations among elements that have neither a history nor development, a system that has no diachronic dimension. This is clearly not Saussure's position.[20] There are no universal and timeless elements of language. It follows that synchronic and diachronic perspectives are in dialectical relation; more important, they compose perspectival differentiations, not divisions given antecedently and timelessly.

Here we note that mechanism, with its elementary constituents, along with any transformational theory of grammar that is based on a strong form of syntactic autonomy, presupposes a synchronic system to which history and time are but incidentally related. Grammar is a system that is "triggered" but not formed. Similarly, the notion of a language competence that is entirely distinct from performance presupposes a synchronic system of relations independent of real-time utterances.

The alternative is that synchronic and diachronic forms of analysis be understood functionally, complementarily and supplementarily, that they represent no uniform, intrinsic, and constitutive structures of language or any other cultural system. Every culture has a present, a system of interrelations that may be interrogated apart from its history, past or future. But only some of these relations may be stable enough to be returned to in other contexts, in other presents; and few of these relations may be understood very deeply without expansion in diachronic terms. Thus, we may understand the relation between synchronic and diachronic perspectives to be similar to the relation between analytical and synthetic perspectives: complementary and dialectical perspectives that only together constitute intelligibility and understanding, but that are not reducible to each other. The dialectic is the manifestation of the aporias that pervade the intelligibility of language.

There remains for consideration the strongest form of the synchronic, mechanistic perspective, that based on a principle of generation:

(g) *Generation.* Complex forms in a language are built up according to principles of composition from elementary constituents.

In this sense, transformational generative grammar, though it professes to be a rationalist rather than empiricist (behavioristic and inductive) theory, shares with classical empiricism and its most extreme descendant, logical positivism, the same assumptions concerning intelligibility. Knowledge is to be understood in terms of the workings of the mind, and the principles governing such workings are as follows:

(*i*) knowledge is composed of internal representations (ideas);

(*ii*) internal representations may be divided into simpler and combined into more complex units;

(*iii*) complex representations (concepts or ideas) are to be understood in terms of combinatorial principles that generate such complexes out of simpler units.

Proposition (ii) is the principle of mechanism. Proposition (iii) is the principle of generation. Simpler units are more intelligible or basic; complex aggregates are generated by some internal procedures, most likely, mechanistic, from these primary, elementary units.

Among the purposes of this discussion is to identify the principles that have been taken to constitute the basis of intelligibility in most contemporary theories of language, and to indicate how certain principles that for the most part have been taken to entail each other are in fact independent. Thus, even if we grant the analytical assumption that intelligibility entails division into elementary constituents, we do not have to accept the stronger form of the principle of generation, that complexes and aggregates are to be understood as rule-governed constructs out of simpler elements. The principle of generation depends on one of two assumptions: (a) internal processing mechanisms are essentially combinatorial (rather than, for example, divisional); (b) there is a synchronic system of elements related differentially, shared by all speakers of a language (in some views, any language).

Each of these assumptions is implausible, not because there are no elementary units and no system of differential contrasts, but because the relationship between complex and elementary constituents in language is neither synchronic nor generative without exception or qualification. To the contrary, to any subject matter, we may bring both synchronic and diachronic considerations, dividing our understanding perspectivally. But it does not follow that there is a direct parallel between the analytical and the synchronic perspectives, nor even between the synchronic and systematic perspectives. For example, a holistic approach, modified to avoid totalization, would entail a continuous movement from simples to complexes, but also the reverse, while no system in language, syntactic or semantic, could be taken to be all-encompassing.

The conclusion of this discussion is that the principles we have considered so far to compose the assumptions of linguistic structuralism go far beyond any domain of plausibility, making any of the stronger forms of structuralism quite implausible. Nevertheless, each of the principles has some domain of application in which we may take it for granted, possesses an important if qualified plausibility. Together, the principles are aporetic, since there is no definite resolution of their differences.

RULES, ARBITRARINESS, AND CHOICE

(h) *Rules*. A language is a system of rules.

In Chomsky's words: "Clearly, a child who has learned a language has developed an internal representation of a system of rules that determine how sentences are to be formed, used, and understood."[21] "The idea that a language is based on a system of rules determining the interpretation of its infinitely many sentences is by no means novel."[22] In Searle's version of speech-act theory: "My knowledge of how to speak the language involves a mastery of a system of rules which renders my use of the elements of that language regular and systematic."[23] We will see that language, along with other cultural forms, is not in any obvious way to be described as rule-governed, that the concept of a rule is, except in connection with games, quite misleading. The notion of a rule seems to have been chosen with games in mind, and in that respect has implications that are unacceptable in connection with language. For example, there is simultaneously a hypothetical and categorical nature to a rule of chess in the following sense: we need not choose to play chess, but if we do, we must follow the rules. Thus, the concept of rule entails both necessity and latitude, but these do not correspond to the necessity and latitude, or arbitrariness, involved in language. That is, we may choose to speak one language or another, but do not "choose" to be "in" language. On the other hand, there are no rules of language that cannot be broken without sacrificing interpretability. In this sense, language is both more lawful and compelling than a game, in that sense not governed by rules, and more open to variation, in this sense not rule-governed. We will neglect, for the moment, the elements of play and seriousness in both games and language.

The view of language as a game is Wittgenstein's, although often overlooked is the force of his argument that rules cannot explain anything in language, for appeal to a rule itself requires a rule for interpretation, entailing a regress, or else we must appeal to something other than a rule to make rules intelligible: a form of life.[24] It follows that meaning and language are not to be interpreted in terms of rules, but to the contrary, rules are to be interpreted in terms of cultural practices. If we think of some simple languages, or uses of languages, as "language-games," we may observe that being able to "play the game"—to continue a mathematical series, to reason effectively—is not a function of "knowing the rules," articulated or not, but is rather a function of being able to "go on," a complex and open-ended capacity that resides in a practice, not in conformity with rules. What is in question is whether a practice can be understood without either understanding or following rules.

Another relevant set of issues is exhibited in Kant's approach to rules in the *Critique of Judgment*. He defines art, aporetically, as purposive purposelessness, which can be described in terms of following (or establishing) rules that, again aporetically, have no antecedent necessity: that is, a necessity that is not necessary, for it is given by the free play of the cognitive faculties, especially the imagination, therefore "as if" necessary but not so. Similarly, Kant defines genius as both a departure from rules and the establishment of rules: "exemplary."[25]

Kant confines genius to the sphere of art, and we might find his view of science too restrictive. He is, however, operating under the assumption that science falls under conceptual categories, and is subject to a mode of objective necessity, while art is the free play of the imagination, subject to the standards of taste, but not objectively necessary.[26]

We may also consider the distinction between rule and law. In politics, rule is an imposed necessity that is not quite necessary, as Hobbes points out, a constraint that leaves freedom unhampered, since we are free not to obey the sovereign, to defy him: but his rule is based on power, and he may cause us to suffer for our defiance. In the case of rules of a game, we are both entirely free to disobey the rules yet altogether unable to play the game while flouting the rules. We have, then, simultaneously, constraint by rule and freedom of choice.

The situation is different in the case of a law of nature, for we are both entirely unconstrained, subject to no force, yet quite unable to choose otherwise. Thus, in the case of natural necessity under law, we do not function in the presence of alternatives and choices, but nevertheless are not "forced" to do what we do.

The concept of rules is therefore situated on the one hand in relation to the concept of a law of nature by expressing a qualified necessity in relation to which alternatives and selections, arbitrariness and choice, are unavoidable and on the other hand in relation to the norms and standards that define any practical or epistemic domain of activity. Rules rule without ruling, so to speak: that is, they demand variations and departures. This complex and aporetic relation to latitude is what calls into question the standard view of language as rule-governed, for linguistic—that is, grammatical—rules do not accommodate the relevant kinds of latitude.

In this context, the concepts of rule, choice, and arbitrariness are closely related.

(i) *Arbitrariness.* Linguistic relations are arbitrary, that is, according to no form of natural necessity.

Saussure claims that in language, the relation between signifier and signified, the sign, is arbitrary, and that this arbitrariness is unique to language. We have seen that the kinds of latitude he describes are relevant to knowledge in general. Knowledge is always accompanied by and interpreted in terms of choices or selections, in terms of alternatives that might have been chosen instead. In relation to language, the principle is:

(j) *Choice.* Every utterance or any of its constituents must be understood to be the result of choices among alternatives.

We have here a theory of interpretation by differential contrast, one of the essential features of any structural theory, except that we do not presuppose primary elements or mechanical or generative principles of composition or analysis. Utterance involves choice, latitude, convention, or arbitrariness in the sense that we can understand what an utterance is only by understanding what it (or some of its constituents) is not and might have been. Nevertheless, on our view such a contrasting relation is not unique to language, but pertains to all semasis on the one hand, and to all things and their truths on the other. This contrast involving latitude is closely related to inexhaustibility and its excesses.

We return briefly to the concept of rules. In simplest terms, we may claim that to say that language is governed by rules is to say precisely and only that language is epistemic, pervaded as are all epistemic domains by necessity and latitude, by alternatives and choices as well as constraints.

However, it is far from clear that rules in Chomsky and Searle contain the range of latitude essential to such a theory of knowledge; instead, they associate knowledge more with constraint. There is a tension between Chomsky's view of the epistemic nature of language and the views of Saussure.

To say that language (or any practice) is rule-governed is to say that, unlike a purely natural event, it is both constrained by common norms and conditions and open to modification: a conjunction of necessity and latitude. A natural event is subject to laws of nature, and as such, contains no degrees of freedom: every event of a certain kind will have consequences of a certain kind, without freedom. The distinction here, between rules and laws of nature, parallels the distinction between "mere causal events" in human experience and knowledge. The latter involves validation and selection and is therefore both subject to conditions and open to variation. The issue is not one of determinism versus freedom, for latitude and variation are equatable with freedom in only the most rudimentary sense, at best necessary but far from sufficient conditions. The larger issue is of determinism together with indeterminism, excess, and supplementarity: inexhaustibility. The more relevant point is that all the concepts that apply to human life and experience in a strong sense—knowledge, inquiry, purpose, intention, meaning, interpretation, and intension—all imply selection and variation, alternatives and validation.

It follows that choice, rules, and arbitrariness are inseparable concepts. We have examined the possibility that the epistemological tradition's pursuit of perfect knowledge is a mistake, that there is no sense of knowledge in which selection and variation, error and indeterminateness are eliminated. Arbitrariness is present in and pervades every epistemic situation: there is no knowledge, no known truth, that is immune to falsification, to misinterpretation, that does not require interpretation and reinterpretation, incessantly. We are not pursuing fallibility here so much as the locatedness of knowledge conjoined with inexhaustible possibilities of interpretation and reinterpretation, discovery and rediscovery.

Chomsky argues for the innateness of grammar on the basis of what he calls the "creativity" of language: "The most striking aspect of linguistic competence is what we may call the 'creativity of language,' that is, the speaker's ability to produce new sentences, sentences that are immediately understood by other speakers, although they bear no physical resemblance to sentences which are 'familiar.' "[27] However, his interpretation of this creativity is that "normal use of language involves the production and interpretation of sentences that are similar to sentences that have been heard before only in that they are generated by the rules of the same grammar."[28] There is a long tradition, going back to Plato and before, in which emphasis on novelty and creativity is accompanied by a demand for explanatory adequacy that is effectively incompatible with novelty.[29] Similarly, the only creativity Chomsky can accommodate in his transformational theory is the production and interpretation of new sentences based on a permanent and unchanging set of rules (at least, unchangeable by choice and intention).

Chomsky speaks of the innate grammar as a "theory," something known by a native speaker of a language, and suggests that his entire view of such a knowledge is based on an ideal speaker-listener.[30] We will later examine this notion in detail. Here we may observe that Chomsky presupposes the intelligibility of the notion of an ideal language-knower. We will discuss the limitations of this view when applied to language in the next chapter. Here we may consider the possibility that the concept of perfect knowledge of any sort is unintelligible and incoherent.

One of Chomsky's examples is the rules of chess. Is there such a thing as "perfect knowledge" of how to play chess? One might know the rules, but this is minor, and in no sense of performance could knowledge of chess be perfect. But suppose one could think ahead so many moves that one never made a mistake, that one won every game by computing every outcome completely. Then, we might conclude, one would not be playing the game, but turning it into a computational exercise: knowing how to play chess is inseparable from making moves and making mistakes.

One can never prove a theorem if one already knows all the theorems and their proofs: one simply writes down a remembered proof. One can never play chess if one already knows the outcome of the game. In the case of language, there is no ideal speaker-listener because language includes, as part of its everyday nature, mistakes, variations, and modifications, and these are features of the effectiveness of language. What Chomsky excludes in the name of errors and mistakes are what gives to language the richness that enables it to function expressively and communicatively.

It is not possible to transgress a law of nature, for it is a condition but not a force. At best, laws of nature may have exceptions, but they may not be violated. Every linguistic rule is subject to selection and validation, and may be modified or varied, interpreted and reinterpreted. If language is subject to law, if grammar is untransgressable, it can be neither epistemic nor arbitrary. If language is governed by rules, it may equally be governed by other rules, and every such rule may be replaced by another at any time. To say that language is a form of knowledge, that we know language, as well as that language itself embodies both knowledge and purpose—is epistemic and intentional—is to acknowledge that language is, in any particular respect, subject to interrogation and variation, to intentional modification. Linguistic rules are optional and variable, in no clear sense, then, "rules" at all.

CONTEXT

We may pause in the midst of our discussion of structural principles to consider another principle of great importance to language and semasis. We are referring to the principle of context:

(k) *Context.* Meaning is a function of context.

This principle, understood functionally, expresses the inexhaustibility and ergonality of language and semasis.

The structural principles that we have discussed, including those below, define non-contextual properties of language: complex strings composed of simple elements combined according to general rules. Yet every structural principle is deeply qualified by what may be the most important and general principle of semasis, that we find a way to express what we mean, somehow, despite any constraints of situation or form, and other people find a way to understand what we mean. From the standpoint of our approach to language, this principle takes precedence over all other assumptions about the nature of semasis, language, and communication, particularly over assumptions concerning specific kinds and qualities of understanding and meaning. It takes precedence over even the sense we may have that certain experiences, like the Holocaust, or the uncanny, cannot be given form in language. They cannot be given conventional linguistic form, but we still speak of them, if only in poetry. And it takes precedence over the unsaid, unthought, and forgotten, the excess and supplement in language and semasis, because these appear in language, if only as traces and heterogeneities.

There is a variability with situation and context that pervades all utterances, and it is important that we are concerned here with utterances, judgments, not with *langue.* The question of the autonomy of language is at issue, since to the extent that meaning is a function of context, it varies from situation to situation, and cannot then be autonomous with respect to either the functions and intentions relevant to those situations or the people involved in them. Thus, Saussure's distinction between *langue* and *parole,* with Chomsky's analogous distinction between competence and performance, are attempts to define a science of language based on its autonomy, and presuppose that some semasic factors are not variable with context.

One of the most important semasic principles that we have discussed is the principle of stability: meaning is stable over different situations and contexts, different speakers and audiences. Like all the principles listed in this chapter, the principle of stability is partly true but greatly qualified, or, to put it differently, is true interpreted in certain ways but not in others, while no formulation of it is quite satisfactory. Moreover, the different principles conflict. Through this conflict we are tracing language's aporias. Contextuality and stability do not compete, as they would if the former simply entailed variability. The principle of context is more than a principle of latitude.

Yet it is commonly interpreted as such, and under such interpretations strongly entails an extreme and implausible form of semasic relativism. The meaning of an utterance is a function of, and entirely varies with, contextual location. In certain respects, this variability is both clear and unavoidable. Grammatical forms vary over time as do the meanings and pronunciations of words. Far more important, however, are variations among different speakers and audiences in a given context, since without individual variations of this kind there would be fewer misunderstandings but also fewer insights into new semasic connections that compose the working basis of every domain of query.

This last observation displays one of the general principles of the semasic analysis we are considering. It is implausible to identify the contextuality of utterances with variability; it is similarly implausible to identify inexhaustibility with openness. Variability is inseparable from stability; moreover, sheer variability is unintelligible. Similarly, openness is inseparable from definiteness, indeterminateness from determinateness. It is not simply that what varies with every context and has no stability could not be understood, which is true enough, but that the notion of unqualified variability is incoherent. There must be something stable to recognize as variable. Conversely, however, stability belongs together with variability in that something altogether and unqualifiedly stable would be incoherent because we would not be able to recognize its recurrence, since every occurrence would be the same. Here stability and variability are semasic and epistemic expressions of the more generic principle that determinateness and indeterminateness belong together. The result is heterogeneity.

Contextuality is then the source not only of semasic variability but of definiteness and specificity. With respect to the former, utterances are always interpreted differently in some respects by different audiences under different circumstances. Yet these differences are a source not only of misunderstandings but of greater understandings. Latitude is not simply destructive variation against a background of stable knowledge, but is the source of any understanding whatever. An utterance can have a precise meaning, and can be understood precisely, only in virtue of its particular context, its speaker and audience.

The principle of context has two forms: epistemological and ontological. The latter is so important for the view of language being developed here that it is worth considering at this time. The epistemological side, however, is more relevant to the present purposes, since what is involved is how we are to understand understanding a language or a meaning.

We will discuss additional epistemological ramifications below; some have already been discussed. What is essential is a view of knowledge, not as a possession that, once achieved, needs no further variation, but a continuing and developing process of interrogation and reinterrogation. We have associated this ongoing process of questioning and answering with query. Query is the interrogative form of the unending play of judgments upon judgments that we have associated with semasis. Query demands interrogation and self-criticism in every location, and that such an interrogation can be provided only through multiple differences in locations and situations.

This view of linguistic contextuality presupposes an epistemic view of language: that it is both something known and a means of knowing and interpreting. So are all forms of semasis and query. What such a view entails is that each context in which a given semiate or semasic field functions provides heterogeneous variations in terms of which any semasic connection or function may be called into question.

This is a very abstract formulation: we can understand a semiate only in the context of potential misunderstandings, and these are clarified and developed only by contextual variation. An even more abstract version is that no semasic relation can be altogether determinate, a specification of more general ontological conditions. Determinateness and indeterminateness are co-relevant. The conjunction is inexhaustibility, heterogeneity, and excess. But the ontological form of the relevant principles should not obscure the specific contextuality of linguistic utterances and how such contextuality shapes both utterance and meaning.

Many linguistic utterances conform to regular syntactical and traditional patterns; others are quite irregular, or, more accurately, conform to different and often incomplete patterns of regularity. Thus, many everyday forms of discourse are syntactically incomplete, employ idiosyncratic vocabularies, and are both morphologically and phonologically distinct from linguistic patterns in other regions and contexts. Social groups frequently develop private codes, unknown to others (but acquirable by them) that are used to mark social acceptance.[31]

While from the standpoint of any one social context others may be described as aberrant or idiosyncratic, each is stable and regular in its own terms. Moreover, within each group, there is no difficulty in understanding utterances, in terms of both overt content and the social status and standing that are implicated in their form. Thus, we may say that from the standpoint of a multiplicity of social and human contexts, utterances can be understood only as a function of context, with the consequence that such utterances are intelligible in both their form and content only in terms of a given milieu, that is, they vary with milieu and are definite in virtue of their milieu.

This last point is crucial: contextuality implies both variation and stability, not just variation alone. Language, now in the sense of *langue*, is common over diverse social and individual contexts of utterance. In this sense, a linguistic expression in the absence of context is incomplete, heterogeneous, awaiting both utterance and interpretation, both multiply contextual. Even if we suppose, as Chomsky and other linguistic structuralists argue, that there is a stable syntactical structure within every natural language, contextuality is not diminished in the least for utterances (performances). Relative to syntactic norms, everyday and status-seeking utterances and codes are unique and incomplete, yet members of the requisite groups have no difficulty in understanding what is uttered. Utterance, then, is heavily contextual, as are other semasic relations, whether or not there are specific and innate linguistic forms. Contextuality and structure are antagonistic alternatives only if one or the other demands complete surrender. If there is a structural core of language, nevertheless there are enormous variations in utterances and their significations with different contexts; if utterances are functions of context, nevertheless not every contextual variation is a variation of semasis: that would make understanding a language or an utterance altogether impossible.

We return, then, to the togetherness of variation and stability and of contextuality and structure. These are to be regarded as conjoint conditions of semasis: utterances vary in form and content with location, but some of their semasic relations must be stable over many (but not all) locations to be intelligible. These conditions are not simply conjoint, but are complementary: that is, every stable linguistic relation admits of variation in utterance for effect and significance—admits and demands such variation; every variation presupposes semasic stability in order that signifying relations may be involved.

The point, practically speaking, is that while different contextual locations promote variations in semasic structures and significations, different locations are required for intelligibility. Heterogeneity is a condition of intelligibility, not its antagonist. It is true that a given (abstract form of) utterance is and must be interpreted differently in different locations; it is equally true that without stability in different locations, no utterance can be understood densely and specifically. Writing is deceptive in appearing to be contextless, suggesting that it may be understood entirely formally. But writing is as contextual, temporally and socially, even individually, as any spoken utterance. The contexts of writing differ from the contexts of speech, particularly in relation to discursive norms. But then, as Foucault argues, formal norms are always means of control, manifesting the structures of power and desire in any discursive context.[32]

This togetherness in variation and stability in discourse is an expression of a deeper ontological, metaphysical, or natural togetherness of determinateness and indeterminateness, and of a deeper ontological condition, that of multiple locatedness. Contextuality and stability are not restricted to human experience or semasis, but pertain to every being: everything is both determinate in certain ways and, inseparably, indeterminate in other ways: indeterminate in being determinate and conversely, a function of multiple contextual locations.[33] We have returned to inexhaustibility, a complementarity and supplementarity of determinateness and indeterminateness, openness and definiteness. Every thing is definite, determinate in certain ways, many ways: otherwise it could not be. But every thing also bears the promise of novelty and change, taking on new properties, surprising us in new relationships and properties.[34] Inexhaustibility is not openness alone, but the belonging together of determinateness and indeterminateness.

We may think of such togetherness in inexhaustibility as the result of multiple locatedness. To be is to be situated in a context, thereby definite and determinate; but also multiply located, in many locations and contexts, and the multiplicity provides alternatives and variations. Everything is multiply located, with the consequence that every determination is opened up to alternatives and variations, is heterogeneous. It is nevertheless determination.

Whatever we mean, or intend to mean, can be expressed in language, though not in language alone or always best in language. As a consequence, language, or linguistic discourse and utterance, is situated within the manifold concerns of human life and experience, pervades both experience and judgment. It follows that language cannot be determinate without being indeterminate, and conversely, in the sense that it cannot serve its manifold functions successfully and specifically without being indeterminate in manifold ways. The creativity of language is inexhaustible to the extent that given particular circumstances and contexts, we can find a way to express any thought or meaning in language by modifying it suitably. In this sense, a language's structures are means of creative expression that we are required by the manifold functions of language to modify where necessary. The principle of expressibility is a principle of heterogeneity and excess.

COMPETENCE AND PERFORMANCE

Chomsky views our relation to language as epistemic, though it is not necessary to linguistic structuralism that such a position be adopted. One could consider the structural systems inhabited by human individuals to be more causal than epistemic. Nevertheless, it has seemed plausible to hold that the structural system we occupy is the only epistemic system we have. Within such a system, we may distinguish competence from performance. "We thus make a fundamental distinction between *competence* (the speaker-hearer's knowledge of his language) and *performance* (the actual use of language in concrete situations."[35] This position embodies several distinct principles:

(l) *Episteme (A)*: a language is something known.

(m) *Competence*: there is a minimal knowledge comprising knowledge of a language.

(n) *Ideality*: language and knowledge of a language are perfectible and potentially ideal.

(o) *Tacitness*: what is known by individuals who inhabit a language may be implicit, tacit: even ideally, such individuals may not be able to articulate what they know about their language.

(p) *Innateness*: competence, or some part of competence, is innate.

(q) *Episteme (B)*: language is a means whereby we acquire and express what we know of things.

Principle (l), that we know a language in being able to employ it, in inhabiting it, is so plausible that we need not defend it. Most of the controversial questions concerning language arise in connection with the other principles listed. Nevertheless, even in connection with (l) there are some questions worth considering.

(i) Is a language a "thing," an object? While individuals who inhabit a natural language know something, they may not know "the language" any more than they know "being": neither may be an object to be possessed or known. Rather, they may know how to produce sentences and longer discourses, how to say what they mean, how to interpret utterances, and so forth. But in the most plausible senses of knowledge, such individuals do not know a language, and certainly do not know "language." Even on Chomsky's view, the theoretical knowledge of a language possessed by the linguist corresponds to but is not the knowledge possessed by individuals who inhabit a language. This is more a question of whether language is an knowable object than of the epistemic nature of linguistic capacities.

(ii) Is knowledge of language something possessed, or is it more the capacity to carry on human activities within and by language? Similarly, is inquiry (or generically, query) something we know and possess, or is it the way in which we understand and reflect upon our surroundings?

It follows from the importance of such questions that we must not too readily identify an epistemic theory of language, in which our rational capacities are directed toward as well as realized through language, with any particular epistemology, particularly one that conceives of knowledge in perfectible form. Is there something minimal that we can identify as largely stable over all persons and utterances that is competence in a language, or is knowledge of language manifold in its variety, rather more like a network of partially overlapping capacities than any stable grammatical capability?

Three comparisons may be fruitful. One, again, is knowledge of how to play a game. Saussure and Searle give the example of chess, yet it is not acceptable to identify knowledge of how to play chess with knowledge of the rules of chess.[36] Rather, we expect certain game-playing capacities and skills: knowledge of how to open, how to checkmate in certain positions, how to build a middle game, and so forth. Both Saussure's notion of *langue* and Chomsky's notion of competence presuppose a stable core of knowledge in a language. Yet "language" is more a fluid concept embodying overlapping capacities but no core or essence, an exemplar of Wittgenstein's view of concepts without essences.

A second example is knowledge of how to perform a musical composition. Here again, although there is a notational system for identifying the work and clear instructions for performance, knowledge of the work is not definable in terms of the notation alone. One may play all the notes correctly and still have no sense of the style of the work, playing Mozart in the style of Brahms. One may also misplay some of the notes and nevertheless perform the work with sensitivity and understanding.[37]

The third is the knowledge required by a social agent to function successfully in a social milieu. Is there a minimal social competence that is distinguishable from performance? It is unlikely.[38] Here to know how to function is to be able to function. We may add that there is a reflexiveness pertinent to social agency missing from the other two examples, but shared in the case of language: agents may raise the question overtly within their sphere of social knowledge, capacities, and functions of what they know and what they need to know. Agents who inquire as to the knowledge they must possess to function effectively as an agent do not leave the realm of social agency, but inhabit it in virtue of their question. When a group defines a secret code to exclude others, we cannot separate the act of legislation from the operations of the group and the knowledge required of its members. There is nothing here that enables us to distinguish competence stably from performance.

It is true that human beings differ in what they know and how effectively they can use their knowledge. Relative to any particular linguistic agents, relative to any particular language, there is more and less knowledge at their disposal. This is clear in relation to acquiring a foreign language. Yet when is one competent in a second language? The question has no stable answer, but is dependent on the uses to which the language may be put, ranging from everyday reading and speaking to proficient discourse.

It follows that the notions of competence in Chomsky and *langue* in Saussure are not separable from the highly implausible notions of an ideal speaker of a language and the notion of ideal knowledge itself. We have repeatedly questioned this notion of epistemic ideality. That we might distinguish minimal from maximal forms and ranges of knowledge within an epistemic field, knowing something of physics as against a physicist's knowledge of physics, does not entail that we could define a particular core, stable through time and social context, comprising such minimal knowledge of physics as to be considered competence. Even more important, in such a field as physics, invention is not merely possible: it is obligatory. And it is unrestricted by any universal conditions. In this sense, knowledge of physics entails inventive capacities incompatible with any unmodifiable rules as well as with any stable core of ideal knowledge. In any field in which such sweeping invention is expected, any field of query, ideal knowledge must be regarded not as a possession but as an activity and a capacity. It is in this sense that we may question the intelligibility of "ideal" knowledge of language: language not only is not something that can be known ideally, but so pervasively involves invention and discovery that greater competence is marked more by inventive performances than any stable structural core.

The point of this discussion is that language is not just an object about which we possess knowledge, but is itself an important form of knowledge and rationality.[39] There is no reason to take the stronger position that language is the only epistemic medium or that it includes all signs and significations, a position that, as formulated here, is false: it is sufficient that language be one of the pervasive embodiments of semasis and reason. It follows that we cannot have knowledge of language without having knowledge of what language provides knowledge of. This way of putting it is Socratic: it is the shepherd or cobbler who knows the language of shepherding or shoemaking, the statesman the language of politics, the comedian the language of humor. We need not deny that language can be an object of knowledge in order to accept the important insight in this claim: that knowledge of language is inseparable from the other kinds of knowledge expressed in language, from the (non-ideal) human activities in which language functions: that therefore the notions of an ideal knowledge of language and of an ideal language are incoherent. Epistemic ideality is a heavily qualified notion.

As a consequence, it is unsatisfactory to equate either competence in a language or ideality in knowledge of a language with grammaticality. One can be ungrammatical yet highly expressive, somewhat crude in form yet highly accurate as well as communicative in expression. Everyday language is very much like this. We do too much with language to equate any particular skills with either competence or ideality. What is ideal in language is, finally, ideal in the diverse and heterogeneous human activities that embody language—which is all human activities, including those in which language is not employed but might be, as well as the activities in which ideality is unintelligible.

A consequence of the discussion to this point is that we cannot separate a theory of language as something known from the epistemic functions of language, in discourse and query. We will discuss the implications of this principle below. Here, however, we may return to one of the most important ramifications of the Chomskian argument: that knowledge of a language may be distinguished into two forms, knowledge$_1$ and knowledge$_2$, knowledge possessed by the speaker-listener-inhabiter of a language, and knowledge possessed by the linguist.[40] In both cases, in all cases in which knowledge is involved, we may divide the language mastered at any time into explicit, formulated, thematic knowledge and implicit or tacit knowledge.[41] What we know at any time is far more than anything we may be able to say or show. More important, there is a dependency relation between what we can indicate explicitly and what we know implicitly. Different arguments may be given to make this point, for example, that knowledge depends on a foreground-background relation, and the background can never be articulated except by becoming foreground, thus entailing another tacit background. A stronger argument is that no derivation of knowledge is possible from a nonepistemic base, so that the emergence of new forms of explicit knowledge conceptually presupposes a domain of unarticulated but known truths.

Some form of tacit knowledge is relevant to any explicit form of knowledge. The controversial issues are the following:

(i) Is there a stable core of tacit knowledge, either in particular epistemic conditions or throughout a discipline, say in language? Chomsky argues that the grammatical core of language, the universal grammar, is both innate and tacitly known. This core is presumably stable over all languages and throughout time. The argument from perception and foreground-background relations suggests that explicit knowledge varies with context and is always dependent on an unarticulated residue.

(ii) One of the most remarkable features of Chomsky's position is that tacit knowledge of deep structure remains tacit even after having been articulated by the linguist. The native speaker "knows₁" his language independent of any knowledge that may be made explicit. This makes language highly anomalous, for in other cases of tacit or implicit knowledge, what is tacit changes its form and nature as we become more explicitly knowledgeable of it. While a structuralist theory must maintain that at least some of the relations that inhabit a system of meaning are implicit, felt but not noticed so to speak, it is not obvious that any particular tacit or implicit relations will continue to be implicit even after having been explicitly realized through a structural analysis.

(iii) Closely related to these issues is the question of innateness. Chomsky argues that there must be an innate core corresponding to ideal competence in a language. This is a strong and implausible reading of an important principle. For no one, however minimalistic, would deny that something is innate in human experience and learning, including language. The issue is what we can show is required for any particular masteries, and whether language is something we can master. Chomsky and Fodor[42] argue that all empiricisms are finally inductive, and that induction cannot give us the rich range of epistemic achievements involved in knowledge of a language. They both conclude that there is a permanently tacit and innate component of language or the understanding of concepts.

The alternatives of a richer empiricism or a less grandiose innatism must not be rejected out of hand. If we agree that some associative and structural principles are innate, then the argument comes down to what principles are required within a theory of language to generate an explanation on the one hand of language acquisition and on the other of the highly segmented, articulative nature of language when compared with other semasic domains. Two ramifications may be considered:

(i) *Caretaker languages.* There is evidence that parents speak to their infants in a modified, highly simplified form of language. Infants are thereby assisted to master simpler linguistic forms, nominal and gestural, by repetition and encouragement. The task involved in mastering inductively such a simplified language may not be beyond the natural capacities of the child. In addition, we may not describe the employment of language here in relation to the child as "instruction" so much as "construction"—construction of a social milieu in which language characterizes both the relations and the persons involved. We may also hesitate to speak of the ways in which individuals inhabit language as forms of "mastery."

(ii) *Overgeneralization.* There is evidence that children tend to overgeneralize linguistic elements, lexical and grammatical: "ball" is an effective substitute for "I want the ball," "that is a ball," "that looks like a ball," and so on. Children probably do not distinguish these precisely until their language becomes sophisticated enough to encourage such distinctions. Yet the style of expression may be an innate form of activity with profound epistemic consequences.[43]

The caretaker-language hypothesis defines a simplified source of linguistic data on the basis of which linguistic hypotheses may be acquired; the hypothesis of overgeneralization defines a means for generating general principles and patterns from rudimentary sensory data. The latter also embodies a striking means for the construction of concepts, overgeneralized but constricted under the pressure of counter-indications, in which no two persons are likely to understand two concepts (or grasp two rules) in quite the same way, though their understandings will greatly overlap. In both cases, some very powerful principles and capacities are innate, but they are highly variable with context and surroundings, not genetically programmed specifically for the determination of language.

Human children acquire language readily; animals do not. At least they do not master human languages readily. Yet there is a growing and controversial body of evidence suggesting that higher animals possess linguistic capacities, even grammatical capacities, along with complex and nuanced rational and emotional capacities. One reason why animals do not speak to us in our language may be their inability to mimic the caretaker language employed by human beings, since animals do not have the same sound-generating capabilities. Another may be the greater power of human processes for generating linguistic hypotheses. No doubt there are also language-specific capacities triggered in human social and epistemic interactions. We should avoid postulating the most restrictive principles pertaining to language without exploring less restrictive and more open ones, or postulating restrictive conditions that justify diminishing the communicative and epistemic capacities of animals to the point where they may be treated as objects. What is innate can be used to explain inventive capacities, but it also constricts them unduly, and innatisms tend to produce theories that are incompatible with the very powers they claim to represent.

EPISTEME

Language is both something known and understood and is a primary means for acquiring and expressing knowledge. We have criticized too sharp a distinction between competence and performance as presupposing a rigid conception of linguistic structures. What is required, on the view taken here, is a richer and more flexible view of the epistemic potentialities of language, based on a finite, located epistemology. We have suggested that such a view of knowledge may be found in Peirce's theory of inquiry with the qualifications that we abandon the requirement that inquiry lead to consensus, as potentially applicable only to certain branches of science, and that we generalize inquiry to query.

Peirce's view of inquiry is developed in terms of the notion of fixing belief.[44] Yet "belief" is not very satisfactory here in its restriction to propositional attitudes. The generic term in relation to query that corresponds with belief is that of "judgment." Beliefs are epistemic insofar as they may be subjected to inquiry, to criticism and confirmation, and insofar as they emerge from heterogeneous and plural alternatives. Judgments are selections from diverse and heterogeneous alternatives that are directed toward some form of validation or truth, therefore subject to query. Query is epistemic, and consequently, if it is rule-governed, it is so contingently. On the view developed here, inherent in Peirce's view of inquiry, latitude and heterogeneity are inherent in truth and knowledge. We have understood semasis as the succession of judgments, later judgments pertaining to earlier judgments, a profoundly epistemic relation. Query in this sense is interrogative semasis, while semasis is ongoing judgment. Meaning as semasis is endless interpretation and reinterpretation, judgment after judgment. Knowledge is the outcome of query, of incessant interrogation, validation, and re-validation. Query here is identified with reason and is the only form reason can take in finite, local terms. On this view, Western rationality has broken the endless succession of judgments by the quest for origins or grounds. Reason, here, is profoundly historical, temporal, and multiple, heterogeneous.

To this view we add that there are typical forms or modalities of judgment and query, multiple and heterogeneous. The multiplicity of disciplines expresses heterogeneity. Not only is there propositional knowledge, "propositional judgment," but multiple forms corresponding to Aristotle's distinction among saying, making, and doing: propositional judgment, but also practical and fabricative judgment. The second of these has been articulated in relation to language in speech act theory; the third includes poetry and humor, building and playing with language, wherever works are produced. Our emphasis on locality, and on the togetherness of determinateness and indeterminateness, evokes a multiplicity of forms of knowledge and semasis, modes of judgment and query, heterogenous disciplines, and the permeability of every form and mode by other modes. Inexhaustibility entails that knowledge and query are multimodal in a triple sense: every judgment may be interpreted in any mode; every mode is open to other modes, through interrogation and query; and every mode is open to other modes excessively and supplementarily. This multiplicity of modalities is reason's heterogeneity.

We will discuss this general view of judgment and query in greater detail in chapter 4. Here we are concerned with the principles that follow from such a local epistemology for our understanding of language. Our starting point is that language is both something known and an important medium of knowledge in our experience. We understand this conjunction as an aporia, giving rise to heterogeneity, not as a closed circle. With respect to language as something known, we have seen that we do not know language in any antecedently specifiable ways, for example, structurally or in terms of competence and performance, but in whatever ways we are able to know anything, through heterogeneous modalities of judgment, including linguistic judgments. That is, we know language in and through judgment and query, in their manifold forms. We must add that language is a means for interrogating itself, is profoundly reflexive, but we can avoid overstating this important principle by noting that language is interrogable from the standpoint of many other modes of judgment and query also, in all the ways in which deeds and words exhibit and define the limits of linguistic expression. Gestures, movements, constructions, and material embodiments are entangled with discourse and both supplement it and delimit it. Semasis includes the play of all of these, as well as other possibilities yet to be realized.

With respect to the epistemic reach of linguistic utterances, we may observe that while language may be the most prominent, pervasive, and recurrent medium of judgment and query in human experience, it is neither necessary to them nor characteristic of them. Despite the importance of language for our epistemic powers and achievements, we can regard language as neither a form of knowledge nor a kind of judgment, not even a mode of judgment. Not only does language admit of any judgmental modality, as does every other epistemic form, but it is employed in virtually all human judgments, throughout query, though no particular form of judgment, not even propositional judgment, requires language. As for whether language is a medium of thought: that is similar to the claim that language is an instrument, a claim with some plausibility, but one that without qualification distorts the nature of our relation to language. For if language is a medium, it is a medium like sound in music and vision in painting: a medium inextricable from the judgments produced in that medium, a medium, but not a vehicle, less something used than an intrinsic ingredient of the judgment. To all of this we may add that animals' understandings and feelings are in no obvious way tied to language. Yet we defy evidence and experience to deny that animals understand and feel.

To what extent do the recurrent forms of thought and judgment require language? A minor ambiguity here should be considered.

There may be judgments of any modality in gesture and form that are not linguistic in nature. In this sense they do not require language. In another sense, more difficult to explicate, it may not be possible to produce complex propositional or even fabricative judgments in the absence of linguistic capabilities. Furthermore, it is not necessary to hold that linguistic capacities are prerequisites to such epistemic capacities, only that the latter cannot be formed in the absence of the former: they may be concurrently developed, as Piaget suggests.[45]

We are in a similar position with respect to the relation between language (or semasis) and knowledge as we have been throughout most of our discussion of linguistic principles: there is sufficient truth to the principle that language is a prominent form of knowledge and truth, an instrument of thought and understanding, that we cannot ignore the connection, but language is both much more than a medium of knowledge, a medium of communication and action, a domain of human habitation, an environment for human development, an opening into nature, and much less, since much of what we know and are able to express can be both known and expressed in nonlinguistic forms. But much of our knowledge—mathematical, logical, scientific, conceptual; abstract and systematically complex—we could not have without employing language. In this sense, language is neither necessary nor sufficient to knowledge, though it is essential to it and characteristic of it. This aporetic relation of necessity and superfluity between language and knowledge, like the relation between language and our surroundings, experience and physical events, is an exemplification and expression of inexhaustibility.

If we suppose that language, if neither a form, mode, nor medium of knowledge, is nevertheless both characteristic of it and one of its prominent forms of expression, then most of the structural principles described above may be taken to be in conflict with fundamental epistemological principles. The two fundamental principles of knowledge that we take to be essential are (1) that any epistemic domain is open indefinitely to further interrogation, at more and more complex levels of interrogation—that is, that nothing is beyond question in any rational and epistemic domain of judgment and query; and (2) that an epistemic domain requires the development of means of validation. These two principles are expressed in the principle that knowledge is the outcome of successful query, that query is successful when it produces validated judgments as the result of ongoing, unterminating, interrogative semasic judgment.

The incompatibility of strongly structural principles with such a view of knowledge and query is far greater with the first than with the second principle above: the openness of query to further interrogation indefinitely, the expectation of invention within query and with respect to any established norms and conclusions, the continued presence of heterogeneity. The principles of autonomy, stability, structure, and generation all entail, in their stronger formulations, effective closure upon interrogation and invention. If language is the means whereby refined and sophisticated forms of knowledge are developed and expressed, then language must be capable of revision and modification indefinitely under the pressures of truth and understanding. That anything within language should be so stable or autonomous as to be beyond revision would make it incompatible with the attainment of truth at least in some areas of investigation, into our own capacities, for example.

We may therefore formulate a number of other general principles to characterize our local epistemology:

(i) *Judgment*: the field of human and natural interaction is the field of judgment, and there are many modes and forms of judgments with many modes of validation. Judgment is epistemic, seeking validation, but not every judgment is valid. Semasis is the play of judgments upon judgments. Query is interrogative semasis.

(ii) *Query*: knowledge is the successful outcome of rational methods, of methods of query.

(iii) *Foundations*: there are no foundations to knowledge although there are reliable, effective, and truthful conclusions.

(iv) *Invention*: knowledge is measured by invention and discovery.

(v) *Inexhaustibility*: knowledge and nature are inexhaustible.

Human knowledge emerges from cultural and social conditions, limited by them but also enhanced and empowered by them. Without such conditions, we would know very little; because of such conditions, we know what we know under limits. Query, the ongoing, interrogative, inventive, and methodic pursuit of valid judgment, is the sphere within which epistemic activities have their fruition, and only within query can we develop our understanding of our surroundings and our own achievements.

The consequences of this understanding for language are that every utterance is regarded as a judgment, while judgments and utterances seek semasis first, then query, for their culmination and validation. Language, however, is generally speaking essential to query, yet not itself always query. Language can be both thoughtless and thoughtful, creative and stultifying, inventive and repetitive, illuminating and confining. Language, then, is more like complex judgment and semasis than it is like query: epistemic in its possibilities and conditions, but not always successful or reflective. Just as judgment expresses something profound about what it is to be human, language expresses a large part of that humanity. But language is not more human than judgment and is not to be equated with either humanity or judgment. And judgment is not to be identified with language or semasis. On the one hand, there are human forms of thought that are not language: visual arts, gesture, even music. If these are language, they are extended forms, quite unlike speech and propositional thought. On the other hand, to make language the fundamental form of humanity is to overlook other profound forms of human expression, and these are not countable, restricted to some determinate number.[46] It is also to neglect other forms of life and being.

It follows that language is both highly specific, distinct from other forms of judgment and thought, and generically pervasive throughout human experience. In this respect, it is no different from other pervasive characteristics of humanity: consciousness, thought, judgment, history.[47] The generic concepts applicable to our humanity have fluid boundaries because they express simultaneously the pervasive features of our being human and particular manifestations given expression by the form in question. The point is emphasized through the principle of invention, for these generic forms both manifest invention and encourage it, thereby exemplifying fluidity and indeterminateness.

In summary, language must be inventive and capable of departing from every rule, where necessary, if knowledge, practice, and art require it; on the other hand it is always bound by tradition and rule. We have seen that no rule can govern without exception, that rules must be susceptible to modification and are an outcome of human social and cultural life. But the epistemic and practical functions of language make such a conclusion far more forceful. It follows that there is a dynamic tension in language between its form and its function, a tension that is in large measure a consequence as well as a source of the inexhaustibility of language.

INTENSIONALITY AND INTENTIONALITY

There remain for consideration some specific principles relevant to the epistemic functions of language. Perhaps the most important of these are the homonyms of intentionality and intensionality.

One of the implications of an epistemic view of a capacity is that it falls under a description, thereby incurring the complexities of intensionality. That is, to the extent that a capacity or condition is described propositionally, extensionally equivalent terms, that have exactly the same range of reference, may not in general be substituted for each other while preserving truth value. Since Mark Twain and Samuel Clemens refer to the same person, then it is true both that Mark Twain wrote *Tom Sawyer* and that Samuel Clemens wrote *Tom Sawyer*. This property, of preserving truth value under substitution, is called "extensionality." However, it is not true that a person who believes that Mark Twain wrote *Tom Sawyer* also necessarily believes that Samuel Clemens wrote *Tom Sawyer*. Similarly, to know that-*p* is not necessarily to know that-*q*, even where *p* and *q* are extensionally equivalent, if they fall under a different description. The same is true for all epistemic capacities, and since the view taken of human being here is that human productions are judgments, and that judgments are epistemic, then the form or mode of utterance of a judgment is inseparable from its truth.

(r) *Intensionality*. What we know is always differentiated by the form in which we express it.

The properties of utterances and the capacities expressed in calling them intensional are clear enough where propositions are involved, where different descriptions characterize a given subject matter. The questions here have to do with: (1) the importance of language to intensionality, expressed by the phrase "falling under a description"; and (2) the relevance of intensionality to epistemic modalities that are neither propositional nor descriptive—practice and fabrication, for example—to which the phrase "falling under a description" does not apply.[48] We will begin with the second of these issues.

There are many modes of judgment, including at least propositional, practical, and fabricative judgment. The notion of falling under a description suggests both language and propositions, so that it may be natural to conclude that intensionality does not apply to practice and fabrication, not even to philosophy. That is, we may identify an action, not with its intention or purpose, nor with a description, but with explicit deeds performed and their consequences. Actions here might be considered equivalent if they were constituted by the same movements or behavior, possibly including the same intentions.

However, movements and behavior, not to mention aims and norms, fall under descriptions. 'The suggested position is equivalent to the view that a single description has final authority, that is, we assume an ideal language. In relation to practice, the notion of the "same movements" is thoroughly intensional. We may consider two mundane examples: (i) upon introduction, one person shakes the other's hand; (ii) that person tells the other that he is glad to meet him.

(i) Hands may be shaken gently or firmly, quickly or slowly, perfunctorily or earnestly. Handshaking is also variable in significance in different cultures and within different subgroups in a given culture. There are secret handshakes and secret forms of handshakes. Handshaking, then, is variable in modality with cultural forms and personal styles. These are the equivalent of different descriptions. We may, of course, describe any of these different actions and styles, but the stronger point is that what a handshake is, as an action, is determinate only relative to interpretations established by social, cultural, and personal variations. A judgment is the judgment it is only relative to, as a function of, context and situation, including personal, social, and cultural variations. It follows that we have the equivalent of intensionality for actions and works in that whatever is known in and of an action is not known of a bare movement (if there is such a thing), but of an action, a judgment, therefore defined by milieu, context, and intention.

As a consequence, whatever we may say about human individuals, what they do, whatever they produce, whatever we regard as a judgment, can have no one description, no one authoritative form, no particular manifestation or expression. Judgments can be known only under particular modalities, and such a modality is a function of the milieux in which the judgment is located. The sense in which we know how to act in a given situation, including our knowledge of what can be said, what it would mean, and the rules of language, is not a function of bare movements and events, but of judgments and their milieux, of perspectives.

(ii) The second example, therefore, of what is said in a social situation, also falls under a description and has different judgmental modalities. A social remark may be a mere formality, a social gesture, a personal compliment, and so forth. It follows that in a social context utterances can be equivalent only in certain respects and cannot be substituted for each other in all or many ways. Utterances are in this respect, and borrowing Goodman's term, dense.

We may conclude, then, that while language manifests intensionality, and does so forcefully, intensionality is a property more of knowledge and judgment than specifically of language. Intensionality is the property that every epistemic act or judgment, including propositions, is doubly reflexive, in that what is known is determined both by what kind of thing it is and what kind of judgment is involved in knowing it. Yet in this formulation, we are not "trapped" within language, because language is not essential to judgment or knowledge.

Perhaps we should think of the situation as being trapped within judgment. The notion of being trapped is severely undercut by the fact that judgment is a natural condition. But the stronger point is that the reflexiveness and inexhaustibility of judgments, manifested in intensionality, is shared in certain important respects by everything. Everything is inexhaustible. Everything is excessive, supplementary. Intensionality is the manifestation of this inexhaustibility in a context defined by judgment and knowing: whatever we know is not simply true, unrelationally true, of an object, as if we could mirror it, but true of it in relation to the forms of human life and judgment. The metaphysical conclusion is that nothing is simply true of anything independent of the milieux to which it and we belong.

A similar conclusion follows from intentionality or purposiveness in judgment and knowing, especially, for our present discussion, in language. Language is a human artifact (though not an artifact alone, insofar as it is a milieu), thereby the result as well as the embodiment of purpose. Human beings and other creatures function with aims and goals, purposes and plans. Language both assists in their formulation and is itself functional and purposive.

(s) *Intentionality.* Utterance, meaning, and judgment are intentional, that is, situated in relation to judgment and directed toward validation.

We reach a conclusion similar to that involving intensionality, that language, in virtue of its intentionality, is subject to human purposes, and is therefore characterized by human social forms and cultural variations. As such, it is incapable of providing unmediated knowledge, but is itself known and provides a knowledge that is always imbued with artifactual and cultural characteristics. For example, to regard utterances as doing work, as speech-act theory holds, regards them as fundamentally purposive, having aims, being subject both to cultural forms and to personal goals or intentions. On speech-act theory, we can understand what individuals mean only by understanding what they intend, that is, what their activity is directed towards. It follows that meaning, in language or in connection with any sign or semiate, is a function of human milieux and activities, purposes, aims, and validations.

Purpose and intentionality here are epistemic, concerned with aims and validations. The implication is that what we know of language is effectively doubly epistemic and reflexive: we can understand what a word or utterance means only by understanding the work it does, which entails knowing it, the language it belongs to, and the social milieux and concerns of those who produce it. The conclusion is that there is no bare meaning or function of language, but the functions of language that are defined by the relevant social milieux and judging agents within them.

We add again that language is not unique in these respects, but shares these properties with all practical judgments. Practical judgments are doubly intentional, imbued with aims that define their criteria of validation and resident within situations that compose the norms of relevant intentions and achievements. The intentions of agents are not complete determinants of the meaning of their utterances, though they are certainly relevant factors: we must include the intentionality of the social contexts in which their utterances are interpreted. This may be regarded as a distinction between public and private contexts of utterance. The point is that intentionality pertains to both public and private milieux, and that every utterance inhabits a wealth of such public and private milieux and serves a multiplicity of different intentions and functions.[49]

SOCIALITY

We may distinguish a number of principles under the general heading of sociality:

(t) *Sociality.* Language is a social product and functions within social milieux.

Five related principles may be noted:

(t-i) Language is acquired within a social environment and betrays a social influence wherever it is employed.

(t-ii) Words and utterances have a social meaning, and there is no meaning that is not public in principle.

(t-iii) Language is a means of communication, and communication depends on social environments and conditions.

(t-iv) Despite all this, language is the primary means we have for expressing our knowledge of things, and there is no knowledge that is not public or social, no knowledge with only an individual character.

(t-v) Language is political, influenced by political events and institutions and an instrument for wielding power.

(i) Language is a social product, acquired within social surroundings, a product of the linguistic activities of other people. This would be true even if certain formal innate conditions were involved in the normal acquisition of linguistic competence. We have examined several of the difficulties involved in the latter view, the assumptions of ideality in knowledge of a language and of the legitimacy of the distinction between competence and performance. Yet it is important to emphasize that we are not forced into extreme positions on innate linguistic capacities. There are innate powers inherent in the acquisition of language, whether or not these are specific to language or more generic human and epistemic powers. There are conditions that produce regular grammatical forms, whether or not these are generic epistemic and logical conditions or whether they are specific to language. Moreover, that we could trace the development of particular morphological developments from generic human powers staggers the imagination.

Nevertheless, whether or not there are specific innate linguistic capacities, language is acquired within a social environment and, in the absence of other people, is typically stunted. Children deprived of a linguistic environment during the period of normal language acquisition do not develop normal linguistic abilities. (They do not develop normal epistemic abilities either.) This does not mean that they are not capable of extraordinary and profound human capacities.[50] A more interesting example is the development of signing among deaf children in schools where sign language has been forbidden: without the presence of generations of signers, these signing activities are mere gestural codes, lacking the richnesses of developed sign languages such as American Sign Language.[51]

Another important consideration is that whether or not there are innate grammatical competences that are triggered in a social environment, every normal language-speaker must also acquire the specific grammatical, phonological, and lexical capacities required by any specific native language, and these require a particular social environment for their development. Thus, a social environment is required both for linguistic capacities triggered by social interaction and for the specific capacities required by any particular natural language.

The implications of the social side of language are much more powerful, for if there are linguistic abilities that cannot be regarded as innate, triggered by the environment, but all such abilities are acquired through social interaction, then the major arguments for strong specific innate capacities break down.[52] Children must acquire the grammatical forms specific to their native language (sometimes, to several); and if they can do this, there appears to be no good argument why it is impossible for them to acquire the more generic forms through social interaction and inculcation. The point here is devastating to all principled (as against empirical and contingent) forms of innatism, including Chomsky's and Kant's. If we can acquire some epistemic capacities through experience, then there can be no principled argument to show that there are epistemic principles that cannot be acquired that way. The proof can only be contingent, that we begin life with certain capacities. Otherwise, it rests on a different assumption: that there are some truths that cannot be acquired from experience either because of the latter's inherent limitations or because the truths are self-evident. But self-evidence and self-validation are indefensible: all judgments require validation from without. Moreover, the entire account rests on assumptions concerning the limits of experience as a source of knowledge, assumptions falsified by the fact that we do acquire such knowledge. Arguments against empiricism always presume certain a priori principles concerning the nature of experience and the nature of knowledge. Thus, a rationalist presumes to know a priori precisely what is in question: the nature of both experience and the knowledge that we can acquire from it. The alternative is that we relinquish all a priori principles concerning the acquisition of knowledge from experience except the principle that we do indeed learn from experience, including in relation to the present discussion that we acquire linguistic capacities and powers. And we acquire such capacities and competences within and from our social environments.

It does not follow that we must take the stronger position on the influence of social activities and forms on our linguistic capacities, that the meaning of all utterances is entirely derived from a public social space and intelligible only in social terms. The distinction between what is public and what is private is a subtle and complex one. Vygotsky and Mead argue that meaning is first of all public.[53] The nature of this priority is unclear, given the nature of human infancy, since the social setting of human infants renders at least one significant interpretation to be largely contingent and effectively negligible: that without a social environment, no person would acquire sophisticated linguistic and epistemic powers. This principle is compatible both with innate conditions triggered by the environment and with subsequent personal and effectively private meanings and powers. Are we to take the stronger position, that only what is given by the social environment can be thought or meant? That would appear to make invention and creative language use impossible.

The theory of judgment we are exploring here as a setting for the theory of language regards publicness and privateness as reciprocal dimensions of experience, therefore of utterances and judgments.[54] There is a public and a private side to every judgment and to every meaning or semiate. This would be true even were a human being capable of inventing a language in private, capable of developing human capacities without the assistance of other people. Such a language would be intelligible to, interpretable by, other people. This public side to meaning and judgment is, in fact, a public side to nature and being, human and otherwise. Anything whatever is public in that there are common determinate forms that embody the determinateness of being-something; yet whatever public forms there may be, there is always something idiosyncratic, individual, private in every being. This is true even for atoms and electrons, though we typically conceive of them as entirely substitutable for each other without individuality. Yet that any one of them might be individualized requires that it be unique though we may not be able to express or even conceive of that uniqueness. This individual uniqueness is privateness though neither reflective or reflexive.

The forms of public and private experience are more obvious: to every thought or experience there is a public and a private side, though there may not be an intrinsically private side, unamenable to public expression. There is the publicly determinate and determined character of experience and the individualized, personal character of our assimilation and reflection. Another way of putting this is that to be meaningful, every experience and form must be publicly determinate, but every such publicly determined meaning is assimilated in personal ways. This is a consequence of the idiosyncratic nature of every personal experience more than of the uniqueness of individual powers. A good example is manifested in any empirical model for the development of a complex concept: presented with public expressions involving that concept, we construct either an inductive generalization based on a public but unique range of experiences, or, perhaps more likely, we overgeneralize from our experiences only to encounter highly personal counterexamples. The consequence is that the principles of sociality and stability interact continuously with the principle of personality: that meaning is always in some ways personal, however social and public it may be in other ways. We will discuss this principle in the next section of this chapter. However, we have been led to the second of our subprinciples of sociality.

(ii) The acquisition of language through social interactions must be distinguished from the public functions language fulfills. We have concluded that while we require a social setting for the acquisition of language, there is a personal and idiosyncratic side to every linguistic semiate, a personal style, but also a personal range of semiates, in and out of language, that are acquired within the social setting of language. That this should be true does not refute a more functional view of the sociality of language, that it always functions within a social milieu, and that whatever can be meant can be meant publicly. There is no wholly private meaning.

Yet the togetherness of the public and private sides of semasis and language suggests that while the principle that meanings are always public is true, it is also misleading, because it is equally true that meanings are always private, idiosyncratic. The point at issue has little to do with language and everything to do with how we understand experience. Are there intrinsically private experiences? If there were, no public discourse would be possible concerning them, although we can discourse on any topic we please. The range and power of language and other semasic domains preclude limiting language to any subdomain of expression. We can talk and write about anything. It does not follow that what we say is true or important. It does not follow that what we say others will understand as we mean it. The public side of certain semiates may be empty. This is not so much true of inner reflective states of consciousness, which may require public forms to be determinate, even personally, but of our inner symbolic life, where representations play highly charged idiosyncratic roles, sometimes of course expressive of profound universal human conditions. It is also true of apocalyptic events and experiences, which we put into words even as we feel and say that they cannot be put into words. That is what poetry is for.

There is no wholly private meaning, and no wholly private experience, in that we can always say something about any experience, and the saying is effectively public. Yet we can imbue every mode of language or speech, every symbolic and semasic mode, with private or idiosyncratic ingredients, and, it seems, cannot help doing so. The interplay of publicness and privateness here is the source of the inventiveness and creativity that language and thought require. This is not simply a creativity of form, but inventiveness of content and uniqueness of discrimination as well as depth of theory and reflection. Every thought, every public semiate, is transformed in personal experience, frequently inadvertently, due to the idiosyncratic, personal elements of individual experiences. This profound semasic truth is particularly evident in relation to writing, that most public form of linguistic expression in which we nevertheless seek the most personal expression. There is no way we could keep all meanings entirely socially stable and universal. Similarly, however, we cannot keep meanings entirely inward and have them function semasically. The reason for this is both the inseparability of the public and private dimensions of experience and the manifold functions played by any semasic form.

(iii) One of these functions is communication, and expression regarded as communicative. Language, along with other symbolic forms of expression, plays a variety of roles in human experience, does work. In this respect, language is a form of practice: we accomplish certain goals through speaking and interpreting what others have said; we produce certain artifacts that inhabit social spaces. As a consequence, language has a social side, since there could be no communication without a social milieu, the presence of other people with whom we communicate.

Yet despite the importance of communication in and for language, and the consequent importance of a speech-act theory of language, the sociality of language and semasis required by such views is no stronger than that there must be a public, social side of language and of meaning in order for utterances to perform communicative functions. There might well be norms of discourse inherent in the communicative side of language.[55] But such norms are neither unconditioned forms of community, taking community to be a political notion, entailing that at least some part of the social side of language and discourse is political, nor do they embody the intrinsic character of language or of any semasic domain. Language may function in communication, though so do gestures, events, and other actions, but language also functions in private reflection and in guiding the course of analysis and thought.

(iv) The conclusion is that the sociality of language is important and prominent, but that it is only one of the important and pervasive characteristics of language and both contributes to and is at odds with other functions of language, especially those that involve personal variations and epistemic development. Language plays a role in communication, but it is also a primary form of epistemic expression. We may hypothesize that not all knowledge can be communicated, not because there are inner states that only an agent can know, but because every communicated insight has an uncommunicated, idiosyncratic side, one that can be communicated subsequently, but only through a communication that again has a hidden side. This is another acknowledgment of the togetherness of the public and private dimensions of experience and meaning. The consequence is that the sociality of meaning is not so much its primary characteristic as one of its pervasive temporal elements.

Here, however, we come to an aspect of language that is important enough to be identified among our major principles: language is an embodiment of power, an instrument of and influenced by relations of dominance and control. We recognize here the influence of Nietzsche, for whom all human life and action is the embodiment of the will to power. Yet the generality and extremity of Nietzsche's position should not lead us to overlook the political nature of all pervasive human institutions and forms of life. Language, along with other symbol systems, is one of the most pervasive of such forms.

Along with myriad less apparent ways, there are at least two prominent ways in which language and semasis involve relations of power, political relations: (1) the manner in which discourse both influences social and political events and institutions and is a symptom of established forms and powers; and (2) the importance and differential nature of the right to speak and the right to listen, the right to produce language and the right (or enforced require- ment) to be an audience or to be silent. Both of these latter rights are closely related to the rights to freedom of thought and speech, clearly themselves fundamental political issues. They are also closely related to widespread and repeated forms of oppression.

The relevant principle is:

(u) *Politics*. Discourse inhabits a public, political world; it influences political institutions and events and is influenced by them. In this sense, no discourse, no utterance, is politically neutral.

The most interesting writer on the politics of discourse is Foucault, partly because of the subtlety of his analyses, partly because of the richness of his interpretations of the relations among discourse, power, and desire.[56] He has made his case in relation to madness, imprisonment, and medical care, but his most far- reaching analysis is found in his treatment of sexuality.[57] This work has been supported, criticized, and supplemented by subse- quent feminist writing, which itself has profoundly influenced our understanding of the social and political nature of sexuality and sexual difference. What we understand sexuality, gender, and sexual difference to be, the forms through which we understand and act sexually, cannot be regarded as entirely or even largely biological in nature, but are both socially shaped and effective forms of political domination.[58] What is permitted and prohibited sexually is a matter of what is said and what is permitted to be said as much as of what is done. Foucault offers us less an analysis of language than of discourse, but we may not separate the two, any more than we may separate the biological from the social forms of sexuality or punishment. Sexuality is doubly social and doubly discursive, in that (1) we always find ourselves within social milieux already shaped by social determinants, in this case already shaping the conventions of sexual behavior and response, and (2) all our descriptions of human activity, however scientific or biological our terminology, are socially influenced and socially influential. What we say and the institutions through which we attempt to realize our understandings of human qualities are both socially determined and politically effective.

There is a relatively negligible respect in which the principle of power is true: that political events are shaped by rhetoric (and description) as much as by events and action. This is the traditional understanding of rhetoric, profoundly influenced on the one hand by Plato's condemnation of such rhetoric as duplicitous and corrupting, influenced on the other by Aristotle's understanding that language has a moral and practical function, and that a practical agent must understand the functional forms of language to be effective. Yet the traditional understanding is profoundly limited, as such Continental writers as Foucault and Derrida on the one hand, and Anglo-American writers like Austin and Searle on the other, have shown (though the latter tradition largely neglects the political dimension). The point is that language is as practical as it is theoretical, that utterances are acts as well as descriptions. Even more important, rhetoric and theoretical discourse are themselves actions. Utterances are at least partly, though certainly not altogether, speech or utterance *acts*, and such acts inhabit public milieux of power relations and political efficacies. Even this account falls short, for legislation, discourse, analysis, all the forms of representational "writing," regarded as the production of texts rather than utterances, also exhibit and inhabit power relations and have political force. In this respect, there is no discourse that is not uttered in a social and political, though also an individual, milieu.

Foucault argues that our understanding of madness and the incarceration of insane people are closely related, and the two are closely related in turn to our views of social normality and criminality.[59] To imprison criminals with insane people, or to incarcerate the latter with those who have committed crimes, not only affects how we regard both of them, but affects our view of the acceptable norms within society, influences those who seek to be normal. If criminals are social deviants, they are both decriminalized by conjunction with the insane and regarded as abnormal, rather than as persons who have chosen to defy social laws. The concept of abnormality both encourages a goal of rehabilitation rather than punishment and suggests that criminals are "different" rather than "normal" human beings who have committed undesirable actions. One of the consequences of such views is that the identities of both criminals and insane human beings are socially constructed by being subjected to such classifications and perceptions.

The conclusion is that language inhabits manifold milieux, locales, frames of reference, perspectives, or states of affairs (these are largely terminological distinctions), including, among many others, social perspectives involving status and esteem on the one hand, individual perspectives involving personal, that is, idiosyncratic, understandings and interpretations on the other, epistemic and theoretical perspectives representing whatever we may know and understand about our surroundings, and political perspectives involving influences, embodiments, and relations of power. At the extremes, we may suppose that the social and political contexts of linguistic production and interpretation so contaminate our understanding of language and other semasic forms that meaning is effectively a function of a local form of life, or that language somehow, together with its social and political variability and functions, achieves and embodies norms derived entirely from objective, scientifically determined forms of knowledge and verification. According to the former extreme, science is itself a social and political form of life and being; according to the latter, the politics and sociality of language are distortions of ideal forms of knowledge and semasis.

Given the two extremes, we may suppose that the truth lies somewhere between, but the concept of "between" here is problematic, as if there were a single spectrum and range of considerations. To the contrary, between may be a point of excess and aporia. The sociality and politicality of language and semasis, along with their epistemic nature and revelatoriness, their humanness, public and private, are profoundly, inextricably, and aporetically intertwined. The striking thing about the politicality of language and rationality is that however thoroughly reason is politicized, it is not contaminated by power, but also enhanced by it. This is the aporetic direction in which our understanding of the conflicts among the semasic principles leads.

PERSONALITY

The principle that the public and private dimensions of experience and semasis are complementary, inseparable, and supplementary, excessive, entails the complementarity and heterogeneity of sociality and individuality. Vygotsky and Mead argue that the social side of meaning is primary, the individual side derived from it. That conclusion is far too strong and incompatible with complementarity. If there is a public side to every linguistic semiate, a consequence of the principles of stability and structure, there is equally a private side, expressed not only in the creativity of language and meaning, but in the transformations that every individual works upon public materials. We have here two additional principles important for our understanding of language and semasis:

(v) *Personality.* Every utterance, every semiate possesses an inexhaustible wealth of individual understandings and interpretations.

This principle closely involves the related subprinciple of invention:

(v-i) Language (along with every form of knowledge) is inventive; its deviations occur not only by chance, contingently, as a result of variability in human life and experience, but as the purposive result of interrogative judgment.

We cannot assign invention entirely to individual rather than social spheres. There are technological and political inventions, among others, that require social resources and institutions. Reason is no more individual than it is social. However, it cannot be understood entirely from a public, social, communal point of view. For example, Vygotsky's strong emphasis on the primacy of the social in human life includes an important role for individual transformations.[60] Individual life consists in the appropriation of public semasic elements and forms, transforming them in inner life and experience, thereafter returning them to a public space. Among these public semasic elements are individual identities, constituted in public, historical and social, thereafter profoundly modified in private spaces. The limitations of such a model are that transformations and modifications of semiates are relegated entirely to the individual side, although important transformations are worked within society. The model is as one-sided as Dewey's in *Human Nature and Conduct*,[61] where he treats the social contribution as largely inertial, the individual contribution as creative and transformative. Rather, and this is certainly what Dewey means, every form and element of human life, social or individual, is inseparably both creative and inertial, transformative and stable. In the domain of language and semasis, there are social codes that are preserved throughout individual variations and new social codes invented by a group; there are individual interpretations of stable social forms and individually inertial judgments and associations that have long outlived their social relevance; there are individual identities constituted in public and public codes transformed in private. Publicness and privateness belong together, are complementary and supplementary, as are determinateness and indeterminateness. Publicness and privateness, congruence and deviance, individuality and sociality, are complementary distinctions, multiple functions of multiple locations.[62]

There is a history of claims to private experience, ranging from solipsism to the peculiar logic (it is claimed) of our knowledge of inner states like pains and images. Yet the life that each individual lives in common with others, in the presence of others, makes the claim to a wholly private experience unintelligible and even perverse, not simply because, as Wittgenstein argues, the forms of language and meaning are based on custom and rule, but because such inner and private experiences are relevant to others, as are any individual's reflections and dreams. Since they affect that individual, they affect others. They are part of others' spheres of relevance because they are part of that individual's spheres of relevance.

This argument depends on the assumption that there is nothing in human life that is irrelevant to other human beings. The public life of judgments and semiates is a manifestation of the openness of relevance to modification in public spheres. We do nothing, dream nothing, think of nothing, feel nothing, that is not capable of affecting others through our responses to it; as a consequence there is nothing in human experience that is not publicly meaningful, a consequence of public relevance.

In this context, we must discuss not only the publicness of particular judgments, but the publicness of the fact of language and of a public language. Wittgenstein argues that there can be no private language, that language depends on customs and rules. He does not consider the fact that a private language would be a remarkable public fact. For example, imagine a private code invented by an individual that no one else understood. One possibility is that while known to only one person, others could understand it if it were explained. Here we come up against considerations of secrecy, certainly not a matter of private spheres alone. A second possibility is that the code refers to private objects such as pains and twinges, inner states. Yet no inner state is without an outer form, and whatever code exists for public manifestation, we will interpret it as we can. Thus, the language of pains and intentions, thoughts and dreams, has meaning because we can understand it, interpret it. It does not matter whether we can break the individual code, but that we can employ our own. Our own code is the public form of the private one.

What is essential here is that we might live among people who employed private codes, involving secrecy and withholding, denial and repudiation. The issue of privacy is less a theoretical than a political one, in that the presence of private spheres within public spheres is something that political institutions may or may not tolerate. Imagine, for example, that every inner state, in a certain society, was given public form in a public transaction. Suppose all individuals in a given society were expected to explain their inner experiences in publicly accepted forms in a public ceremony. There would be no private codes here because they would not be considered publicly acceptable. It is nevertheless a fundamental political and social fact, relevant to all public activities including language and semasis, that every public product has a private, individual side, though the form in which it is expressed is influenced politically.

The social side of language is as political as it is pervasive. Conversely, however, the individual side of language is as moral as it is common. Morality here refers to the relevance of issues of right and wrong as well as to human rights and to a conception of what it is to be human. And with this topic, we come to the most important of the aspects of individuality for semasis and meaning. This is the close relation between our understanding of language and our ethical understanding of humanity. It is particularly important to the extent that we identify humanity with some form of linguistic capacity.

This identification is historically of grave importance. There is little doubt that animals know, think, and signal, and they are able to acquire rudimentary linguistic abilities. How we describe the achievements as well as the limitations of dogs and cats, apes and porpoises, is not simply a theoretical matter—no such complex description can be merely theoretical, merely propositional—but has moral and political implications. We might have obligations to animals we were not prepared to meet if they were fully rational, fully language-speakers. Somehow it is more important that we define who we are by excluding animals than that we consider the possibility of expanding ethical rights to animals. The "gift of language" denies animals our respect far more than it grants respect to humanity.[63]

The issue here is one of a rationality that engenders moral rights and obligations. Can we imagine that the test of rationality is grammar? Can we imagine that we are morally justified in killing animals because they have no grammar? What is at stake is the creativity of language and the inventiveness of reason. We ascribe reason to ourselves and not to animals (to the extent that that ascription is not simply political) because we take the absence of language both to signify and to have as a consequence a corresponding absence of epistemic and emotional capacities. Without language, one cannot investigate mathematics or physics, write poetry or reflect on oneself. Self-consciousness, self-knowledge, and self-discovery all appear to depend on the powers of language. Yet in every such case there are deep intuitions that manifest themselves non-linguistically.

We must distinguish here two different claims. One is that creatures without language cannot reveal their inner thoughts and self-reflections, that we cannot verify their rationality. The other is that language is required for more sophisticated forms of thought. The first is implausible, since there are other signs of reason than self-revelation. The second is also implausible but far more important, for it emphasizes both the epistemic nature of language, without identifying knowledge and rationality with language, and the inventiveness that belongs to both language and reason.

A subprinciple of the principle of personality, then, is what may be called the principle of mind:

(v-ii) Language profoundly involves the mind.

This may be divided into several parts:

(i) In order that a creature be capable of knowledge, it must be able to represent internally what it knows of external things. Moreover, this system of internal representations must be public, at least in part, if this knowledge is to be shared and shareable. Language is the primary system of such representations in human life.

It does not follow, however, that there are not other systems of internal and external representation, nor that they are not very powerful forms of knowledge. We are referring to pictorial representations, musical symbolic forms, and gesture (in dance and everyday life).

(ii) Language is a primary manifestation of the epistemic powers of the mind; conversely, without language, the powers of the mind would be severely stunted.

(iii) The human mind has both a public and a private side. These are manifested in language in the public and private forms of linguistic utterance and interpretation. Every utterance has an idiosyncratic side, sometimes given largely by context and intonation, sometimes in variability of expression; every utterance has a public, common side, available for interpretation by many audiences. Mind here along with language possesses the two significant dimensions of reason: invention and stability.

Language may or may not be highly specific in its relation to other epistemic capacities. But it shares with our understanding of reason and thought the congruence of invention and stability that marks the important characteristics of our understanding of being human. The notion of personality, then, has at least the double character, in relation to language, of joining the public, social side of language and semasis with the private, idiosyncratic, creative contributions of individual human beings, and of manifesting the close kinship of language and mind, not in structural affinities, which are largely negligible where they exist, but in the affinities of language and reason, expressed in the inventions and discoveries that are essential to both. Language is not the only form of reason or knowledge, but it is the paramount embodiment of the complexities of query, both in the inventions and variations essential to reason, and in the mixture of technique and everydayness that all rational forms possess.

All of this is so plausible that we must remind ourselves repeatedly that we find ourselves deeply involved in ethical and political issues when we think of the relation between language and reason.

INEXHAUSTIBILITY

We may begin to collect the multiplicity of principles we have discriminated within language and semasis (as well as within other domains of nature and judgment) by emphasizing that they entail the inexhaustibility of semasis and being, that there is no totalization of or closure upon meaning and understanding, and certainly not upon nature and being, that can limit it in antecedently determinable ways. Language, like being and knowing, is and must be both determinate and indeterminate, in myriad and inexhaustible ways.

The argument can be made in two different ways. One is by considering the principles of semasis in their interrelation. Here we find multiplicity and heterogeneity, complexity and interaction, fluidity and diversity. There is inexhaustibility within the semasic interplay of language and other semasic fields. The second argument is given by considering the epistemological and ontological roles assigned to language and other forms of semasis. If being is inexhaustible, then in that sense knowledge is inexhaustible, inexhaustible in the forms of query, inexhaustible within any particular form of query.

We may consider, then, the principles above, classified into two major groups. One group emphasizes the formal and structured nature of language and its peculiar relevance within human life. Here we emphasize the autonomy of language, the stability of meaning and linguistic forms, the various structural characteristics that generate the forms of language with which we are acquainted—articulation, mechanism, generation—and the ways of regarding language that emphasize stability and structure, synchronicity and innateness. The paradigm that confronts us here is that of grammar, and we may take Chomsky's view to represent the challenge to which our view of inexhaustibility is a response. There are relatively stable grammatical forms in language, along with other stable elements, lexical and phonemic, and a language without stability would be unintelligible, not "language" at all. The autonomy and specificity of language is plausible to the extent that we emphasize structural elements such as grammar and both morphological and phonological stability. All we need to add here is Nietzsche's claim that we will not get rid of God until we get rid of grammar.

But language is also a primary means whereby we express and

conceive what we know about our surroundings and ourselves, and to the extent that we may grant such knowledge authority and respect, to the extent that we acknowledge rational powers and judgmental validation, to that extent language, along with other semasic mediums, must be capable of the revelation of the truth and significance of what can be known, even of the revelation of what cannot be known. In that sense, language must be open to whatever modifications are required by our experiences and our surroundings, inexhaustibly open and modifiable.

In this second group, therefore, we emphasize the principles that express the ontological nature and epistemological powers of language and semasis: the second principle of episteme, that language is a medium of knowledge, along with both intensionality and intentionality, but especially the principles of contextuality and sociality, of personality and politics. And especially within the latter, we begin to see, as we cannot easily tell from other principles alone, the togetherness of determinateness and indeterminateness that is the mark of inexhaustibility.

The contexts in which human life and experience are located, including the complex interactions of the public and private dimensions of experience, of individuality and sociality, especially of politics, are simultaneously limiting and unlimiting, heterogeneous, in inexhaustibly manifold ways, and exhibit this inexhaustibility within themselves. This is what is meant by claiming that locality is identical with inexhaustibility. A good example again is politics. The fundamental fact of politics, we may say, is that we always are faced with political undertakings, of great moment, with grave consequences for many people, from within political circumstances, enmeshed within the influences and consequences of prior political events. There is no innocent political mind, nor any pure and ideal principle: all principles, viewpoints, understandings, are political in the sense that they benefit some and deprive others, that they are already adjudications among competing considerations.

The point, then, is that political circumstances simultaneously define and confine the contexts of political thought and action. We are both enabled to inquire into and act upon political concerns and limited to those possibilities of thought and action that circumstances make relevant to us. "Liberation" and "theory" are not terms external to political circumstances, but are themselves enmeshed within such circumstances.[64] The conclusion is that political action and thought are context- and situation-relative, that there is no political thought that is not radically relative.

Yet the argument applies equally well to all forms of knowledge, including the physical sciences, and to language. There is no modification of or development within language that is not already from within language, no knowledge that is not derived from other knowledge. There is, then, no pure knowledge, no derivation of knowledge from non-epistemic principles or conditions, no pure speech or form of expression.

This side of language, knowledge, and semasis is expressed in the principles of arbitrariness, surplus, and invention, and expresses those qualities of inexhaustibility. It is important to emphasize again that inexhaustibility is not simply openness and variation, but is the complementarity of openness and determination, of determinateness and indeterminateness that marks the presence of finite limits. The principle of inexhaustibility is a principle of limitation, provided we understand that every limit has two sides, both an inside and an outside, that every limit is limited. Limitation here is an ontological principle. In the context of the politics of discourse, it expresses the simultaneous significance of the determination of political activities from within established political circumstances and the openness to modification required by any activity regarded as political. The ontological condition is that of locality: every being is multiply located and a function of its locations, varying with them, determined by them and open inexhaustibly to new locations.

The principles to which we have been led, then, are three, two of which deserve formal recognition.

(w) *Surplus.* There is always more that is meant in any semasic situation than any utterance can express, though the latter utterance itself has its own surplus of meaning.

This principle is closely related to the principle of inexhaustibility:

(x) *Inexhaustibility.* Meaning, truth, and nature are inexhaustible.

We have considered two of the corollaries of this principle:

Complementarity. The major determinants of being, knowing, and meaning are complementarily related to their indeterminants.

The second repeats the principle of surplus.

Supplementarity. The major determinants of being, knowing, and meaning are supplementarily related to their indeterminants.

The various principles we have discerned collectively manifest the inexhaustibility of language. Language is both highly specific and largely autonomous yet an important instrument of understanding and meaning. In the latter role, it must be capable of modifying any of the conditions that determine its specific autonomy. Another principle is involved here that we may note briefly before considering it in greater detail.

(y) *Expressibility.* Whatever is meant can be said, can be expressed in or out of language.[65] Similarly, whatever is known can be expressed.

As a rational and epistemic medium, and it is both far more and far less than this, language cannot be intrinsically limited in any particular ways, as if there were some forms of knowledge that we cannot express because of the weaknesses of language. Language is simultaneously and complementarily both confined by its circumstances and history and inexhaustibly open to modification. The principle of expressibility does not oppose the principles of surplus and supplementarity, but fulfills them.

We have concluded that the arbitrariness of language is a manifestation of a far more general quality of experience and nature: the openness to modification of every being and the irrelevance of some aspect of every being to any particular determination. We are speaking, then, of one side of inexhaustibility, but not of its entire nature. For the other side of inexhaustibility and limitation is that of determinateness.

Nature is inexhaustible because every being is multiply located and locality always involves a togetherness of determinateness and indeterminateness: that of being circumscribed or defined by a location while open indefinitely to modification in virtue of other locations. The fundamental principle here is that of multiple locatedness: every being is multiply located, situated, and limited. The interactions among the multiplicity of limits provide the openness essential to being.

Being is inexhaustible;[66] so are meaning, language, and knowing. So, particularly, is judgment: inexhaustible in diverse modalities and forms of validation, inexhaustible also in the locality of truth. Every judgment may be interpreted in any mode; any mode is pervasive throughout judgment and experience. In query, judgment becomes not only truthful, but interrogative and inventive. Here inexhaustibility becomes manifest, not only in its applications and relevance, but in our understanding of it, and in its surpluses, arbitrarinesses, and supplements. In query, we recognize inexhaustibility in manifold ways: in the uncertainties of all proofs and arguments, the incompleteness of all evidence, the limits of every situation in which query obtains, and especially in new and emerging forms of query.

How does all this apply to language and semasis? That is the burden of the subsequent discussions. We will see that even the most autonomous and specific characteristics of language are functions of inexhaustibility and multiplicity. Here, however, we may emphasize not these specific factors—structural characteristics, morphological, phonological, and syntactical differentiations—but the diverse, manifold, inexhaustible functions language must serve, epistemic, social, expressive, communicative, and so forth. The inexhaustibility of language here is a direct expression of the inexhaustibility of nature and experience, for there is nothing in nature that is not linguistic, not expressible in language, knowable through language, influenced by language, even within the limits of language. Despite all this, language is not the only and not even the most authoritative symbolic and expressive form through which we understand our surroundings and ourselves. Inexhaustibility in relation to thought is manifested as aporia, and the inexhaustibility of language is manifested in the aporetic tensions among the principles and functions that constitute our understanding of it.

We may conclude the immediate discussion by noting that the principle of inexhaustibility, with its corollaries of complementarity and supplementarity, is the ontological principle in our theory of language and meaning analogous to epistemological principles (A) and (B). The latter express the fact that language is both a knowing and a known, a means or way of knowing and an object of knowledge. Many of the other principles above are consequences of this double epistemic condition. It is because we have interpreted knowing in terms of query that the principles of arbitrariness and surplus of meaning follow as corollaries from the epistemic conditions of language.

Similarly, the principle of inexhaustibility, interpreted by its corollaries of supplementarity and complementarity, expresses the ontological truth of language that it is both a being (or many beings) itself and revelatory of being, located and locating. Here the principles of arbitrariness and surplus are not epistemic so much as ontological, expressions of the supplementary indetermination that is inseparable from every determination. Language here, along with every mode of symbolic expression, is situated within and among beings and is both relevant to them and revelatory of them. The sense of revelation here is the sense that is defined by judgment and query.

We have, then, in this ontological locality of semasis an explanation of the primary aporias in our understanding of language: a being itself yet expressive of any being, including itself; capable of saying anything, yet permeated by an unsaid. The former condition entails the specificity of language as a being, its uniqueness of character; the latter entails the inexhaustible heterogeneity of language that enables it to serve its epistemic and revelatory functions. The two belong together, producing the aporias, tensions, arbitrarinesses, and surpluses of meaning and being. The latter are the properties of semasis that require the most complex analyses of which we are capable.

SEMASIS

We may conclude our list of linguistic and semasic principles with two that define paramount features of our understanding of how language is situated within human experience. We restate the principle of expressibility.

(y) *Expressibility.* Whatever is meant can be said; whatever is said is meant.

Searle formulates the principle of expressibility as that "whatever can be meant can be said."[67] He explains that although we often mean more than we actually say, we can always in principle add to or modify our language to express ourselves exactly.[68] Given the difficulties we frequently experience in saying what we mean so that we will not be misunderstood, Searle's formulation is implausible. This point may be made in two ways: one is that to claim that I can say "exactly" what I mean presupposes that there is no gap between intention and execution even in cases where what is being expressed is extraordinarily complex, as in theoretical discussions or political contexts. Given the history of legislation and courtroom cases, it would be remarkable if any complex thought could be expressed exactly. The point is that the notion of exactness of meaning is not applicable to any practical semasic situations.

Closely related to this contingent point is the more general observation that the ideal of exactness presupposes something about singleness of meaning that is incompatible both with our semasic experiences and with Searle's own understanding of utterance acts—in particular, that every utterance is at once many acts: propositional, phonemic, phatic, illocutionary: many different illocutionary acts at once. If so, then saying exactly what one means in one respect is almost certainly not saying exactly what one means in another. The point has important implications for translation, since no translation of a complex thought can succeed in carrying all the semasic implications of the original: translation is therefore a complex balancing act trading gains and losses.[69] It inhabits the aporetic regions of language and expression.

Searle's formulation of expressibility is so implausible that we must reject it as a description of any linguistic or semasic state of affairs, and must interpret it instead as a methodological postulate. We could regard it as an idealization, the notion that though we may mean more than we say in a particular case, we can in principle expand our linguistic resources to say what we mean, but an idealization that is, practically speaking, both empty and unintelligible. Methodologically speaking, however, the principle expresses the far from trivial truth that in relation to any particular failings of expressibility, we may always say more and elaborate upon what we have already said to make it more intelligible. Closely related to this point is the assumption that there is no semasic field, no domain of experience, knowledge, or meaning, that is intrinsically incapable of expression in any particular semasic form, here in language. This is an affirmation of the locality of experience in relation to language: we are so located that we cannot seriously entertain the possibility that language is deficient in principle. That is, we cannot define anything outside of language against which language is systematically deficient. Yet we cannot think of or within language without a continuing sense of what we cannot say, of silence and the forgotten.

We may interpret the principle of expressibility to carry the following implications:

(i) There are no intrinsic limits to the expressibility of language, only the limits that every event and every being have.

(ii) There are no intrinsic limits to the epistemic powers of language, only the limits that every judgment has.

(iii) We can in principle say "exactly" what we mean, but there are no entirely independent senses of exactness of meaning. We say what we mean in the sense that language, along with other semasic domains such as gesture, painting and drawing, or facial expression, is the field in which expressibility is to be found.

(iv) The other side of exactness of meaning is that no particular utterance can be regarded as altogether satisfactory in any specifiable respect (nor altogether unsatisfactory).

(v) We can express anything in language but what we express always indicates what we have failed to express.

The principle of expressibility carries the force of one side of the inexhaustibility of semasis and language: that utterance is determinate in precisely the ways that make it effective, and that its effectiveness cannot be challenged in totality, only in certain particular respects. We say what we mean, and when we mean something and say it, or mean something and exhibit, show, display, indicate, manifest, or reveal it, what we say is what we mean. There is no other sense of meaning, independent of saying or showing, that can be a standard against which the latter is measured. In practical terms, we do not think one thing and say or show another, but the thought is shown by the saying and displaying to be what it is.

Nevertheless, we often have the overpowering sense that what we say is not what we mean, that we understand something but our words do not express our understanding, that what we have said fails to express something deeper, inexpressible, that "words break off."[70] The one side of inexhaustibility in relation to meaning and language is that there is no meaning that cannot be expressed; the other side, expressed as the surplus of meaning, is that no meaning is ever exactly or completely expressed in any particular form or constellation of forms. Inexhaustibility is a togetherness of determinateness and indeterminateness, and the principle of expressibility captures only the former; we must supplement it by the principle of the surplus of meaning: that meaning always transcends any expression. The two together manifest inexhaustibility:

(i) Whatever we mean we can express (say, show, reveal, manifest).

(ii) We always mean far more than we express.

We will attempt to express the overwhelming inexhaustibility of language and meaning in terms of a semasic field theory that expresses the two sides of inexhaustibility: the irresistible surplus of meaning in any utterance and the precise and definite semasic connections that are present in any effective utterance. This, then, is our final semasic principle:

(z) *Semasis*. Language is situated within an inexhaustible range of semasic forms and semasic fields.

We have been emphasizing the two sides of being, determinateness and indeterminateness. The principle of semasis gives us a more precise interpretation of this interplay in relation to human experience. Every utterance, linguistic or otherwise, is a judgment, and judgments are interpretable in manifold ways, variable both in modality, as the kind of judgment they are—propositional, practical, fabricative, etc.—and in relation to the kinds of truth relevant to them. In this sense, any utterance, and any component of an utterance, inhabits a complex semasic field comprising whatever is relevant to it as a semiate, whatever is relevant to its semasic functions, including other utterances, other words and gestures, experiential relationships, and even objects and complexes of objects in our surroundings. Semiates function in complex ways and in virtue of complex relations: these relations define a complex field, or nebulous mass of overlapping fields.[71] Semiates also function in complex successions of judgment upon judgment.

Such a view borrows part of Saussure's view of language, that semasis functions in virtue of complex differential relations, but rejects both his systematic holism and the restriction of the domain of signs to language. The principle of semasis locates language amidst a wider domain of semasic relations, including other forms of utterance, gesture and display, but also including the wider domains or fields of culture and experience that enable semasic connections to function. In this sense, structuralism is supplemented by forms of life, but the latter are interpreted in terms of the heterogeneity of cultural practices and forms that inhabit human life and experience. We reject the generality of Peirce's theory of signs along with Saussure's structuralism, but not the principle of generality involved. Language cannot be understood as something in itself, apart from its cultural locations, its epistemic and theoretical or its communicative and social functions. It follows that our fundamental problem is to locate a theory of language within a semasic theory, to the extent that language is autonomous, in the ways it is unique, and commonly in terms of the semasic properties it shares with other forms of semasis. That we will be forced to consider some of the most pervasive features of human life and experience in our discussion is not a deficiency of our theory, but a manifestation and revelation of the inexhaustibility of language and semasis, nature and experience.

Summary

We have discriminated an English alphabet's worth of principles relevant to language and semasis. The principles could have been expressed in a number appropriate to any alphabet, an expression of the arbitrariness of semasis. It may be worth listing all the principles together in one place, in their most acceptable formulations:

(a) *Autonomy.* Language is, in some respects at least, independent of its functions, epistemic, social, expressive, or semasic.

(b) *Stability.* The meaning of any semiate is stable over a variety of its uses and contexts.

(c) *Structure.* Meaning implies structure.

(d) *Composition.* Language is composed of distinct elements that are conjoined in complex utterances.

(e) *Mechanism.* There are procedures or rules for generating elements from complex linguistic utterances, or complex utterances from elements.

(f) *Synchronicity.* Language, along with other semasic domains, may be regarded synchronically as well as diachronically, as comprising a system or network of semasic relations at any particular time.

(g) *Generation.* Complex linguistic utterances and forms are generated from simpler forms by the repetition of certain patterns or rules.

(h) *Rules*. Language, at least some part of language, is governed by rules.

(i) *Arbitrariness*. The relation between sign and signifier, semiate and any of its relevant constituents, is always arbitrary in some respects.

(j) *Choice*. In any utterance situation, what is uttered, any semiate present, must be regarded as an outcome of selection or choice.

(k) *Context*. Semasis and meaning vary with contexts of utterance.

(l) *Episteme (A)*. Language, along with any semasic domain, is something known, not merely present.

(m) *Competence*. There is, within knowledge of a language, a minimal knowledge comprising competence in that language as well as the actual performance of linguistic utterances. The latter always requires additional knowledge beyond the minimum required for competence.

(n) *Ideality*. Language, like all other semasic utterances, is an idealization, general in certain respects even when applied to specific and individual things. In this sense, differentia are always recessive in any semasic expression.

(o) *Tacitness*. Explicit knowledge always depends on implicit knowledge. Knowledge of a language is always in important respects tacit or implicit. We always know far more about a language (or anything else) than we have articulated or can articulate.

(p) *Innateness*. Some aspects of linguistic competence must be innate; not all aspects of semasic and linguistic functioning can be acquired.

(q) *Episteme (B)*. Language is a means whereby we know things. More precisely, language is a medium of both judgment and query, therefore involves creativity.

(r) *Intensionality*. Language, meaning, and semasis are intensional; that is, what we know is always differentiated by the form in which we express it.

(s) *Intentionality.* Utterance, meaning, and judgment are always characterized by selection and validation.

(t) *Sociality.* Language has both a public and a private side, a social and an individual side, inseparably.

(u) *Politics.* Language, judgment, and query, along with other semasic forms, are always irresistibly political, immersed in human conditions, influenced by them and influential.

(v) *Personality.* Every utterance has both a public, common side and personal, idiosyncratic elements. Semasis is always permeated by individual variations.

(w) *Surplus.* There is always more in any utterance or semasic situation that is meant than can be intended or revealed by any interpretation.

(x) *Inexhaustibility.* Language and semasis along with being are inexhaustible. The corollaries of inexhaustibility are finiteness, complementarity, and supplementarity. Inexhaustibility is a corollary of locality.

(y) *Expressibility.* Whatever is meant can be expressed.

(z) *Semasis.* Language is one of manifold forms of semasis, each of which is inexhaustible.

On our analysis, each of these principles is true and important in some formulation, though many plausible interpretations are false. More important, however, the principles conflict without contradiction or acceptable resolution or synthesis. There are unresolvable aporias among the principles of autonomy and structure—including mechanism, generation, rules, synchronicity, and competence—on the one hand and the functional epistemic principles of language—supplemented by intentionality, intensionality, sociality, contextuality, and personality—on the other. Important considerations support some versions of these principles, and all are important and true in some respects, but there is no satisfactory resolution of their differences. The reason is that language embodies the inexhaustible, aporetic nature of human being. Language along with human being and being itself is inexhaustible.

Epistemological principles (A) and (B) express the epistemic conditions of language and semasis, to be both knowing and known. The principle of inexhaustibility, with its corollaries of supplementarity and complementarity, expresses the ontological conditions of semasis and language, both to be and to be expressive of nature. Inexhaustibility entails the inseparability of determinateness and indeterminateness that is part of all locatedness: specificity and limitation on the one hand, arbitrariness, variation, and surplus on the other.

The most important issue facing us is of the specificity of language together with its inexhaustibility, a specificity inherent in the concept of inexhaustibility. This specificity, marked by autonomy and structure, is one of the most important consequences of inexhaustibility. That is, inexhaustibility is not to be identified with vagueness and indeterminateness, but with the two sides of being: limitation and openness, the two sides of locality. Language (like other semasic domains) is both highly specific and heterogeneous. This is precisely the nature of a semasic medium, analogous to the notion of a medium in art. To make this point, we will begin our subsequent discussions with consideration of grammar and syntax in language, the subject that presents the greatest difficulty for any theory that would situate language within a wider field of human life and semasis. We will see that the principle of the surplus of meaning has two important consequences: one entailing the incompleteness and openness of any semasic interpretation, the other entailing the highly specific and determinate nature of any semasic utterance. The two together compose the joint complementarity and supplementarity of determinateness and indeterminateness inherent in locality and inexhaustibility, the fundamental traits of every being.

NOTES

1. "Language is a system of interdependent terms in which the value of each term results solely from the simultaneous presence of the others, . . ." "[I]n language there are only differences *without positive terms*" (Saussure, *Course in General Linguistics*, pp. 114, 120).

2. "Language . . . is a self-contained whole and a principle of classification. . . . These are the characteristics of language: 1) Language is a well-defined object in the heterogeneous mass of speech facts. . . . 2) Language, unlike speaking, is something that we can study separately. . . . 3) Whereas speech is heterogeneous, language, as defined, is homogeneous. . . . 4) Language is concrete, no less so than speaking.

Language, once its boundaries have been marked off within the speech data, can be classified among human phenomena, whereas speech cannot . . ." (ibid., pp. 9, 15–16).

3. "The bond between the signifier and the signified is arbitrary. Since I mean by sign the whole that results from the associating of the signifier with the signified, I can simply say: *the linguistic sign is arbitrary. . . .*

"Unlike language, other human institutions—customs, laws, etc.— are all based in varying degrees on the natural relations of things. . . .

"Language is a system whose parts can and must all be considered in their synchronic solidarity" (ibid., pp. 67, 75, 87).

4. Ibid., p. 23.

5. See Chomsky, *Aspects of the Theory of Syntax*; *Cartesian Linguistics*.

6. Michael Polanyi, *Knowing and Being: Essays by Michael Polanyi*, ed. Marjorie Grene (Chicago: The University of Chicago Press, 1969), pp. 80, 133; see my *Learning and Discovery* (London and New York: Gordon and Breach, 1981); and *Inexhaustibility and Human Being*, pp. 4–5.

7. See Margolis, *Persons and Minds*, for extended discussions of a sophisticated empiricism and related criticisms of Chomsky and his followers. See also note 42, below.

8. See Paul Feyerabend, *Against Method* (London: New Left Books, 1975); Willard Von Orman Quine, *Ontological Relativity and Other Essays* (New York: Columbia University Press, 1969).

9. Wittgenstein, *Philosophical Investigations*, pars. 265ff., esp. 269.

10. David McNeill, *The Acquisition of Language: The Study of Developmental Psycholinguistics* (New York: Harper & Row, 1970); also Breyne Arlene Moskowitz, "The Acquisition of Language," *Scientific American*, 239 (November 1978), 108.

11. See the discussion of the stability of meaning in John R. Searle, *Speech Acts: An Essay in the Philosophy of Language* (London: Cambridge University Press, 1969), pp. 137–38.

12. Dewey distinguishes means from ends, where the former are relational and public meanings, the latter the uniqueness of things "just what they are." He also maintains the continuity of means and ends, so that means are themselves ends, uniquely, and ends are always relational. See John Dewey, *Experience and Nature* (New York: Dover, 1929).

13. This metaphysical principle is found in Alfred North Whitehead, *Process and Reality*, D. R. Griffin and D. Sherburne (New York: Free Press, 1978), pp. 289–90; Dewey, *Experience and Nature*; Stephen David Ross, *Transition to an Ordinal Metaphysics* (Albany: State University of New York Press, 1980); *Inexhaustibility and Human Being*; *Metaphysical Aporia and Philosophical Heresy* (Albany: State University of New York Press, 1989) and *Ring of Representation*.

14. See Lev S. Vygotsky, *Thought and Language*, edd. and trans. Eugenia Hoffman and Gertrude Vakar (Cambridge: The MIT Press, 1962); *Mind in Society*; and see Harré's discussion of Vygotsky in *Social Being*.

15. See Searle, *Speech Acts*, pp. 16–17.

16. Hilary Putnam, *Realism and Reason* (Cambridge: Cambridge University Press, 1983), esp. chap. 13; see also Margolis, *Persons and Minds*.

17. See Philip Pettit, *The Concept of Structuralism* (Berkeley: University of California Press, 1977); Saussure, *Course in General Linguistics*.

18. Compare Jürgen Habermas, *Communication and the Evolution of Society*, ed. Thomas McCarthy (Boston: Beacon, 1979), p. 62; Searle, *Speech Acts*.

19. See Pettit, *Concept of Structuralism*.

20. See Saussure, *Course in General Linguistics*, Part III.

21. Chomsky, *Aspects of the Theory of Syntax*, p. 25.

22. Ibid., p. v.

23. Searle, *Speech Acts*, p. 13.

24. Ludwig Wittgenstein, *The Blue and Brown Books* (New York: Harper & Row, 1958), pp. 25, 81.

25. "We thus see that (1) genius is a *talent* for producing that for which no definite rule can be given; it is not a mere aptitude for what can be learned by a rule. Hence *originality* must be its first property. (2) But since it also can produce original nonsense, its products must be models, i.e., *exemplary*, and consequently ought not to spring from imitation, but must serve as a standard or rule of judgment for others. (3) It cannot describe or indicate scientifically how it brings about its products, but it gives the rule just as nature does. . . . (4) Nature, by the medium of genius, does not prescribe rules to science but to art, and to it only in so far as it is to be beautiful art" (Immanuel Kant, *Critique of Judgment*, trans. J. H. Bernard [New York and London: Hafner, 1966], par. 59).

26. "The *beautiful* is that which without any concept is cognized as the object of a *necessary* satisfaction" (ibid., p. 77).

27. Noam Chomsky, *Topics in the Theory of Generative Grammar* (The Hague: Mouton, 1966), p. 10.

28. Ibid.

29. Whitehead argues that Platonic Forms are essential to explain novelty: the consequence is that there are new actualities and new actualizations of eternal potentialities, but there can be no new potentialities ("no novel eternal objects") (*Process and Reality*, p. 22).

30. "Linguistic theory is concerned primarily with an ideal speaker-listener, in a completely homogeneous speech-community, who knows its language perfectly and is unaffected by such grammatically irrelevant conditions as memory limitations, distractions, shifts of attention and

interest, and errors (random or characteristic) in applying his knowledge of the language in actual performance" (Chomsky, *Aspects of the Theory of Syntax*, p. 3).

31. See Goffman, *Forms of Talk*; Harré, *Social Being*.

32. Michel Foucault, "The Discourse on Language," trans. Rupert Swyer, Appendix to *The Archaeology of Knowledge*, trans. Alan M. Sheridan Smith (New York: Pantheon, 1972); *History of Sexuality. I. An Introduction*, trans. Robert Hurley (New York: Vintage, 1980).

33. See works cited in note 13, above.

34. See works cited in note 6, above.

35. Chomsky, *Aspects of the Theory of Syntax*, p. 4.

36. Saussure, *Course in General Linguistics*, pp. 22–23; Searle, *Speech Acts*, pp. 33–42.

37. This is a criticism of Goodman's view of the relationship between a notational system and the identity of a work of art (see *Languages of Art*, chap. 4).

38. See, however, Harré's view of social competence in *Social Being*.

39. This is precisely the burden of Foucault's discussion in *The Order of Things* of what he calls "man and his doubles" and "the analytic of finitude": "Man appears in his ambiguous position as an object of knowledge and as a subject that knows: enslaved sovereign, observed spectator, he appears in the place belonging to the king" (p. 312). "Man" throughout is a recurrent figure of ambiguity. See the extended discussion in *Ring of Representation*, chap. 3.

40. Chomsky, *Aspects of the Theory of Syntax*, pp. 8–9.

41. See my *Learning and Discovery* for a detailed discussion of tacit or implicit knowledge.

42. Jerry A. Fodor, *Representations* (Cambridge: The MIT Press, 1981). Fodor's position has gone through a number of variations and developments.

43. See Moskowitz, "The Acquisition of Language"; Harré, *Social Being*.

44. Peirce, "The Fixation of Belief."

45. See *Language and Meaning: The Debate Between Jean Piaget and Noam Chomsky*, ed. Massimi Piatelli (Cambridge: Harvard University Press, 1980).

46. See Lorna Selfe, *Nadia: A Case Study of Extraordinary Drawing Ability in an Autistic Child* (New York and London: Harcourt, Brace Jovanovich, 1977), for an exceptional case study of alternative forms of expression. Also see Oliver Sacks, *Awakenings, A Leg to Stand On, The Man who Mistook his Wife for a Hat and other Clinical Tales, Seeing Voices* (New York: Quality Paperback Book Club, 1990); Susan Curtiss, *Genie: A Psycholinguistic Study of a Modern-Day "Wild Child"* (New York: Academic Press, 1977).

47. See my *Inexhaustibility and Human Being* and *Ring of Representation*.

48. See Margolis, *Persons and Minds*, for a detailed analysis of intensionality, propositional attitudes, and "falling under a description."

49. A useful list is offered by Searle: "belief, fear, hope, desire, love, hate, aversion, liking, disliking, doubting, wondering whether, joy, elation, depression, anxiety, pride, remorse, sorrow, grief, guilt, rejoicing, irritation, puzzlement, acceptance, forgiveness, hostility, affection, expectation, anger, admiration, contempt, respect, indignation, intention, wishing, wanting, imagining, fantasy, shame, lust, disgust, animosity, terror, pleasure, ahorrence, aspiration, amusement, and disappointment" (John Searle, *Intentionality* [Cambridge: Cambridge University Press, 1983], p. 4); see also Searle, *Speech Acts*.

50. See McNeill, *Acquisition of Language*, and Curtiss, *Genie*. For a little while, Genie seemed to be the exception. See also Selfe, *Nadia*.

51. Moskowitz, "The Acquisition of Language."

52. This argument is from Joseph Margolis' *Persons and Minds*.

53. See Vygotsky, *Thought and Language*; Mead, *Mind, Self and Society*.

54. See Whitehead's view of the complementarity of publicness and privateness, in this chapter, note 13; see also chap. 5, note 27.

55. See Habermas' view of the norms of reflexive communication, in *Communication and the Evolution of Society*.

56. See Michel Foucault, *History of Sexuality* and *Discipline and Punish*, trans. Alan M. Sheridan Smith (New York: Vintage, 1979).

57. Foucault, *History of Sexuality*.

58. "The central issue, then (at least in the first instance), is not to determine whether one says yes or no to sex, whether one formulates prohibitions or permissions, whether one asserts its importance or denies its effects, or whether one refines the words one uses to designate it; but to account for the fact that it is spoken about, to discover who does the speaking, the positions and viewpoints from which they speak, the institutions which prompt people to speak about it and which store and distribute the things that are said. What is at issue, briefly, is the over-all 'discursive fact,' the way in which sex is 'put into discourse.' Hence, too, my main concern will be to locate the forms of power, the channels it takes, and the discourses it permeates in order to reach the most tenuous and individual modes of behavior, the paths that give it access to the rare or scarcely perceived forms of desire, how it penetrates and controls everyday pleasure—all this entailing effects that may be those of refusal, blockage, and invalidation, but also incitement and intensification: in short, the 'polymorphous techniques of power' " (ibid., p. 11). See also my "The Limits of Sexuality," *Philosophy and Social Criticism*, 9, No. 3 (Spring 1984), and *Inexhaustibility and Human Being*, pp. 173–83.

59. Michel Foucault, *Madness and Civilization: A History of Insanity in the Age of Reason*, trans. Richard Howard (New York: Pantheon, 1965); *Discipline and Punish*.

60. Vygotsky, *Thought and Language*; Harré, *Social Being*.

61. John Dewey, *Human Nature and Conduct* (New York: Holt, 1922).

62. Several pairs of categories express complementarity and supplementarity generically, in relation to nature and being, to locality and inexhaustibility. I have discussed these in a number of works, with a number of different terminologies. They are discussed again in chap. 5 below. The latest expression of these categories, from *Ring of Representation*, representing locality, inexhaustibility, and ergonality, is as follows: "A *locus*, located and locating, in spheres of relevance: a *locale* of its *ingredients*; an ingredient of other locales. An ingredient, one among many other ingredients in a locale: as one, a *unison* with many *resonances*, the other ingredients relevant to it in that locale. A unison including many other unisons: a *superaltern unison* located in a *superaltern locale*. An ingredient with a superaltern unison in a superaltern locale *belongs* there, otherwise it *departs*. Every ingredient belongs to and departs from any of its locations in *harmony* and *disharmony*. An ingredient together with other alternatives ingredient in a locale: such an ingredient works there in *polyphony*, otherwise in *stillness*, lacking possibilities. Every ingredient echoes stilly and polyphonically in any of its locations." In *Inexhaustibility and Human Being*, these categories were expressed as locus-constituent, unison-ramifications, belonging-departing, situality-availability. The sonant categories express the music of language.

63. A striking example, discussed at length by Derrida, is where Heidegger speaks of the hand as bearing upon thinking by denying the possibility of hands to animals: "Apes, too, have organs that can grasp, but they do not have hands. The hand is infinitely different from all the grasping organs—paws, claws, or fangs—different by an abyss of essence. Only a being who can speak, that is, think, can have hands and can handily achieve works of handicraft." Heidegger speaks of "the gift" of language. (Martin Heidegger, "What Calls for Thinking?", *Basic Writings*, ed. David Farrell Krell (New York: Harper & Row, 1977), p. 357. See also Jacques Derrida, "*Geschlecht* II: Heidegger's Hand," in *Deconstruction and Philosophy*, ed. John Sallis (Chicago: The University of Chicago Press, 1987), and my discussions in *Ring of Representation* and *Injustice and Restitution: The Ordinance of Time* (Albany: State University of New York Press, 1992).

64. See my *Inexhaustibility and Human Being*, esp. chap. 4; Habermas, *Communication and the Evolution of Society*; and all of Foucault's works, but esp. *Order of Things*.

65. We have noted Searle's version of this principle in *Speech Acts*.

66. See my *Transition to an Ordinal Metaphysics* and *Inexhaustibility and Human Being*.

67. Searle, *Speech Acts*, p. 19.

68. "[E]ven in cases where it is in fact impossible to say exactly what I mean it is in principle possible to come to be able to say exactly what I mean. I can in principle if not in fact increase my knowledge of the language, or more radically, if the existing language or existing languages are not adequate to the task, if they simply lack the resource for saying what I mean, I can in principle at least enrich the language by introducing new terms or other devices into it" (ibid.).

69. See my "Translation and Similarity" and "Translation as Transgression," *Translation Perspectives*, 5 (1990), 25–42.

70. See Heidegger, *On the Way to Language*.

71. This image of a nebulous mass is from Wittgenstein, *Blue and Brown Books*, p. 81.

3

GRAMMAR

THE SENSE OF "GRAMMAR" in this chapter is closer to the older, traditional sense in which it "came to embrace the whole study of language, so far as this was undertaken by the Greeks and their successors,"[1] than to the more recent, though still traditional, sense in which "the grammar gives rules for the construction of sentences out of words, and the dictionary tells us what the words mean."[2] The phenomena with which we are concerned are the segmentation and differentiation of languages, closely related to the principles of composition and generation, as they fall under the principle of structure. If we are to portray the inexhaustibility of languages, we must be able to represent the specificity of the repetitive forms and differential elements that constitute known languages.

We have to this point spoken sometimes of language, sometimes of languages, as if the distinction were of little theoretical importance. Yet the issue of *Language* is very important: language as against a plurality of languages, linguistic universality—syntax and rules, innate principles of language—in contrast with a plurality of languages and other forms of representation. It is an issue of the autonomy of language, but also of ontology, of the being of language as against the many beings of many languages, of the difference between being and a plurality of beings.[3] The question of Language is analogous to the question of Being.[4] We have addressed it metaphysically in relation to the inexhaustibility and heterogeneity of nature and the world. Heidegger asks whether there is a difference in language corresponding to the difference between Being and beings.[5] To make these issues explicit, we will henceforth speak of "languages" except where it is specifically appropriate to raise the question of Language.

We will see that in an important sense there are languages, but not Language. This is so despite the fact that we find it natural to speak of language as well as languages and that there may be something common among the many human languages. In a similar way, there are beings but there is not Being. The reason is that the generic term tends to draw all inexhaustibility and heterogeneity into itself, effectively denying the inexhaustibility of beings. The difference between beings and Being falls into every being, pervades nature, as locality and inexhaustibility.[6]

The point is that languages are inexhaustible, in that sense not demarcated objects of understanding or thought. Yet every being is inexhaustible, technical and instrumental things no less than human or natural things. Here we depart from Heidegger's and many post-Heideggerian critiques of Western rationality. To be in any way is to be multiply local and inexhaustible. To be is to be heterogeneous. Our discussion explores what it is to belong to and to know, to judge within and to judge, inexhaustible and heterogeneous spheres of relation. The question for us here is whether languages are uniquely inexhaustible, perhaps in the ways that nature is inexhaustible in contrast with the particularities of individual beings. And if languages are distinctive in this respect, the further question is how we are to understand the particular segmentation of linguistic elements and patterns.

The latter question may be reformulated: if languages are inexhaustible in the sense that they are inexhaustible means for understanding inexhaustible things, then is not the presence in languages of patterns and regularities, differential elements, segmentation and generation, that we may identify and understand, incompatible with a radical sense of inexhaustibility in which every feature and element is heterogeneous and contingent? The answer is that inexhaustibility is openness and indeterminateness on one side, but specificity and determinateness on the other. It is the purpose of this chapter to address the challenge posed to inexhaustibility by the grammar of languages, to consider the testimony of modern linguistics that our understanding of languages is based on pervasive structural differentiations and segmentations, on repetition and recurrence, and to show that such patterns are not incompatible with inexhaustibility, but are profoundly if aporetically part of its nature.[7] The inexhaustible difference between language and a multiplicity of languages lies in each of them.

DIFFERENTIATION

If the ways in which languages are inexhaustible appear incompatible with the regularities and patterns, the differentiations and segmentations, that inhabit languages, the ways in which languages are differentiated themselves appear to be inexhaustible. This includes not only their manifold diversity of forms, but the dividedness within them that characterizes how they are differentiated and segmented, phonologically and syntactically.[8] The phenomenon is particularly striking with respect to phonemes,[9] since differentiations within different languages do not correspond, and all native language-speakers must learn to recognize and produce the sounds that mark the unique differentiations in their own language.[10]

We have noted several principles relevant to this phenomenon in languages, most of them incorporated into Saussure's principle of difference, overstated to be sure, that in languages there are only differences among the elements of a system. In the immediate context, the differentiation of sounds into phonemes is language-specific to the point where speakers of one language cannot without special training hear or mark certain differences relevant within another. Thus, a phoneme is a function of differences among elements in a system of differential relations. We may extend this point from phonology to morphology and even to semantics: a significant difference is defined systematically by and within a language, and the language is a system of such differentiations. Elements here serve to differentiate; they do not represent prior differences as much as they constitute them.

The relevant principles formulated in the last chapter may be considered in the present context. The most germane for our present purposes are the following:

(b) Stability
(d) Composition
(e) Mechanism
(f) Synchronicity
(g) Generation
(h) Rules
(i) Arbitrariness

as well as, of course, the principle of

(c) Structure

We have introduced in this chapter two additional terms, segmentation and differentiation, to express the relevant properties of languages. By segmentation we characterize one important aspect of composition, mechanism, and generation: that complex utterances are composites of a finite array of elements, that there is, synchronically speaking, a specific range of elements at any level of linguistic analysis, phonological or morphological. Only certain differences are relevant; these characterize the elementary constituents of the language. In this sense, every language is segmented by structures and rules into elements; these elements are uniquely differentiated from each other; complex utterances are composed of these elements according to the rules of that language.

It is important to emphasize that segmentation and differentiation do not entail any particular kind or degree of stability beyond that required for utterance (as contrasted with the stability of a language). What this means can be indicated by considering expressive gestures before we take up the special case of a language. A gesture can be expressive, we may say, following the principle of stability, only if the gesture can be identified and if its identification is stable at least over the utterance situation in which it is expressive. But we need not postulate that any other person, in any other situation, would either produce the same gesture or interpret it similarly. And we certainly need not assume that a gesture is segmented, differentiable into its elements.[11]

The principle of stability is plausible only in its weakest forms, in relation to the minimal requirements that enable an utterance to be determinate and interpretable, and is far less plausible in relation to stability of structure throughout a language, elements of a language, or segmented components. However, in its weaker form, the principle of stability is no stronger than the principle that an utterance can be expressive only if it is determinate, if it possesses a (stable) identity, and the identity need possess no more stability than required by the utterance situation. An expression of condolence or reassurance need be neither reproducible nor specifically remembered to serve entirely adequately.

Languages nevertheless appear to be grammatically stable over a greater range than that of a particular utterance situation or speaker-audience interaction. Despite almost continual variations in phonological and morphological, not to mention semantic, conditions of linguistic utterances, there are relatively stable lexical and phonological units as well as rules of formation. Several different kinds of questions are related to the principles above defining linguistic structure:

   a. Is the principle of stability anything other than a necessary, and in this form, negligible, condition that a language and its component elements be recurrently identifiable and reidentifiable?

b. Are the principles of composition and mechanism anything other than generic conditions for recurrence and repetition? If there were no repeatable units and no procedures for combination and division, linguistic utterances would not be recognizable as "the same utterances" in distinct appearances.

c. Is there a valid synchronic state of a language (or of any other evolving and developing large-scale process), or is there simply a synchronic perspective that can be brought to bear upon and within any process, with consequent limits and achievements? Alternatively, is a synchronic perspective on a language or on any other highly mobile form of human life not a misrepresentation of a developing, historically variable process, a "spatialization" in Bergson's sense?

d. There is potentially an unlimited number of sentences, novel sentences, in a language. Chomsky argues that this creativity of language requires a set of generative rules biogenetically defined in the internal repertoire of all language-users and speakers. We have concluded that such an argument effectively denies or explains away the fact of creativity.[12] It is worth observing that the sense of "generation" here is ambiguous as to whether native language speakers themselves generate strings following certain rules, or whether the transformational grammarian generates strings according to a grammatical model.[13]

Several related points are worth considering.

(i) The sense in which the rules generate acceptable sentences is not in most theories, though it is in Chomsky's, a theory of how either language producers or audiences generate or interpret acceptable utterances. The rules generate acceptable complex sentences in a logical or mathematical but not in a procedural or empirical sense.

(ii) There is no plausible sense in which we may expect a generative grammar to produce all the acceptable sentences in any natural language, largely because the distinction between grammatical acceptability and other forms of acceptability is marginal and tenuous.[14]

These issues are controversial.[15] What must be added is that they are obscured by many standard accounts of linguistic grammar. We may, however, make the following observations:

(iii) The sense in which a language is segmented and rule-governed is largely expressed by a formalization of the language.

(iv) Generativity is a formal property of a grammatical representation of a language, not of an actual language.

(v) To argue that because a formal theory of a language is generative the language is generative depends on assumptions of what a native speaker "knows" implicitly about his language even though he cannot articulate that knowledge and may not accept the linguist's account. That is, he may accept the applicability of the rules to the utterances he takes to be acceptable and not acceptable without accepting the rules as part of his repertoire of linguistic understanding.

(vi) Even more important, the entire account depends on the concept of an unexamined, unarticulated "rule."

Thus, further questions to which we are led are:

e. Is the concept of a rule applicable within a natural language as well as within a formal, codified game, such as chess?

f. Expressed from the other side, to what extent is the arbitrariness of languages captured by, or compatible with, the idea that languages are rule-governed?

g. Generically, is the principle of structure in languages strong enough to overcome the arbitrariness and indeterminateness of linguistic structures? This question will be the focus of the ensuing discussion.

RULES

Before we consider different types of structure and their importance to language, we must consider in greater detail the concept of linguistic rules. One of the most remarkable considerations in this regard is that the concept of a rule is often embraced as the primary notion through which we may understand the concept of linguistic structure, but it is seldom carefully defined.

We have noted that Chomsky begins *Aspects of the Theory of Syntax* with reference to an ideal speaker-listener, a homogeneous speech-community, and his essential distinction between competence and performance.[16] The crucial properties in Chomsky's account are the notions of an "ideal speaker-listener" in a "completely homogeneous speech-community, who knows its language *perfectly* [my emphasis]." The concept of rules is closely related to these quite remarkable and implausible theoretical and episte-mological assumptions.

Chomsky does not mention rules until a few pages later, largely in passing.[17] He goes on to say that such rules are "known" (tacitly) to a speaker-listener even where the latter is "unaware" of them.[18] The term "rules" has several entries in the index of *Aspects of the Theory of Syntax*, but it is never defined. Chomsky takes for granted that the concept of rules is clear, even in its application to natural languages and even in their quite distinct differences from games like chess and poker.

In *Speech Acts*, Searle similarly refers to rules, and compares rules in language to games, but also never defines rules or considers the defects of the concept applied to languages.[19] He compares knowledge of a language with knowledge of baseball and chess.[20] But the rules of baseball are codified: there is a rule book. And even if there were not, there would be the role of rules in defining the game: one plays the game "wrong" if one does not follow the rules. It is far from clear, and a striking assumption, that there is a similar sense of "wrongness" in relation to a language, though there is an important sense of acceptability.

Searle's reliance on rules is as strong as, but in certain respects very different from, Chomsky's, for without defining them, Searle regards rules as belonging to a sphere of action, while Chomsky regards them as belonging to a sphere of form.[21] Nevertheless, Searle does discuss rules explicitly, devoting an entire section to them, and offers an important and useful distinction between regulative and constitutive rules.[22] But he neither defines rules nor considers language complexly, and reaches the highly implausible conclusion that the structure of a language is to be regarded as a system of constitutive rules.[23]

The question before us is whether we can say that languages are rule-governed:

(a) if we cannot say what the rules are;
(b) if there is no rule book;
(c) if the rules change constantly;
(d) if there are exceptions to every norm;
(e) if there are no authorities who decide whether the rules have been followed.

We may consider two additional views of rules before undertak-ing a detailed discussion of this issue. One of the most important discussions of rules is to be found in Wittgenstein, and he is often appealed to as an important authority on the concept of rules in language. Yet we have noted that he explicitly rejects the possibility of basing our idea of language on rules.[24] Moreover, he describes ordinary language as "a nebulous mass," an idea largely incompatible with a rule-governed view of language.[25] In addition, he carefully describes the limitations of rules as explanations of meaning in language. Rules do not interpret themselves, but depend on how they are interpreted to function as they do, in the life of the tribe.[26]

Wittgenstein leads us to two important considerations concerning languages: (1) that the concept of linguistic rule explains nothing, but only expresses the presence of a norm; (2) that rules belong to explicitly codified systems that may bear structural or predictive analogies with languages, but that also possess very different characteristics.

Suppose we visited a society whose practices and languages we did not understand. We go to the park and find many people engaging in highly repetitive practices. We might want to say that they were playing games according to some unknown rules, and we might try to figure out these rules. Suppose, however, the "games" that were being played contained the rule that every rule could be changed upon announcement that that rule was being changed. That might still be playing a game according to rules.

We may imagine another case. Suppose the game contained the rule that any rule could be changed at any time, without announcement, simply by departing from it. (a) Is this still rule-governed activity? (b) Is it possible that a language is more like the latter case than any of the former cases? Yet it is indistinguishable from activities that conform to no rules whatever, that are performed for whatever reason the agent takes to be valid.

When and why do we employ the concept of rules? In one clear case, we give the rules of a game to people who do not know how to play the game, effectively explaining the game to them. Here we are speaking of what Searle calls "constitutive rules." He presupposes a clear contrast with those moves in the game that are not direct applications of the rules, strategic, tactical, intelligent moves. Of course, rules require intelligence for their application, but a different kind of intelligence.

Constitutive rules explain how to play a game in a sense analogous to Chomsky's notion of competence: what one must know to play a game as against playing it well. Yet even here there is a difficulty, since one might know the rules of chess, that is, how to move the pieces, how to set up the board, and that the game ends when the king is threatened with capture and cannot move to escape, without being able to play the game—knowing how to make an opening move, to reply to attack, to checkmate an opponent. The point is that chess is a game defined by rules, but is not played by following the rules. And we cannot then explain a game of chess by giving the rules, indeed, no explanation of a particular game would be satisfactory if only the rules were referred to.

Two conclusions follow from this: that competence is not definable in terms of rules alone, but includes heuristic, tactical, and strategic considerations, all only loosely distinguishable from performance; and that rules themselves belong to the practice of playing the game, and in this sense do not explain it. Rules may delimit certain conditions relative to a game, and must be referred to when certain points are called into question, for example, whether a certain move is legitimate (but not whether a certain move is effective or brilliant), but largely explain very little relative to the nature of any particular game.

All of this is in relation to the relatively clear case of rules of a game. We may consider some more difficult examples by way of contrast. Consider walking down the street: one walks forward, not backward, because walking backward risks bumping into other pedestrians. Is this a rule? It would be considered strange to walk backward, or to walk by hopping on one leg, or to walk on one's hands, or to wear one shoe and one sandal. All of these may be considered unacceptable, but not necessarily the flouting of rules.

Consider running a red light while driving an automobile, or driving seventy miles per hour in a thirty mile-per-hour zone. This is risky, dangerous, illegal, possibly unwise and thoughtless, but it is not the breaking of a rule, not in the sense that the act of driving an automobile would somehow be unintelligible if either of them were done. Perhaps these are not constitutive but regulative rules. Yet the concept of a regulative rule may be the point at issue. For laws regulate without being rules, and rules appear not to have the force that is required for the activity in question.

Two additional examples may be considered. One is Searle's example of promising: he claims that one cannot promise to do something for another person while intending in one's heart not to do it. Now promising is doing something: it is not, for example, scratching one's nose. The question is whether the distinction between them is characterizable in terms of a rule. Scratching one's nose is not promising to pay back money one owes, but not in any obvious sense because there is some rule that is being broken, any more than that riding a bicycle is not walking because walking conforms to certain rules. We need a distinction between rules and a practice, and the latter is the fundamental concept, for rules can be rules only within a practice, and there are conditions in practices that are not rules (Wittgenstein's point precisely).

Promising is as close to a normed, rule-governed activity as we can find in human life. Closely analogous to it are social codes and group conventions: for example, shaking hands upon being introduced to someone, saying "goodbye," smiling upon passing. Are these governed by rules, so that one can be said not to understand how to act in social surroundings if one does not do these things? If one knows that other people do these things, but chooses not to do them? Or is the point much more that a practice is defined by certain subpractices, and that one's actions are interpretable only in relation to practices with their subpractices? Thus, not to smile upon passing is interpreted as an affront or (to weaken the sense of offense) as a sign of distraction. Rules here are not conditions of social life as much as they are ways in which we understand our own relationship to that social life, if we accept or deny the relevance of rules. For no social milieu is so closed that one belongs to it only upon following certain rules; rather, one's actions within that milieu are interpretable by virtue of certain conventions and norms. The social remark "one does not do that sort of thing" does not define a rule so much as a practice that a member of a group must relate to as a member of that group, but every social practice accommodates deviations from norms.

We come, then, back to language, with the possibility that there are no rules in a language, grammatical or phonological. There are practices with constitutive conditions, but the conditions are both fluid and responsive to changing social surroundings, thereby accommodating within themselves the possibility of deviation, and they define the basis for interpreting individuals' actions, not so much the actions themselves. Put another way, the conditions of human practices are definitive of styles more than rules. They provide the interpretive framework for understanding what people do, not for determining what they do. In the case of language, grammatical norms define how we are to understand what people say or write, particularly the latter, far more than they define how people are to write and speak. Rules here govern less than they make intelligible. And in this sense, it is far from obvious that we are speaking of rules at all, since any practice or norm may be departed from provided there are good reasons for doing so relative to what we are trying to say, understand, or communicate; if we are able to understand something about the nature of the departure, then it involves some alternative sense of intelligibility.

What of people who do not understand a particular language, or who enter a culture foreign to them? Can we not say that they do not know the rules of this society or language? Far more important, we may say that they do not understand the practice itself, in that we cannot interpret what they do from within the practice as intelligible either in conformity to it or in departure from it. This notion of our interpretation of the actions of others includes our interpretations of our own actions. We cannot interpret our own actions within a practice if we do not understand the practice. The question is whether understanding a practice is understanding rules. We are exploring considerations against that interpretation.

Similarly, however, human practices are not structured the way crystals and geological strata are, nor do they conform to natural laws the way molecules and billiard balls do. By this we refer to two features of human practices: that they include their own variations, unlike natural laws, natural structures, or constitutive rules; and that they define how actions within a practice are to be understood, both in conformity with and in departure from certain subpractices. This conjunction of conformity and departure is essential to intelligibility within a practice.

And it may bring us back to the notion of a rule, if not to constitutive rules. The concept of rules defining language must be relinquished, but perhaps not the notion of regulation by force, here taken to include deviations as well as conformations. Thus, we may appeal to the notion of a regulative rule to delineate the legitimate variations within a practice as contrasted with the notion of natural law. We have, then, two contrasts relevant to the concept of rule: a contrast with natural law, and a contrast with arbitrariness or unintelligibility. Practices are intelligible because they involve rules instead of laws, because actions may depart from rules and practices without becoming unintelligible.[27]

We might agree to call a language (and every facet of social life) "rule-governed" if this were understood not only in a sense involving social practices, conformity and variation, and reasons for one's actions, but also in the sense that what is involved is the notion of understanding or interpreting an action, that is, against a range of conditions definitive of and defined by a practice, where the practice itself includes departures from any or all of its conditions. Here grammar is less an intrinsic condition of language—that would effectively be a natural law of language—than a norm of intelligibility, and intelligibility is certainly fundamental to language and expression. Chomsky's (as well as Saussure's) view of rules in language is effectively a theory of natural law. Chomsky might reply that no science of language is possible without its natural laws. But rules and natural laws are only one pole of the contrast that defines the concept of rule; the other is that of unintelligibility. There are norms in languages both because languages do certain things—communicate, inform, express—and because we must interpret what people say and do relative to certain practices. We are led to the position that rules do not explain the interpretive practices we employ, therefore do not explain language, as Wittgenstein argues, but are effectively explained as a consequence of the demand for intelligibility in relation to linguistic utterances. This is precisely the conclusion that structure in a language, including syntax and phonology, is both intrinsic to particular languages (definitive of their particularity: human "finiteness"), and a consequence of a far more pervasive and profound human condition, that intelligibility resides in languages (and other human practices), an intelligibility that includes both the possibility and the actuality of departure from any particular conditions of intelligibility.

If these be rules, then a language is governed by rules. But it does not seem clear that this view of rules is the one that prevails throughout most theories of language.

LINGUISTIC STRUCTURES

As we have framed it, the question of structure in languages is two questions in one. One is whether a language could be understood if it were not structured, that is, whether a linguistic theory requires structure; the second is whether a language can accomplish its tasks, do what it is supposed to, without structure, that is, whether communication, meaning, and action require structure. The two questions merge in our realization that a language is, among its other attributes, a pervasive and fundamental form or medium of understanding.

We have noted Merleau-Ponty's remark that language is both immanent and transcendent;[28] structure also is profoundly immanent and transcendent. The structure of a language is both specific to it yet transcended where necessary, where expressiveness demands transcendence; similarly, language is immanent in the life of human beings, structured by them and transcended by them, virtually inseparably.

A more explicit and specific account of how languages are typified by structural conditions yet transcendent of them can be found in Gadamer. He emphasizes the possibility of conversation and dialogue that languages encompass. Structure here masks the unsaid features of conversation that make communication and understanding possible.[29] Gadamer is careful to emphasize, repeatedly, that language is not simply an instrument, but a milieu, an environment.[30] This contrast of language with instrumentality and tools is unpersuasive, for we never find ourselves over against the world, toollessly, any more than wordlessly. We may say that technology and instrumentality are, with language, dimensions, primordial aspects, of human being. Nevertheless, Gadamer offers us an important insight into language. Two elements in his account qualify any view of structure we may bring to languages (with or without an association of structure with meaning). One is that a language does more than represent overtly, says more than can be said explicitly, but speaks in silence, speaks of a silent unsaid, forgotten. The other is that a language is more than an instrument (even if we agree that every instrument is more than an instrument), that it is one of the immanent forms of human being, thereby transcending any particular roles we may assign it. Language, with being and human being, with truth, power, and desire, exceeds its limits even as it is limited by them. A language is transcendent in two ways: it goes beyond any structural analysis because it constitutes the milieu of understanding within which any sentence can convey meaning in virtue of its form; and a language is not simply an instrument of understanding, but a pervasive characteristic of human being, in which anything may be said and anything may be known. These two "beyonds" represent excess.

These insights have been described as a "surplus of meaning." Whatever is said carries with it a double surplus: what has been said in silence in virtue of the fact that something has been said overtly; and the multiplicities and complexities of any linguistic utterance, its vagueness, ambiguity, and multiplicities of reference, denotation, significance, and implications. We may now note a third, perhaps ironic surplus, that of structure. Gadamer, with Heidegger and Merleau-Ponty, virtually all major Continental writers with the possible exception of Foucault, emphasize the ways that language transcends the specific characteristics of particular languages, the surplus in language beyond any particular culture, world, milieu, or form, the excess of meaning in silence and understanding beyond grammar, reference, or specificity of utterance. What they neglect is the reciprocal inexhaustibility of structure in relation to meaning and understanding, an inexhaustibility closely akin to that of instruments and tools in relation to any particular human purpose. Inexhaustibility belongs to language, but it also belongs to technology, instrumentality, and structure. It belongs to nature and to being.

Referring to Bataille, Foucault speaks of the limit of limit as "transgression"; we are pursuing this transgression into the heart of grammar as its excess, unlimit:

> Transgression is an action which involves the limit, that narrow zone of a line where it displays the flash of its passage, but perhaps also its entire trajectory, even its origin; it is likely that transgression has its entire space in the line it crosses. . . .
> The limit and transgression depend on each other for whatever density of being they possess: a limit could not exist if it were absolutely uncrossable and, reciprocally, transgression would be pointless if it merely crossed a limit composed of illusions and shadows. But can the limit have a life of its own outside of the act that gloriously passes through it and negates it?[31]

We are exploring the possibility that grammar, which Nietzsche associates with God, belongs together with transgression, that is, with limits and their limits, with excess and heterogeneity. The specific structures of language, thought, and being represent something excessive, something that flashes beyond the limits of understanding. We add that understanding also is transgressive, that every truth flashes beyond the limits of any truth.

Gadamer claims that we are never outside of language, though we are frequently able to master more than one particular language. He thus specifically contrasts language with languages, and denies that language is merely an instrument. We have repeatedly emphasized that instruments are also not "merely" instrumental, but inhabit and characterize human life, and provide environments for human purposes. The source of Heidegger's and Gadamer's concern with technology is that it is effectively inexhaustible, quite like language, but appears to deny itself and its inexhaustibility, appears to deny difference, excess. Its form of life seems to bring everything under the rule of perfectibility. Yet we can neither step outside of instruments and technology, though we may reject or overcome any particular form of technology, nor think and exist as human beings in a non-technological or non-instrumental way, only in some other technological way. And technology is no more perfectible than any language, or language in general. Language marks the inexhaustibility, the locality and excess, of languages. *Technē* marks the inexhaustibility, the locality and excess, of instrument and techniques, of practice.

There are, in this way, analogies among the proposed relations between Language and languages, Being and beings, *technē* and tools. In every case, there is a specificity to a particular language that Language mediates, but also disrupts, to a particular being that Being appropriates and makes available, but also disturbs. One way of characterizing the criticism is that language and being are abstract compared with the specificity of particular languages and beings. Another is that language and being neglect the specific structures and essences of words and things in making possible the very nature of words and things. An alternative, which we are exploring, is that Language and Technology, like Truth and Being, express the inexhaustible heterogeneities in utterances, instruments, and things.

An illuminating contrast may be drawn here with Chomsky's innatism. One of the implications of Chomsky's position is that languages uniquely and specifically characterize human thinking and understanding, so that the theories we are capable of developing, like the languages we are capable of acquiring as native speakers, are specific in their grammatical and structural properties. Unlike Kant's argument, which suggests that he is providing the a priori grounds for any rational, cognizing subject, Chomsky's is a contingent innatism. One of the consequences of this contingency is that we are simultaneously enabled to develop theories and languages by the innate forms of our intelligence and effectively limited by them. Limitation and power are two faces of the same capacities.

We have taken Chomsky's account of what is specific to human thought to be implausible. Especially implausible is his view that the syntactic structures that define linguistic competence are enabling as well as confining, since abstract forms of knowledge do not eliminate the need for case by case inductive reasoning and other complex forms of inference. Kant faces the same problem: the transcendental forms of understanding—time, space, and the unity of apperception—do not enable us to understand anything whatever about atoms and molecules or the curvature of space and the measurement of time. The Schematism acknowledges this abyss; it does not cross it. Judgment is required, without criteria and rules. Crudely put, there is no avoiding the need to make fallible and contingent inferences based on whatever finite information we can acquire, and there are no methods for overcoming the finiteness or the contingency. The first two *Critiques* give way to the third.

So crudely put, the point is that foundational, structural, even dialectical and hermeneutic theories all share a profound limitation. They acknowledge finiteness and specificity, inexhaustibility and excess, in terms designed to overcome them, and cannot do so. The finiteness and specificity here are both epistemic and ontological: we are so located among finite things that we cannot overcome our locality, and our inferences are characterized and limited by our historical traditions while exceeding them; similarly, beings are finitely located among other beings and are characterized by their manifold relations without being exhausted in them. Human experience and its surroundings are inexhaustible where finiteness is inexhaustibility. But inexhaustibility is a complex and far-reaching condition, and even those who would acknowledge finiteness in certain terms do not acknowledge its far-reaching nature, especially including those who interpret it to entail skepticism.

Foundational theories would overcome the finiteness of human conditions and every condition by unqualified methods of reason and inference. I include here both rationalist and empiricist foundationalisms. Nature and truth are conditioned and qualified, especially the methods we employ to acquire understanding and to relate to other creatures and things. And even these conditions are conditioned. The limits of limits yield inexhaustibility and excess. Contingent structuralist theories acknowledge the specificity of particular forms of understanding and meaning as a consequence of the specificity of human biological and evolutionary conditions, but effectively deny the capacity of such conditions to provide means for their own transformation. Structures become confining because they are not themselves limited. What may be surprising is how similar skepticism and structuralism are, since if structuralism can be successful either as a theory of knowledge or of human being, it presupposes capacities of inquiry that go beyond any particular structures. This going beyond is to be understood as heterogeneity.

Here hermeneutic theories are important, for they overcome the weaknesses of narrow structuralist theories by emphasizing that understanding and inquiry always presuppose the possibility of mediation. We may characterize a hermeneutic theory as one that depends on two conditions: the unrelenting presence of otherness, requiring unterminating interrogation, and the continuing possibility of mediation. Both of these conditions are inexhaustible; together they are aporetic: the otherness is never entirely overcome and mediation is always possible, whatever otherness exists. From a hermeneutic point of view, what is unacceptable in foundational or structuralist positions is that they deny mediation somewhere, somehow, as if by doing so they would make understanding more rather than less possible. Every unmediatable position is a closure on understanding.[32] Rather, understanding presupposes what Gadamer and Rorty call "conversation" and Dewey and Peirce call "inquiry." We have spoken of "query" to emphasize that we are including more than language and propositional assertion: unending judgment and semasis.

Nevertheless, hermeneutics, at least in its best-known formulations, effectively rejects limits at another level, the level at which Chomsky's approach excels. While there may be inexhaustibly manifold conditions of openness and interrogation, mediation and understanding, these cannot be characterized generically, that is, as Language, Being, Nature, or the World. In fact, they cannot be characterized at all except in virtue of inexhaustibility, and inexhaustibility involves both openness and transcendence—mediation—and specificity of location—heterogeneity. Every finite horizon is both inexhaustibly other to another and inexhaustibly mediatable in relation to it. But this means that every generic condition contains a multiplicity of heterogeneous others within it, is permeated by difference. The continuing possibility of mediation is inseparable from the continuing impossibility of measure. Language here is not simply a generic condition of thought, to which effectively there is no other; rather, every language is permeable but recalcitrant, mediatable but resistant. We find this togetherness strongest in poetry, where translation is most resistant, or else in the encounter with another sensibility, an alien culture. We find it, that is, in silence, in what we cannot say even while we are saying all we can and even while what we say is sufficient for any particular purpose.

Every language is permeable to any other: this is the reply to unqualified linguistic relativism. Every language is also specific, idiosyncratic, different from every other. This is the reply to homogeneity. Every difference can be mediated; every mediation leaves a residue, a supplement. The surplus of meaning lies on both sides of this relationship: a surplus of mediation over the specific structures of any particular language; a surplus of particular structures over the mediating forms among languages and human experience. One of the most important of Gadamer's arguments is that finiteness is what makes understanding possible. One of the consequences of this position is that every understanding is a finite understanding, that is, finite and local in some of its peculiar ways that no translation can entirely capture. Understanding is heterogeneous. It does not follow that every finite understanding is enclosed in its own insular domain, impermeable to any other.

What this analysis allows us to conclude is that the structures of languages contain the heterogeneities of inexhaustibility within themselves, that in so doing, they manifest both the inexhaustible powers that languages have to do human work and to inhabit human life and the specific, idiosyncratic, typifying characteristics of every local human condition. Human life and thought are profoundly and pervasively linguistic, but language is one of the specific forms of human expression and thought in contrast, for example, with imagination, intuition, visual expression, musical expression, gesture and dance, human habitats—in short, all the manifold forms of human representation and achievement to which words may be brought, but that do their work with or without words. The permeability of these forms of thought and expression entails that while each is specifically other, different from, any other, each is open to interrogation and modification from the standpoint of the others. Only in their multiplicity and interaction do we have the richness of human life, inexhaustible in its shared forms and achievements and the heterogeneous specificities of any particular conditions. We speak particular languages, employ particular grammatical forms, emphasize and understand particular phonemic differences; all are part of the inexhaustible fabric of human existence. What the story of the Tower of Babel tells us is that one language would be no language. It would annul the inexhaustibility of judgment and the heterogeneity of semasis. The story tells us that every language is many languages, since it contains this heterogeneity within itself.

The presence of structure in languages and in other forms of human life then marks the poles of inexhaustibility of being and of human being, the origin of universality as mediation and permeation, also the origin of specificity and individuality of perspective. Query depends on permeation and mediation, but also on the individuality and specificity that any particular encounter or condition brings before us. Finiteness is heterogeneity, specificity and excess. The consequence is that every understanding, every inquiry, every interrogation, every interpretation, is both public, in common with other understandings and interpretations, and private, idiosyncratic, a consequence of particular individual situations. Structure marks both of these poles, and we neglect either at our peril.

LINGUISTIC DIFFERENCE

We wish here, like Derrida,[33] to mark a difference, to contrast the principle of differentiation inherent in a strong theory of the structure of languages, which holds that the elements of a language are uniquely differentiated and that complex structures are built up from combinations of the differential elements, from a more generic principle of difference, that being and meaning are local, thoroughly pervaded by differences as well as similarities, supplementarities and complementarities. This generic principle is a reformulation of the principle of inexhaustibility: everything is pervaded by differences as well as similarities, by differences among its similarities and similarities among its differences, therefore by the togetherness of determinateness and indeterminateness that defines locality and inexhaustibility.

Some important and pervasive differences are readily noticeable in relation to languages. Most striking is the multitude of human languages and the differences among them. Here differences are clearly inseparable from similarities, for every language is translatable into other languages, but only so far and in certain respects.[34] Translation shows us that what can be said in one language can be said in any language.[35] Conversely, however, nothing can be translated from one language into another without significant differences. Similarities and differences are bound together within the nature of translation. For a translation that does not disclose that its original was written in another language, however brilliant an accomplishment it may be, suffers from the defect that it has lost some measure of its unique differentiations.

Why are there many languages? One answer is that there are many cultures and many practices, many human beings, that the multitude of relevant differences—among cultural practices and concepts of humanity, and therefore among languages as well—is an important mark of our locality and historicality. Similarly, there might be a world government, but there is not. The reason we may give is that there are many histories, involving many different human beings, practices, and cultures, and these cannot be reconciled into a single form of community without doing violence to important differences. Here history marks a genuine condition of humanity. For from the point of view of humanity taken without its histories, from the standpoint of general principles of reason and self-interest, a world government is profoundly plausible, even attractive. And similarly, those who would advocate a world language have humanity and reason on their side, except that both aspirations depend on an unpersuasive understanding of humanity and rationality.

If history counts profoundly, if locality is a profound condition of human being, then differences also count profoundly. But this does not mean that universality and infinity are still the dream while differences are marks of human frailty. Frailty and power are themselves local; reason belongs to local, not absolute, conditions; political boundaries are expressions of local, not absolute conditions of human togetherness. Finiteness is not the dark side of human being, Gadamer's most important insight, but includes the radiant side as well. For it includes whatever can be included in a human being that is thoroughly local.

This pervasiveness of finiteness and locality gives rise, therefore, to a certain unlimit in limitation inherent in inexhaustibility. It is the inexhaustible play of differences (along with similarities), a play from which we cannot exit, but to which human beings contribute inexhaustible complexities. It follows that to be "only finite" is to be inexhaustibly multifarious, but not infinite, meaning without conditions, without determining and indetermining locations.

The story of the Tower of Babel is a story of a collapse from universality into multiplicity. Most golden age myths share this vision, and provided we understand their visionary nature, we may learn profoundly from them. They speak of a collapse from order to chaos, rationality to conflict. Similarly, one may read Plato's *Republic* as the representation of a golden age, culminating in the myth of Er, in which a perfect society collapses into anarchy and tyranny. Yet an important principle is inherent in the decline of the perfectly just state ruled by a philosopher-king: that the affairs of a state cannot be controlled by any rational knowledge that is outside time. Politics is entirely immersed in temporality, concerned finally with managing, making do, passing its legacy on to future generations.[36] Not only must the philosopher-king know the Good, but he must know how to ensure the moral and psychological as well as physical superiority of future generations. It is difficult to see how such knowledge might be available to the philosopher whose knowledge is understood to belong to eternity.

Languages, similarly, are finite through and through, and, as a consequence, are inexhaustible. But inexhaustibility is the condition that there are always conditions and qualifications, limits limiting and unlimiting themselves, and these pervade languages throughout, inexhaustibly. We may listen again to the story of the Tower of Babel, imagining that all of humanity spoke one language and all belonged to a single society:

> And the whole earth was of one language, and of one speech. . . .
> And the Lord said, Behold, the people *is* one, and they have all one language; and this they begin to do: and now nothing will be restrained from them, which they have imagined to do.
> Go to, let us go down, and there confound their language, that they may not understand one another's speech.

So the Lord scattered them abroad from thence upon the face of all the earth: and they left off to build the city [Gen. 11:1–8].

Suppose there were a single language in a single society that all human beings inhabited. Would this make humanity more powerful, able to accomplish any task? Would this bring human beings closer to godhood? It depends, of course, on one's view of the latter. We recall Nietzsche's remark that we will not get rid of God until we get rid of grammar. Yet the Judeo-Christian tradition's monotheism should not blind us to more pluralistic traditions, and the Greek tradition, with its only too human gods, manifests a deeper sense of the differences within even the divine, gods with conflicting passions and purposes, understandings and intentions. Would humanity remain one within a single society? The latter question is a political one, seemingly irrelevant to our immediate concern with language. And it is a question that has no definite answer. But while we cannot answer it, we can consider what history suggests. It is where language meets God and power.

There have never been periods in human history where all human beings inhabited a single society under a single form of government. The greatest empires, Rome, Alexandrian Greece, and China, were local both historically and geographically. Moreover, all of these empires understood the important concept of exile. Prominent throughout history are human beings who left the societies of their birth to seek to form or to join another. A related phenomenon in contemporary life is the resurgence of ethnic groups, an emphasis on national, religious, and racial identifications. It has given rise to bloodshed and death.

We may regard this multiplicity as a confusion of tongues and humanity, a manifestation of the inadequacies of finiteness and the consequences of divisiveness. That is what the Biblical version suggests, for with one tongue and composing one society, humanity could accomplish whatever it imagined and desired. The multiplicity of societies and languages has seemed throughout recorded history a deficiency in human life and nature, the conflicts among nations and tribes and their cultures and languages a deficiency in human relationships. We may imagine instead that the truth is more complex than this, that multiplicity and diversity, while on the one hand manifestations of the limitations of human perspectives, are on the other hand manifestations of excess. Difference, here, is as much part of greatness as is commonality, as much part of the good.

The conviction embodied in Gadamer's understanding of hermeneutics is that finiteness is not simply limitation, but includes transcendence, a transcendence and universality embedded in local conditions. Another way of putting this is that finiteness does not entail the closure of every finite perspective: locations are indefinitely permeable, open to other locations and points of view.[37] Still another way of putting this is that finiteness is not simply a negative condition, expressing how human life and human beings fall short of some form of perfection, but contains within itself a positive side that is incompatible with perfection. Obvious examples are that only a finite being can learn, reason, or plan, can be a moral agent concerned with the good and avoidance of evil. We may go further, to say that only a finite being can be conscious, can engage in rational activities, can be critical and self-critical, can have purposes and achieve them.

Finiteness, limitation, and difference are closely related concepts, effectively inseparable, and together inseparable from heterogeneity and inexhaustibility. Still another concept inseparable from all of them is locality: we always inhabit particular horizons, speak particular languages, understand things in particular ways, and every particular here has local properties and conditions. Perhaps the most striking local condition for our immediate purposes is the specificity of human languages, a specificity inseparable from their multiplicity. Why are there many languages? One answer is Gadamer's: "The truth is that because man is always able to rise above the particular habitat in which he happens to find himself, and his speech brings the world into language, he is, from the beginning, free for variety in the exercise of his capacity for language."[38] Yet that humanity is free for variety is not equivalent with the impulse inherent in languages toward variety; that humanity is changeable and free, unsatisfied with permanence, is not equivalent with a pressure in life and thought, even in nature, toward political and communal heterogeneity. The testimony of history is that one tongue becomes many; one group divides into many subgroups, one nation divides into many communities. There is, in Gadamer, a suggestion of another consideration, that the multiplicity composes the world: "what the world is is not different from the views in which it presents itself."[39] If the world is its many views, if viewpoints make up the world, and viewpoints are both different as well as similar, opposed as well as permeable, then a multiplicity of viewpoints is required in order to understand

and have the world. This expresses both multiple locality and inexhaustibility, with the qualification that these are pervaded by aporia. Similarly, if a language is not a mirror of reality, but a form of habitation in which selfhood and community are constituted, then to the extent that no model for selfhood and community has priority over all others, nor could have such priority if everything including humanity was finite, then both selfhood and community demand a multiplicity of languages. In this sense, finiteness entails inexhaustibility.

It is a pervasive experience of modern life that, almost in reciprocal relation, as states, governments, societies, institutions, even populations grow larger, there is greater division among the composing subgroups: minorities, neighborhoods, geographical regions, institutional divisions with special loyalties. There is a political and economic trend toward uniformity and growth in scale; at the other end of the spectrum there is greater variety of styles of dress and communal identifications. Closely related to this phenomenon are increased demands for reestablishing linguistic traditions, Welsh, Gaelic, Québecois, Flemish. In some cases, local identities are based on blood and promote bloodshed. Either reason does not lead to uniformity and universality, to world government and world language, or there is an irresistible urge in human beings away from unity toward heterogeneity. We should not accept the second of these conclusions without considering the first, that reason is, like all other human forms, finite and therefore multifarious and heterogeneous. A natural consequence is that languages and other voices are then also inexhaustible and multifarious.

We may return to Nietzsche's understanding of God as imposing the Law of Grammar by recognizing the hold of grammar upon us as a necessity within reason and culture, against which heterogeneity must wage endless war, against its oppressions. Irigaray attacks grammar for its role in silencing women under the law of the Father:

> Turn everything upside down, inside out, back to front. *Rack it with radical convulsions.* . . . Reinscribe them hither and thither *as divergencies,* otherwise and elsewhere than they are expected, in *ellipses* and *eclipses* that deconstruct the logical grid of the reader-writer, drive him out of his mind, trouble his vision to the point of incurable diplopia at least. *Overthrow syntax* by suspending its eternally teleological order, by snipping the wires, cutting the

current, breaking the circuits, switching the connections, by modifying continuity, alternation, frequency, intensity.[40]

The hold of syntax repeats the hold of God's law and necessity under which women and others cannot speak, lack the voice in which to speak in public. Grammar, here, is political; so are all languages, semasis, and representation. Languages and their grammars are always caught up in surplus and excess, even within and because of the hold of grammar. The hold of law, of mastery, is irresistible. Even so, if aporetically, the mastery of language and semasis requires heterogeneity; the heterogeneity of languages requires grammar. Those who write and speak always rack human life with radical convulsions, overthrowing the hold of some mastery even as they submit to the forms of its inscriptions. God always plays a double role, of mastery and of heterogeneity. Our understanding, based on locality and inexhaustibility, is that mastery entails heterogeneity, and reciprocally.

SPECIFICITY

One of the most important implications of Chomsky's view of language, not entirely absent from Kant though largely incompatible with Cartesian rationalism, is the suggestion that what composes linguistic competence, what is innate in human linguistic powers, determines at least in part what human beings are capable of knowing and understanding. The sense of "determining" here is specific and contingent, local, and it is this specificity that we are emphasizing. In Cartesian forms of rationalism, rational principles express the nature and conditions of any rationality, any cognizing subject. In traditional interpretations of Kant, the a priori conditions of the understanding compose the epistemic conditions of any rational subject. What can be known and understood is defined by a priori conditions, and these determine it necessarily and universally, therefore neither contingently nor, in any significant practical sense, differentially. Such conditions are unqualified by the historical, contingent, biological, and social events of human life, and are not then finite but infinite.

Finiteness is closely related to contingency and specificity. That human beings and human life are finite not only entails a historical temporality involving past, present, and future, but a contingent specificity of influences and consequences, circumstances and conditions, that pervades any human activity, including understanding and interpretation. In Chomsky's version, the suggestion is that because we are biologically determined, specifically and contingently, to certain grammatical forms, our languages are characterized and limited by these forms. A universal grammar here is both facilitation and limitation. That grammatical principles might be universal has the consequence that our specific linguistic competences embody principles that uniquely and specifically characterize the languages of which we are capable. It follows that only some languages are acquirable as native languages by human beings, and similarly, only some theories are acquirable by human beings.

Similarly, though Kant is often interpreted, in relation to both theoretical and practical reason, as suggesting that the a priori conditions of the understanding and practical reason render science and morality necessary, this is far from plausible when one considers particular explanations in complex cases. In reality, nothing whatever follows from any a priori conditions of pure understanding for the specific and contingent facts that science requires to be successful. It is plausible to suppose that Kant was fully aware that universality in knowledge is always a specific universality, about forces and masses, not being generically. That is why the *Critique of Judgment* was required, for judgment provides the essential link between universal a priori conditions and the contingency and specificity that knowledge requires in finite conditions. It provides this link, as Lyotard says, without criteria or rules.[41]

With respect to language, then, we may characterize the issue as one of human specificity, that we as human beings are located within languages (though not languages alone) that are always specific, contingent features of human thought and expression. In Chomsky's version, these contingent features are universal, but the universality is no less contingent and specific for its generality over all human languages. It follows that the languages we can acquire and inhabit delimit specific conditions of human experience, that locality entails that what we can know is specifically linguistic, and specifically human. Fancifully, we may construe the point to be that there might be rational beings—we might have difficulty grasping their rationality—who understood things very differently from the ways we understand them, possibly with a different ontology, certainly with very different languages.

We are exploring some of the ramifications of the principle of locality, entailing contingency and specificity. Human beings along with every other being are finite and contingent, therefore local and specific in particular ways. This locality requires us to understand understanding itself as finite and contingent in certain ways. It follows that among the local determinants of human life, along with particular traditions and cultural practices, are the particular differential features of the particular languages human beings speak, write, and inhabit, in which they think. Specificity is one of the consequences, one of the poles, of inexhaustibility in language.

There is, by way of contrast, an emphasis on the universality and primordiality of language in Heidegger and Gadamer that, within a continual emphasis on finiteness, seems to abrogate it, at least not to reflect its specificity and locality. We may emphasize Gadamer's treatment of the issue, for it is somewhat more direct than Heidegger's. It may also lack the certain radicality expressed in Heidegger's claim that "Language is the House of Being."[42] This radicality is even more forceful in Heidegger's reading of Stefan George's line "Where word breaks off no thing may be" as "An 'is' arises where the word breaks up," commenting: "This breaking up of the word is the true step back on the way of thinking."[43] This theme of breaking up is much closer to the locality and inexhaustibility of heterogeneity.

We find two related themes in Gadamer, not sharply differentiated.

> Language is the fundamental mode of operation of our being-in-the-world and the all-embracing form of the constitution of the world.[44]

> The basic misunderstanding concerning the linguistic nature of our understanding is one of language, as if language were an existing whole composed of words and phrases, concepts, points of view and opinions. In reality, language is the single word whose virtuality opens up the infinity of discourse, of discourse with others, and of the freedom of "speaking oneself" and of "allowing oneself to be spoken." Language is not its elaborate conventionalism, nor the burden of pre-schematization with which it loads us, but the generative and creative power unceasingly to make this whole fluid.[45]

Essential to both themes is a distinction between Language and any language, that is, a distinction involving language generically, *logos* and thought, and any natural language, an emphasis on the creative, transcendent, universal possibilities of Language (but possibly not of every local language). We may characterize Gadamer's position as follows:

1. Language is not confining, but contains within it the inexhaustible openness of possibilities of understanding that interpretation requires.

2. Any horizon is open to, mediatable by, any other horizon: language is the medium within which these possibilities lie.

3. Language is essential to human being.

These important theses of the openness of understanding and interpretation within languages may be contrasted with the following:

1'. Language is all-encompassing.

2'. Language is absolutely free from capturing us within it.

3'. Anything whatever can be expressed in language.

The first set of theses embodies the important property of mediation. Interpretation presupposes that differences are mediatable, that we can overcome differences in culture, time, and language. Texts can be interpreted and can be translated. To suppose otherwise is to deny mediation. But it does not follow that every difference can be mediated, that any text can be entirely interpreted or entirely translated without profound loss. An achievement in one respect may be accompanied by a loss in another. Gadamer fully understands this. The question is whether finiteness and mediation must presuppose all-encompassing universality, whether mediation can supersede locality.

The principle that anything can be expressed in language is a version of the principle of expressibility. We have concluded that the principle is true, but under qualification, and we cannot say what the appropriate qualifications must be, for that would be to be able to say in advance what we can understand and what we cannot, in a particular way. Thus, we must accept some of the following qualifications:

a. Anything can be expressed in language, but perhaps not as well as in some other form, gesturally, pictorially, musically. Similarly, anything can be understood, but perhaps not entirely (though we cannot entirely specify how understanding must in principle be incomplete) nor in any particular form, including language. Some things we understand imagistically, viscerally, emotionally. Some things we understand heterogeneously.[46]

b. Anything can be expressed in any language, but perhaps not as well as in some other language, not as effectively, not as precisely, not in as great detail, not as profoundly.

c. Human beings are immersed within, belong to, inhabit language. But every human being is specifically located within some languages and not others, thinks in some languages and not others, lives within some cultures and not others, belongs to some groups and not others. Locality is always finite and specific, situated. It follows that how human beings live, what they do and what and how they can understand things will have specific determining and supplementary features expressive of this immersedness, not all of which can be mediated or overcome.

Gadamer claims that there is "absolutely" no captivity in language. Similarly, we may suppose that there is "absolutely" no captivity in understanding, that we may understand anything and understand it in any way. These conclusions are far too strong. The locality of understandings entails inexhaustibility. If things are inexhaustible and human experience (including language and understanding) is inexhaustible, then what things are is understandable and interpretable in manifold ways, some of which involve major differences. We can acknowledge inexhaustible mediation without requiring absolute universality. Every language is translatable into another, but not as if the two were not different: differences as well as similarities are involved. There can be captivity in language despite pervasive mediatability. Supplementarity and excess are "captivities" in language.

We are led to the principle, shared by hermeneutics and pragmatism, that inquiry is unlimited, that anything may be interrogated, and that only through inquiry or query are interrogation and understanding possible. Does this require a universal principle or ground? We are exploring the possibility that it does not, that inexhaustible possibilities of mediation, interrogation, and understanding do not entail a generic openness incompatible with specificity, but specific "captivities" that coexist with inexhaustible openness to interrogation. These captivities are local and heterogeneous. We have understood the concept of query as enforcing this conclusion: query has manifold forms, each of which is specific relative to the others, but each of which is also inexhaustible and pervasive. Disciplinariness expresses the heterogeneity of judgment and query. To hold that every horizon is mediatable by any other horizon does not entail that all horizons rest on a common ground of mediation, linguistic or otherwise.

That things are heterogeneous, indeterminate as well as determinate, does not entail a common horizon. While anything can be expressed or understood in any language, what and how it is expressed is a specific function of the particular language, and varies from language to language. There is no absolute captivity in language or thought, but there is an inexhaustible specificity that no shared understanding can eliminate, the specificity belonging to locality and inexhaustibility.

Our conclusion is that the differential, structural elements of different languages are a manifestation of the limits that make understanding possible on the one hand and delimit its possibilities on the other. We can understand something because we have some language, or other form of thought, in which to express our understanding. But no particular version can be complete or free from specific determinants defined by the particular mode of expression. And new languages, translations, other forms of expression—pictorial, imagistic, gestural—supplement these limits but do not overcome them. We are speaking here less of language than of judgment and query. Query is inexhaustible because it is multimodal, while each mode possesses important specific determining features. Another way of putting this is that query presupposes indefinite openness and interrogation, but every form of query is resistant to the others. Resistances and openness together compose the inexhaustibility of locality.

SYNTAX AND QUERY

If, as Gadamer and Heidegger suggest, language is the voice of reason or thought, then language is the voice of query. But query has many forms, as there are many languages; moreover, query, like language, has both an outside and an inside, an outside marked by judgments that are not query as well as judgments that belong to query. Language is only one of the voices of query and judgment; reason possesses many voices.

If we associate language with reason, then we appear to regard a language as an instrument of rationality. Yet we inhabit a language as much as employ it.[47] And we are encompassed by technology and instrumentality as much as by language, by politics and society, by acts as much as words.

Query is inexhaustible, as is language. For query, this inexhaustibility is revealed in manifold forms as well as in the incompleteness of any interrogation, the limits of every answer. It is more profoundly revealed in the exteriority that belongs to every interior (and the interiority that belongs to every exterior). Outside and inside are both complementarily and supplementarily related, each requiring the other and becoming the other with a change of location. Thus, there is no absolute inside or outside, no absolute truth or absolute identity. We may call this inexhaustible qualifiedness "arbitrariness," closely related to Saussure's and Derrida's view of language and writing.

Nietzsche suggests that we will not be rid of God until we are rid of grammar. He implies in this suggestion the contingency of both grammar and God, a contingency entailed by inexhaustibility. But we cannot have a language without a grammar, though we could perhaps have a different one and though we might manage with other forms of semasis; we cannot have a language without its excesses. There are two reasons for this. One, every language is specific and contingent, imposing its character on those who inhabit it, all the while open indefinitely to modification and variation, following the principle of expressibility. Two, every language embodies a surplus of meaning that follows from its inexhaustibility. To serve its multifarious functions, every language must transcend any antecedent standards of perfection or determinateness, leading to one or another form of excessiveness if not to God. God is then one of the arbitrarinesses of our languages and dreams, and no language can avoid its own peculiar forms of arbitrariness.

What is arbitrary in any sign? We understand this arbitrariness or difference to be relevant to every being, not simply a function of judgment, but it is particularly evident in the limits of knowledge. To be is to possess certain ingredients and traits in certain locations or contexts, certain configurations, and other ingredients in other locations. There is a superfluity or arbitrariness that is essential to the inexhaustibility of every being. In signs, arbitrariness manifests the mediated nature of signification, of meaning, that no sign can refer or signify wholly naturally. What would be an entirely natural relation? Presumably, one that manifested only the signified, in all its glory, without deceit or distraction. But not only are signs and languages deceitful and distracting, that is, containing features of their own, essential to signification, that constitute the sign but not the signified, but such superfluity is inherent in any understanding, in all query and judgment. Local understanding, and there is no other, is inextricable from misunderstanding except through time and by continuing interrogation, contingently extricable. Reason demands its future, incessantly demands another point of view. To all of this we add that nature itself cannot be entirely natural, but is divided by multiple locality and inexhaustibility. These compose its plenitude.

Query is divided into different modes and forms, and located within judgment. Judgment is divided into manifold modes and forms, and is typically located within the locales of human experience. The play of judgment upon judgment is what we have called "semasis." To say that language is the embodiment of reason entails that reason as query possesses many other embodiments that are not language (though they may be expressive) and that the multiplicity of languages is the only possible embodiment of language. There is no language that we are unequivocally within any more than we are unequivocally within our bodies and our understandings. The different modes of query are the outsides or exteriors, the surpluses and heterogeneities, of any particular mode's inside; different languages and different non-linguistic forms of expression are the outsides of any inside of language, any particular language or language in general. It follows that such generic terms as query or language are not anything at all except divided into manifold modalities.

Our conclusion is that the grammar, the structure and articulation, of languages is a manifestation of locality and inexhaustibility. The definiteness of syntax is a qualified definiteness, qualified because it changes through time, because other languages possess other syntaxes, because there is arbitrariness in the very specificity of any particular syntax. Given any function of language, syntax is too specific to be a consequence of optimizing that function. Given the habitational and encompassing nature of languages, syntax is too definite and specific to be a consequence of the generality of language.

We are exploring the possibility that syntactic structure is part of the arbitrariness of languages, that its very definiteness is a superfluity. Though this may sound paradoxical, it is entailed by inexhaustibility. Similarly, the particular forms of cultural life of any tribe, the rituals and ceremonies, are not just utilitarian functions of social life, optimizing the production of food or social bonding, but take on a life of their own. This notion of a life of their own is analogous to that of contingent variation in evolutionary theory. Certain variations are not selected under adaptive pressure, but belong contingently to clusters that are selected as a group, but not item by item. Similarly, social forms may be grossly adaptive but articulated through highly definite and specific forms that manifest the uniqueness and identity of a particular culture.[48] Similarly again, there is a wide range of expressive forms in social life that are not adaptive or utilitarian as much as they are ornamental, defining status and reputation rather than productive or epistemic relations.[49] Syntax is required for the propositional and communicative functions of language, but once established, syntax itself becomes susceptible to ornamentation and expressive variations.

Thus, we not only inhabit our native language, with its differential phonemic elements and syntactical relations, but participate in its possibilities of variation in at least the following typical ways: (a) in the existence of thousands of other languages and sublanguages with different sound elements and syntactical relations; (b) in the invention of artificial languages; (c) in the complex variations introduced within linguistic expressions by regional and class variations, dialects, creoles, sign languages, etc.; (d) in literary variations and other stylistic developments, such as philosophy, history, and psychoanalysis; (e) in immense capacities for knowledge and expression only rudimentarily related to language, to syntax and grammar.[50]

Suppose the Tower of Babel had been completed, and there were a universal human language; suppose we were all taught Esperanto; suppose we lived under a world government; suppose ethnic, cultural, and linguistic variations disappeared. In a universal human language, we would find that we had reasons to say different things and that these required different linguistic styles, dialects, or sublanguages. The reason for this is the intimacy between our understanding of ourselves and things, personally and socially, and the languages we speak.[51] A universal Esperanto would fail to capture individual, political, and cultural variations. These variations might disappear: a world government is not unimaginable. But a successful world government would have to include within itself the prospect of unresolvable political conflicts; a successful world language would have to include the possibility of inexhaustible linguistic variations. These are only possibilities here, but possibilities that display the inexhaustibility of languages and of what they speak, the relation between languages and inventive variation, and the reciprocity of publicness and privateness in all our cultural conditions.

The specificity of grammar—structure, segmentation, articulation—marks the specificities of languages as contrasted with other forms of expression such as painting and sculpture or dance. The specificity of grammatical forms marks the generic structures of languages over their manifold variations: different languages and dialects, regional variations. The specificity of grammatical forms defines the project of understanding and interrogating the conditions of human life and experience together with its recurrences, especially the forms of understanding themselves. We may summarize this situation by an analogy: just as sexuality is rooted in biology, but is not determined by it, for the forms of sexuality are cultural and ornamental, political and expressive, languages are rooted in biology and utility, but not determined by them.[52] The structure of our bodies determines our sexuality only to the point that we regard it as an unavoidable condition; but we may respond in inexhaustibly manifold ways, and we find ourselves responding in socially constructed ways. The structure of our languages determines the forms of our understanding only insofar as we cannot escape some form of understanding, but we may also accept the project of calling any particular forms into question by interrogation and query, in or out of language.

We must avoid the conclusion that there are no specific syntactical and grammatical forms: to the contrary, we may expect such forms, even universal ones. Semantics entails syntax; function entails form; milieu entails specificity. Yet we must interpret these specific forms simultaneously if aporetically as defining limits and dissolving them, must recognize that limits circumscribe and open, that mediation is part of every limit, including the possibility of unmediatable conditions. This understanding of limitation is what we mean by locality. For a language to be local, and therefore inexhaustible, is not for it to be indeterminate in all or any respects, but to be determinate, specifically so in its grammar and structural forms, but even in the limits of what can be said in it, accompanied in every case by latitude, alternative possibilities, and heterogeneity. Specificity is not then only determinateness but indeterminateness as well; relative to any function of language, particular syntactical forms are both impedances and conditions of plenitude. Linguistic creativity both belongs to its structure and transcends it.

NOTES

1. John Lyons, *Introduction to Theoretical Linguistics* (Cambridge: Cambridge University Press, 1968), p. 133.

2. Ibid., p. 53.

3. See Heidegger, *On the Way to Language.*

4. See my discussion of the multiplicity of modes of being in *Transition to an Ordinal Metaphysics*; also in *Metaphysical Aporia and Philosophical Heresy, Inexhaustibility and Human Being*, and *Ring of Representation.*

5. Heidegger, *On the Way to Language.*

6. See note 4, above; see also chap. 6, below.

7. Merleau-Ponty characterizes this complex relationship as follows: "Language is neither thing nor mind, but it is immanent and transcendent at the same time. . . . One could say about language in its relations with thought what one says of the life of the body in its relations with consciousness. Just as one could not place the body at the first level, just as one could not subordinate it or draw it out of its autonomy (S. de Beauvoir), one can say only that language makes thought, as much as it is made by thought. Thought inhabits language and language is its body. This mediation of the objective and of the subjective, of the interior and of the exterior—what philosophy seeks to do—we can find in language if we succeed in getting close enough to it" (Maurice Merleau-Ponty, *Consciousness and the Acquisition of Language*, trans. Hugh Silverman [Evanston: Northwestern University Press, 1973], pp. 6, 102).

This "immanence," and the ways in which "language makes thought," are the specific structural and segmented traits of languages that both express (what we think of) things and influence them. The complementarity of language and thought requires that thought and language be in close affinity without losing their distinctiveness. Similarly, we are exploring the possibility of a complementary relationship between language and many particular languages in which language is both transcendent and immanent in every language without becoming the ground or essence of these languages.

8. "[L]anguage is patterned, or *structured* . . . on a number of different levels. In every language there are regular principles according to which sounds combine with one another to form words, and regular principles according to which the sounds may be pronounced somewhat

differently in different positions of the word or sentence. At the same time there are regularities in the formation of words and sentences from the point of view of their grammatical function . . ." (Lyons, *Introduction to Theoretical Linguistics*, pp. 36–37).

9. "Two phonetically different 'sounds' in the same environment which have the effect of distinguishing different words are recognized as different phonemes" (ibid., p. 112).

10. " 'It is difficult to demonstrate to a speaker of English that his pronunciation of an element like *p* does vary quite widely. But it is easy enough to demonstrate comparable irrelevant ranges of variation in other languages. For example, if we listen to a Menomini Indian . . . we hear in the middle of the word now a sound something like our *p* and now a sound more like our *b*. We hear the difference because English trains us to hear it. But the Menomini does not hear it, because in his language this particular difference of sound never functions to keep utterances apart . . .' " (Charles Francis Hockett, *A Course in Modern Linguistics* [New York: Macmillan, 1958], p. 25, quoted in James M. Edie, *Speaking and Meaning* [Bloomington: Indiana University Press, 1976], p. 25).

11. Some of these observations are related to insights expressed by Goodman in *Languages of Art*: if notational systems and languages are syntactically or semantically differentiated, there are nevertheless forms of expression and symbolism that are systematically ambiguous and "dense": we cannot differentiate the symbols into elements that have a grammar or a "compliance class."

12. A more useful expression of what we may conclude from such a view of linguistic creativity may be the following: "Every native speaker of a language is able to produce and understand, not merely those sentences which he has at some time heard before, but also an indefinitely large number of new sentences which he has never heard from other speakers of the language. . . . And the 'new' sentences will satisfy the same operational test of acceptability to other native speakers as 'old' sentences, which might have been produced simply from memory. They will exhibit the same regularities and can be accounted for by the same rules. In other words, it is the class of potential utterances which we must identify as the sentences of the language. And the number of potential utterances in any natural language is unlimited. Any given collection of utterances, however large, is but a 'sample' of this unlimited set of potential utterances. . . . It is the linguist's task therefore in describing a language to establish rules capable of accounting for the indefinitely large set of potential utterances which constitute the language. *Any linguistic description which has this capacity of describing actual utterances as members of a large class of potential utterances, is said to be* generative" (Lyons, *Introduction to Theoretical Linguistics*, p. 139).

13. "When we say that a grammar generates the sentences of a language

we imply that it constitutes a system of rules (with an associated lexicon) which are formulated in such a way that they yield, in principle, a decision-procedure for any combination of the elements of the language. . . . This second, more or less mathematical sense of the term 'generate' presupposes, for its applicability to grammar, a rigorous and precise specification of the nature of the grammatical rules and their manner of operation: it presupposes the *formalization* of grammatical theory" (ibid., pp. 156–57).

14. Lyons calls this "the indeterminacy of grammar": "In describing a given language, the linguist will draw the limits of grammaticality at a particular point. His decision to draw these limits at one place rather than another . . . will tend to be determined by two main factors. . . . Sooner or later, in his attempt to exclude the definitely unacceptable sentences by means of the distributional subclassification of their component words, the linguist will be faced with a situation in which he is establishing more and more rules, each covering very few sentences; and he will be setting up so many overlapping word-classes that all semblance of generality will be lost. . . . In fact, one does not have to go very far with the grammatical description of any language before one finds disagreement among native speakers about the acceptability of sentences generated by the rules tentatively established by the grammarian. There is therefore a real, and perhaps ineradicable, problem of indeterminacy with respect to acceptability and unacceptability.

"It would seem to follow from these considerations that the grammatical structure of any language is in the last resort indeterminate. . . . We may therefore restate as a general principle which governs all grammatical description . . . the following fact: whether a certain combination of words is or is not grammatical is a question that can only be answered by reference to a particular system of rules . . ." (ibid., pp. 152–53).

15. "Most writers on grammatical theory . . . would seem to reject this principle. They suggest that the grammatical structure of any language is determinate and is known 'intuitively' (or 'tacitly') by native speakers. This appears to be an unnecessarily strong assumption. [Such] 'intuitions' . . . are an important part of the linguist's data . . . But he need not assume that there will be any direct correspondence between the 'intuitions' of the speakers and the statements made by the linguist" (ibid., p. 154).

16. See chap. 2, note 30; also: "A grammar of a language purports to be a description of the ideal speaker-hearer's intrinsic competence. If the grammar is, furthermore, perfectly explicit—in other words, if it does not rely on the intelligence of the understanding reader but rather provides an explicit analysis of his contribution—we may (somewhat redundantly) call it a *generative grammar*" (Chomsky, *Aspects of the Theory of Syntax*, p. 3). This definition closely conforms to Lyons's

acknowledgment that the generativity of a grammar is a property of its formalization or theory more than of the language.

17. "[B]y a generative grammar I mean simply a system of rules that in some explicit and well-defined way assigns structural descriptions to sentences" (ibid., p. 8).

18. "Obviously every speaker of a language has mastered and internalized a generative grammar that expresses his knowledge of his language. This is not to say that he is aware of the rules of the grammar or even that he can become aware of them . . ." (ibid.).

19. "By reflecting on linguistic elements I can offer linguistic characterizations which do not record particular utterances but have a general character, deriving from the fact that the elements are governed by rules. The 'justification' I have for my linguistic intuitions as expressed in my linguistic characterizations is simply that I am a native speaker of a certain dialect of English and consequently have mastered the rules of that dialect" (Searle, *Speech Acts*, p. 13).

20. "An analogy: I know that in baseball after hitting the ball fair, the batter runs in the direction of first base, and not in the direction, say, of third base or the left field grand stand. . . . My knowledge is based on knowing how to play baseball, which is *inter alia* having internalized a set of rules" (ibid., p. 14).

21. "[I]f my conception of language is correct, a theory of language is part of a theory of action, simply because speaking is a rule-governed form of behavior" (ibid., p. 17).

22. "[C]onstitutive rules do not merely regulate, they create or define new forms of behavior. The rules of football or chess, for example, do not merely regulate playing football or chess, but as it were they create the very possibility of playing such games" (ibid., p. 33).

23. "[T]he semantic structure of a language may be regarded as a conventional realization of a series of sets of underlying constitutive rules, and . . . speech acts are acts characteristically performed by uttering expressions in accordance with these sets of constitutive rules" (ibid., p. 37).

24. "Remember that in general we don't use language according to strict rules—it hasn't been taught us by means of strict rules either. We, in our discussions on the other hand, constantly compare language with a calculus proceeding according to exact rules. This is a very one-sided way of looking at language" (Wittgenstein, *Blue and Brown Books*, p. 25).

25. "The picture we have of the language of the grown-up is that of a nebulous mass of language, his mother tongue, surrounded by discrete and more or less clear-cut language games, the technical languages" (ibid., p. 81).

26. "How does one explain to a man how he should carry out the

order, 'Go *this* way!' (pointing with an arrow the way he should go)? Couldn't this mean going the direction which we should call the opposite of that of the arrow? Isn't every explanation of how he should follow the arrow in the position of another arrow?" (ibid., p. 97). "What characterizes an order as such, or a description as such, or a question as such, etc., is—as we have said—the role which the utterance of these signs plays in the whole practice of the language. That is to way, whether a word of the language of our tribe is rightly translated into a word of the English language depends upon the role this word plays in the whole life of the tribe; the occasions on which it is used, the expressions of emotion by which it is generally accompanied, the ideas which it generally awakens or which prompt its saying, etc., etc." (ibid., pp. 102–103).

27. An explicit definition (or near-definition) of rules can be found in Margolis' *Persons and Minds*. "Rules must be instituted or at least develop in some recognizably social way; must be capable of being viably replaced by alternative systems of rules; must be capable of being followed and violated by beings themselves capable of recognizing that rules obtain and that rules are followed or violated; and must be capable of being conformed to and reformed or revised for reasons to which the beings affected subscribe." Margolis goes on to suggest that, "Conceivably, some relatively weak qualification under these conditions would count as rule-following behavior. But a theory of rules is inseparable from a theory of societal life in which common norms and purposes, criteria for discriminating conforming and non-conforming behavior, and evidence for a sufficiently advanced level of intelligence among the beings affected may be specified" (*Persons and Minds*, p. 115). Yet these conditions, important as they are, do not constitute a definition of rules precisely because they are mute on the distinction between practices and rules. Put another way, it is an important part of our common practice as human beings that we distinguish rules—for instance, the rules of chess—from other norms, whether legal, social, conventional, or individual. A New Year's resolution, however binding, is not the imposition of a rule (except in the sense that "as a rule" I usually do so and so). And this latter sense is the point at issue, distinguishing the usual practice from the regulative character of the rules of a game.

28. See note 7, above.

29. "The merit of semantic analysis, it seems to me, is that it has brought the structural totality of language to our attention and thereby has pointed out the limitations of the false ideal of unambiguous signs or symbols and of the potential of language for logical formalization. The great value of semantic analysis rests in no small part in the fact that it breaks through the appearance of self-sameness that an isolated word-sign has about it. . . . The concept of synonymity becomes more and more attenuated. Ultimately, it seems a semantic ideal emerges, which

stipulates that in a given context only one expression and no other is the right one.

"Accordingly, a certain limitation is placed on semantics. It is true that one can approach all natural languages guided by the idea of a total analysis of the semantic deep structure of language and can view these languages as forms in which language as such appears. But in so doing, one will find a conflict between the continuing tendency toward individualization in language and that tendency which is just as essential to language, namely, to establish meanings by convention.

Hermeneutical inquiry is based on the fact that language always leads behind itself and behind the façade of overt verbal expression that it first presents. . . . Let us turn first to that which is said in spite of not being said. . . . No statement simply has an unambiguous meaning based on its linguistic and logical construction as such, but, on the contrary, each is motivated. A question is behind each statement that first gives it its meaning" (Hans-Georg Gadamer, "Semantics and Hermeneutics," *Philosophical Hermeneutics*, trans. David E. Longe. [Berkeley and Los Angeles: University of California Press, 1976], pp. 83, 85, 88–89).

30. "[A]ctual speaking is more than the choice of means to achieve some purpose in communication. The language one masters is such that one lives within it, that is, 'knows' what one wishes to communicate in no way other than in linguistic form" (ibid., p. 87). "Language is by no means simply an instrument, a tool. For it is in the nature of the tool that we master its use, which is to say we take it in hand and lay it aside when it has done its service. . . . We never find ourselves as consciousness over against the world and, as it were, grasp after a tool of understanding in a wordless condition. Rather, in all our knowledge of ourselves and in all knowledge of the world, we are always already encompassed by the language that is our own" (ibid., p. 62).

31. Michel Foucault, "A Preface to Transgression," *Language, Counter-Memory, Practice*, ed. Donald F. Bouchard, trans. Donald F. Bouchard and Sherry Simon (Ithaca: Cornell University Press, 1977), pp. 33–34.

32. See my *Learning and Discovery*.

33. Especially in *On Grammatology* and *Speech and Phenomena and Other Essays on Husserl's Theory of Signs*, trans. David B. Allison, (Evanston: Northwestern University Press, 1973), where difference becomes *différance*, in "Differance," pp. 129–60.

34. See my "Translation and Similarity," and "Translation as Transgression."

35. This is a formulation of the principle of expressibility. See pp. 86–91, chap. 2.

36. Socrates describes the decline of his aristocracy as follows: "Hard in truth it is for a state thus constituted to be shaken and disturbed, but

since for everything that has come into being destruction is appointed, not even such a fabric as this will abide for all time, but it shall surely be dissolved, and this is the manner of its dissolution. Not only for plants that grow from the earth but also for animals that live upon it there is a cycle of bearing and barrenness for soul and body as often as the revolutions of their orbs come full circle, in brief courses for the short-lived and oppositely for the opposite. But the laws of prosperous birth or infertility for your race, the men you have bred to be your rulers will not for all their wisdom ascertain by reasoning combined with sensation, but they will escape them, and there will be a time when they will beget children out of season" (*Republic*, 546; p. 775).

See the discussion of politics in my *Inexhaustibility and Human Being* and *Locality and Practical Judgment*. See also *Metaphysical Aporia and Philosophical Heresy* and *Injustice and Restitution*.

37. "While we live wholly within a language, the fact that we do so does not constitute linguistic relativism because there is absolutely no captivity within a language—not even within our native language" (Gadamer, "The Universality of the Hermeneutical Problem," *Philosophical Hermeneutics*, pp. 15–16)

"The historical movement of human life consists in the fact that it is never utterly bound to any one standpoint, and hence can never have a truly closed horizon. . . . With the nuances of the linguistic views of the world, each one contains potentially within it every other one, ie every one is able to be extended into every other one. It is able to understand, from within itself, the "view" of the world that is presented in another language" (Gadamer, *Truth and Method*, pp. 271, 406).

38. Gadamer, *Truth and Method*, p. 403.

39. Ibid.

40. Luce Irigaray, *The Speculum of the Other Woman*, trans. Gillian C. Gill (Ithaca: Cornell University Press, 1985), p. 142. See chap. 6 for a detailed discussion of the political side of semasis, under the heading of "discourse." Irigaray pursues several different voices seeking to overthrow the hold of the law of grammar. A few examples from *This Sex Which is not One* are "The Looking Glass, from the Other Side," "The 'Mechanics' of Fluids," and "When Our Lips Speak Together."

41. Lyotard, *Differend*.

42. Heidegger, *On the Way to Language*, p. 63.

43. Ibid., p. 108.

44. Gadamer, *Philosophical Hermeneutics*, p. 3.

45. Gadamer, *Truth and Method*, p. 493. Also: "Hence language is the real medium of human being, if we only see it in the realm that it alone fills out, the realm of human being-together, the realm of common understanding, of ever-replenished common agreement—a realm as indispensable to human life as the air we breathe" (Gadamer, *Philosophical Hermeneutics*, p. 68).

"Language is the universal medium in which understanding itself is realized" (Gadamer, *Truth and Method*, p. 350).

"Language is not just one of man's possessions in the world, but on it depends the fact that man has a world at all" (ibid., p. 401).

"The phenomenon of understanding, then, shows the universality of human linguisticality as a limitless medium that carries *everything* within it—not only the 'culture' that has been handed down to us through language, but absolutely everything—because everything (in the world and out of it) is included in the realm of 'understandings' and understandability in which we move" (Gadamer, *Philosophical Hermenetics*, p. 25).

"Language is not a delimited realm of the speakable, over against which other realms that are unspeakable might stand. Rather, language is all-encompassing. There is nothing that is fundamentally excluded from being said . . ." (ibid., p. 67).

46. See my *Inexhaustibility and Human Being*.

47. See Introduction, note 5, and note 45, above.

48. Stephen Jay Gould, *The Panda's Thumb* (New York: Norton, 1980); see also Melvin Konner, *The Tangled Wing* (New York: Holt, Rinehart & Winston, 1982). But see my critique of the limits of Gould's understanding of contingency in *Injustice and Restitution*, chap. 6.

49. See Harré, *Social Being*; Goffman, *Relations in Public: Microstudies of the Public Order* (Harmondsworth: Penguin, 1972).

50. Again see Selfe, *Nadia*; Sacks, *Awakenings*, and Curtiss, *Genie*. All these studies indicate how powerful human forms of expression are, even where language "proper"—grammar—fails.

51. See Rom Harré, *Personal Being: A Theory for Individual Psychology* (Cambridge: Harvard University Press, 1984).

52. See my "The Limits of Sexuality."

4

KNOWLEDGE

THERE IS A POWERFUL TRADITION in philosophy, matched in our time by a glorification of scientific method, that locates understanding and meaning entirely within discourse and language, in a preferred, "proper" form. There is something both preposterous and irresistible in this view that reason and truth have preferred forms, and that the most privileged are to be found in language. Derrida calls such a view "logocentric," a label that would be more effective if it were not applied to the entire Western tradition, in which thought and speech have been as maligned as writing.[1]

The major goal of this chapter is to explore the fact that a primary function of languages is to be epistemic in the context of a pluralistic and multidimensional understanding of knowledge and truth. Among the subordinate purposes of this chapter is to develop further the argument that the structures of languages are in important respects in tension with their social and epistemic functions, that the varied functions of languages make a structural and grammatical account both essential and of limited value. Similarly, however, the multiplicity and diversity of functions of languages make an epistemic account of languages also of limited value. Between grammar and judgment, languages are aporetic. What must be added is that this aporia is a reflection of the extraordinary powers of languages, their ability to serve so many human functions well despite the continuing presence of obtrusive limits.

INTENSIONALITY

In order to have intensionality, we must have extensionality. Otherwise intensionality is but another surplus of meaning. Its nature and significance depend on its contrasts with extensionality. We have discussed the principle of intensionality and its epistemological significance. We have not included on our list of linguistic principles in Chapter 2 a comparable principle of extensionality. It is time to discuss the reasons for the omission and to rectify the oversight, for there are features of extensional views of language and propositional discourse that we cannot ignore.

If there are intensional contexts in which we cannot substitute identical expressions and preserve truth value, then there must analogously be extensional contexts in which substitution does preserve truth value. However, these may not be generic. To construe the relation as one of dependent contrast obscures several important considerations. One is that the substitution of identical expressions preserving truth values may not accommodate a systematic criterion, so that we may sometimes make such substitutions, sometimes not, without a general criterion establishing which contexts are extensional and which are intensional. Extensionality may be a function of context more than form. A second is that we are presupposing a criterion of identity independent of intensionality and extensionality, and such independence may not be defensible. A third consideration is whether it is reasonable to expect entirely formal criteria to establish semantic relations involving truth and falsity.

There are other considerations. We may begin with the notion of extension. Let us describe words and expressions as "labels" and that to which they apply as "objects." If we suppose that some labels have extensions, we presuppose more than syntactic domains and compliance classes (to use Goodman's terminology),[2] namely a stability of denotation defined by a strong principle of identity. It is interesting to note that Goodman is required, by his expanded notion of world-versions in the context of an extensional theory, to introduce a view of metaphor in which any semantic domain may be expanded into any other domain, figuratively or metaphorically. Thus, we may effectively have our cake and eat it too, since we preserve extensionality while also presupposing that every label may have inexhaustible extensions without ambiguity.[3]

It is frequently claimed that extensionality is required by Leibniz's law, essentially a formal, not a substantive criterion. Yet there are at least two related considerations that mitigate the force of this position. First, we presuppose a certain ontology in an extensional theory, an ontology not only of the "individuals" that are the extensions of the labels we employ in describing them, but an ontology of both individuals and the kinds of beings that individuals are taken to be: stable, reidentifiable, and without qualification identical with themselves, therefore individuals that are not inexhaustible.[4] More is at stake in extensional theories than logical criteria, more than the effectiveness and utility of logical systems. What is presupposed is that the identity (identifiability and reidentifiability) of the individuals to which labels apply are stable and independent of the labels themselves.

Second, in an extensional theory, while every label, with its extensions, is indeterminate at its margins, there always is a relatively stable core. Every concept is indeterminate with respect to certain applications, to some region of its extension. But there is always a core of settled cases, the precisely and unambiguously determined extension of a label. A label, we say, "applies" to certain objects. Every expression that includes labels is satisfied by certain objects. These are its extension. Yet every application is vague to some degree; every extension is indeterminate in some ways, and fortunately, we may say, since without this indeterminateness of extension or denotation, we could never make novel discoveries. The creativity and novelty of thought and language work against purely extensional theories.

We may say that the extension of a concept or label is a function of the rules of language and denotation. Yet rules do not interpret themselves, and there is an important sense in which even the value of *pi* is indeterminate.[5] An extensional theory is too much a "mirroring" theory, the logical theory on which a mirroring epistemology depends. If we accept a mirroring theory, in which words and propositions mirror the way things are, then it is plausible to hold that the things are the extensions of the words. We presuppose that vagueness and indeterminateness of reference are defects of language. Alternatively, however, we may suppose that things do not in general lend themselves to determinate reference, a consequence of the inexhaustibility of both things and language.

There is a wonderful passage in *Gulliver's Travels* where Swift satirizes an extensional view of language. In the grand academy of Lagado, there is

> a scheme for entirely abolishing all words whatsoever; . . . since words are only names for *things*, it would be more convenient for all men to carry about them such *things* as were necessary to express the particular business they are to discourse on. . . .
> Another great advantage proposed by this invention was that it

would serve as an universal language to be understood in all civilised nations . . . [III.5].

This is only the second of the Lagadan schemes: "The first project was to shorten discourse by cutting polysyllables into one, and leaving out verbs and participles, because in reality all things imaginable are but nouns."

Swift here satirizes both all great schemes to improve languages by eliminating their excesses and any identity theory of the relations of words to things. If we accept an identity theory, then either words may somehow be identical with things, as a naming theory of nouns might suggest, one name for each object, or only the things themselves can be identical with themselves. But things are not knowledge of themselves and cannot symbolize themselves (without introducing arbitrariness, since if a thing stands for itself, then it can do so only in certain respects). It is the differences between words and things, symbols and referents, that introduce intensionality, and without intensionality and difference, there cannot be knowledge. Once we have such differences, however, then any knowledge we have of any object can only be in certain respects, and the respects are inexhaustible.

Swift suggests that in order to transact any complex business in the manner described, one would have to carry about a great many things. A more accurate description is that either one could not do very much with such a language or things themselves would, here, be a language, effectively bearing the complexity of a language. A common view of language suggests that we require it to make present what is absent. On this view, making things themselves present would be an effective alternative. The deeper point, however, is that even when present, things are not altogether present, that is, knowable in all respects in virtue of their presence. The reason for this is that presence is not as such intelligible. Nor are things entirely available under the particular circumstances in which they are present. We frequently know little about the objects that surround us. We frequently can do relatively little with the things surrounding us. We can express what we know through language, but not through things themselves, because there is a distance to presence that utterance can overcome, but only through its own forms of distance.[6]

Are things so determinate that we may refer to them determinately as the extensions of words? Are words so determinate that they are capable of referring to things altogether determinately? What is evident is that every thing may be known, described, or represented in countless different ways. In addition, in every language, any truth may be expressed in innumerable ways. Leibniz's law does not settle the issue but rather begs the relevant questions. Extensionality, identity, and reference are all interrelated. In this sense, we presuppose both an ontology and an epistemology when we adopt an extensional theory of language.

There are tables with four legs and a horizontal surface. There are also three-legged tables, multiplication and water tables; there are drafting tables and low tables that we use as benches. One description of this state of affairs is that the word "table" is ambiguous; another is that there is no fixed extension of any word or label, that the very ordinariness of the word "table" gives it a complex, largely indeterminate extension. The interpretation that emphasizes ambiguity presupposes an extensional view of language that fits the facts less than it bends them to its prior view.[7] We have noted the phrase Wittgenstein uses to describe ordinary language: it is a "nebulous mass" with technical languages or language games attached.[8] Another image we may employ is that ordinary language is a snarl of references inseparable from intensionality and indeterminateness of reference, resolvable in real conditions of communication and understanding by context and by technical and ideal simplifications. If we follow the latter image, which may also be an oversimplification, then we must define a theory in which it is possible to simplify linguistic utterances by context and practice, albeit proximately or temporarily. We will explore a semasic field theory that includes propositional and other semasic cores.

We have not, however, finished with extensionality. What is presupposed in an extensional theory, even one that supports only contextual extensionality, is both a determinate ontology and a foundational epistemology. The ontology is required by the assumption that words have extensions, that is, that a definite class of objects, things, or individuals defines the denotation of a label. Suppose instead that labels in some respects constitute the ontology in which they function, that is, that we cannot define the extensions of labels except by using other labels, and that therefore, extensions are but a certain way of interpreting how we understand the references of labels. Suppose that a language less matches or applies to things than that it suits our purposes and activities, including epistemic and communicative activities.[9] A language plays so many different roles, fills so many different purposes, and participates in so many different kinds of activities, that it is inexhaustible, in both form and activity.

Must we, once we allow for the limitations of extensional theories, carry the position through to an unqualified relativism, without stability? The question is how the relativism is to be qualified. In the extreme, the claim is that we cannot agree, and have no good reasons to agree, on any accounts of the referents of labels, but simply give an account from within a language, one that cannot be understood except within that language. However, we do understand what people say in other languages, just as we understand what they say in our own, even if we sometimes find what they say and how they say it rather peculiar. This peculiarity and alienness is sometimes regarded as the problem that a theory of meaning must overcome. Such an interpretation is analogous to the view that an adequate theory of knowledge must overcome skepticism. Yet skepticism has a genuine function, if in most forms it is overstated: to bring to our attention the limits within any understanding. It is overstated when it suggests that the presence of such limits bars understanding. To the contrary, understanding depends on both limits and the limits of those limits. Similarly, that shared communication is incompatible with strangeness is implausible. Rather, sharing and alienness go together within any communication, however intimate. That is how we understand heterogeneity.

We return to the arbitrariness of signification from the standpoint of the hypothesis that arbitrariness is not a defect that characterizes the inadequacies of meanings but is intrinsic within the condition that there may be understanding at all. Part of this insight is found in Gadamer's version of hermeneutic theory: that only one side of the limits of understanding is expressed in emphasizing the limits of horizons. Every limit is permeable, but it is still a limit. Thus, we do understand what others say and mean, even over distant times and places, but never completely. To understand is to understand incompletely. More precisely, the notion of completeness here is both impracticable and unintelligible. Things are inexhaustible, referents and labels both, in that they may always be known in other ways, told about in other words, thought about in other forms. This condition is intrinsic to things as well as to understandings and words: an ontology that would accommodate extensionality as well as intensionality is one that regards extensions as inexhaustible.

An extensional view of language requires us to hold that labels have denotations or referents, that we can have a propositional theory of truth only if we can understand what propositions may be true about, in some respects determinately and unambiguously. Intensionality indicates that the form of propositions, therefore of any linguistic expressions, is not the sole determinant of either their truth values or their truth conditions. We have seen that we may interpret intensionality as a consequence of the many ways in which we may express any truth and of the many truths that are relevant, in extremely complex ways, to any thing, natural and human. Thus, intensionality is a consequence of epistemological inexhaustibility. It may be regarded as a form of arbitrariness only if we disallow the possibility of unqualified arbitrariness, that is, if we complement intensionality by extensionality. The combination of the two is expressed by inexhaustibility.[10]

Every truth may be expressed in many different ways, in many different languages and in many different propositions (and other expressions) within a given language. Shall we suppose that there might be a wholly unambiguous language, a language without synonyms or alternative expressions? Is the multiplicity a feature of our inability to agree on a common language, or is the multiplicity of languages and of alternative expressions within any given language a function of the inexhaustibility of truth and meaning? We have concluded that it is only because we are able to express a given truth in many different forms, producing intensionality, that we can express it precisely in any form. Precision is a function of semasic heterogeneity.

Every label is extensional, if only proximately and by context. This is shown by our ability to introduce new labels, to develop new concepts, and to change the meanings of traditional words. Words are indeed about particular things, have particular referents. But that we should go further, and require logical and formal criteria that relate reference to form, is another matter. For though every label is extensional, every label is equally intensional, that is, replaceable by other labels with almost the same extensions (but not quite, and we cannot "quite" define the differences) and where substitution does not quite preserve truth value. Moreover, every description of the truth value is itself intensional. Ascription of truth values is epistemic, and every epistemic language is both implicitly and explicitly intensional.[11]

This relation between intensionality and ascription is inherent in every language that can include itself. Intensionality is a condition of all forms of knowledge rich enough to include themselves, all forms of knowledge rich enough to contain an epistemology. Every ascription of a proposition known or a truth affirmed is intensional. But this is to recognize many ways of knowing anything, with no unconditioned privilege to any way of knowing something or expressing that knowledge.

Among their other uses and activities, languages are mediums of understanding and expression. There are other such mediums, such as gesture and pictorial imagery, and forms of thought that are not linguistic. But far more important, and decisive in the present context, is the multiplicity of languages and of synonyms within a language. From the present point of view, synonymy is equivalent with translatability: any truth, anything known, may be expressed in many ways, in many languages and many forms in a given language, many of which are equivalent in certain respects, but none of which are entirely equivalent in all respects. An extensional language would be unable to express subtle semasic variations where there were no extensional differences.

Could there be a wholly extensional language? Such a language could not describe itself nor ascribe linguistic competences. Moreover, such a language would presuppose precisely those linguistic and epistemic competences that it could not itself describe. It would presuppose, for example, that those who developed and employed the language to make claims could have employed alternative labels. It would presuppose further that labeling errors are possible—effectively, that alternative forms of expression are relevant even in an extensional language. It would presuppose the kinds of alternatives it could not itself describe extensionally. Finally, one can exclude near synonyms in a purely extensional language only by prohibition, that is, presupposing the possibility of synonymy while legislating its denial.

There is, therefore, and can be, no wholly extensional language in the sense that intensionality is excluded in principle. We could invent a wholly extensional language, but intensionality would both surround it and permeate it as a possibility in every utterance. There is, however, no wholly intensional language, for words and labels do apply to things and propositions assert truths about things. Intensionality and extensionality express the heterogeneity within languages that is the manifestation of inexhaustibility, the co-presence of determinateness and indeterminateness that engenders the arbitrariness of language. The immediate question is how we are to incorporate this arbitrariness and indeterminateness of meaning into a theory of language that accommodates semantic reference and propositional ascription.

SEMASIS

Saussure's structural view situates every linguistic element within a system of differences. We must reject Saussure's notion of pure differences as a misrepresentation of the differential character of a semasic system; we must also reject the synchronic assumptions that define his view of differences. Instead, we emphasize that difference is as much a condition of being and judgment as sameness. Saussure's view depends heavily on the assumption that a unique system can be defined, *langue*, that is the object of a linguistic science. Our analysis has shown that a language is multiply, inexhaustibly situated, that no one system defines a language, that *langue* is a conceptual aberration, and especially that no nontemporal view of a language can be adequate to it although a synchronic perspective may provide valuable insights concerning it. Every linguistic element inhabits a complex field of similarities and differences, a "linguistic field." Every sign, linguistic and otherwise, similarly inhabits a complex field of similarities and differences, a "semasic field." Such a field is pervasively temporal, diachronic, but not without important synchronic relations.[12]

We understand the term "semasis" to represent signs and meanings in general, to be equivalent to judgment following judgment inexhaustibly. The coinage has an etymological basis, and it avoids the complex and in many cases misleading traditional connotations of a narrowly semantic view of meaning on the one hand and of semiotics or a general theory of signs on the other. The notion of semasis is elaborated by the notion of "semiates," which function semasically, and "semasors," who utilize semiates and inhabit semasic fields. Finally, we avoid a narrow view of discourse, restricted to propositional discourse, and define discourse generically, based on a multiplicity of modalities of judgment.

Our argument to this point has been that languages are inexhaustible, that they pervade human experience and, by extension, pervade whatever human beings do and think, including their views of what surrounds them. This pervasiveness does not suggest equivalence: language is not equivalent with being or human being, but pervades any conception we may have of them and of any relation we may take toward them. Similarly, the pervasiveness of language is not to be understood to entail that language is identical' with semasis. There are imagistic and visual semiates, musical semiates, thought and practice that are not in words. This pervasiveness conjoined with difference is the mark of inexhaustibility. Every being and every semiate is inexhaustible. Every language and linguistic semiate is similarly inexhaustible.

The inexhaustibility of semasis can be expressed in terms of a multiplicity of semasic fields. Every semiate inhabits inexhaustibly many inexhaustible fields of semasic relations, including whatever contributes to its semasic functioning. We emphasize that nothing is in principle irrelevant to such semasic functioning, that anything can be an ingredient of a semasic field. Every discovery we make about some of the obscure complexities of human life—dreams, memory, childhood experiences, self-deception, and so forth—displays undisclosed semasic elements and relations. The semasic field of a linguistic symbol, then, includes not only the structural relations, syntagmatic and associative, that for Saussure define the value of linguistic elements, but anything that can be relevant to the semasic functions of a semiate, diachronically and semantically. This includes other semiates that are related by similarities and differences—"rook" and "crook"—but also semiates that have more propositional relevance—castles and crows, turrets and cheats. We need not regard semasic relevance as dependent on a system of language, for similarities and differences are relevant even within a "nebulous mass" of relations, a snarl of associations, an inexhaustible network of connections. And we need not regard semasic relevance as restricted to either languages or some specific domain of signs, for epistemic and propositional relevance involve objects and things. That is, things surrounding us as well as prominent and subtle features of our experience contribute to semasic relations and are included within semasic fields.

If the inexhaustibility of thought and meaning leads us to the notion of a multiplicity of semasic fields, the capacity of words to take on literal meanings and of utterances to possess syntactic properties requires us to avoid an undifferentiated view of such fields. Thus, it is implausible either (a) to restrict our view of semasis to propositional utterances or to grammatically well-formed strings when many common semasic relations of words are neither propositional nor grammatical; or (b) to ignore the structural, grammatical, and propositional capacities of languages as irrelevant when there is so strong a sense of both form and literalness in many linguistic utterances. What should be avoided is too narrow a view of what is primary or most fundamental in a language.

We may therefore consider the idea of propositional or literal cores within a more complex semasic field, emphasizing here a linguistic semasic field. Every semiate inhabits a semasic field including whatever is relevant to its functioning as a semiate. This field, with its inexhaustible range of relevance, is what makes creativity and invention both possible and desired within a language or other mode of semasis. Yet while invention is both desirable and expected in a language, every language has other conditions to meet, in certain contexts, of accuracy, precision, structure, and synonymy. Again, similarity and difference are generic categories: languages and other semasic forms are pervaded by both similarities and differences. The former are required by repeatable truths and recurrent understandings; both are required by communication and acts of language, that is, by the possibility that utterances can serve intentional as well as epistemic functions.

It follows that every semasic field includes a multiplicity of semasic cores, some of which are typically semantic or propositional. We are emphasizing the inclusion of multiple cores within a multiplicity of larger semasic fields to express the inexhaustibility of semasic relations. Typically, the semasic field includes variable and indeterminate relations at its boundaries. Such a view is distorted to the extent that it suggests that the semantic cores are entirely determinate or that they are not the source of the variability that may transform the entire semasic field or render its peripheries indeterminate. We may consider, for example, well-defined, technical scientific semiates, scientific concepts that, under the pressure of anomalous experiments, dynamically transform an entire network of semasic relations, theoretical connections, and semantic implications. We must suppose, then, that semasic fields, centers and peripheries, and semasic cores, including propositional cores, are in constant dynamic interaction. Grossly speaking, the semasic field is in dynamic movement, the propositional core frequently more stable. But this difference can be overstated and exaggerated, since semantic relations can sometimes be placed under greater stress, becoming the focus of violent transformations while the semasic field may be ruled by inertia.

There are other cores than propositional cores; there are multiple semasic fields for any semiate, a function of human personal and social life. Different semasic cores are the relatively limited spheres of semasic relations that enable a semiate to function in a particular way, relative to a particular mode of judgment. For example, there is a communicative or practical core of every semiate that inhabits the fields of human practice and purposes. Each mode of judgment is defined by certain limits, certain constraints, and a semiate can function within that mode only insofar as it meets those conditions. Thus, there is something to the notion of a "literal" meaning of a word that plays a role in assertive judgment: the meanings that inhabit a propositional or semantic core. Every semasic field contains one or more propositional cores: different cores, relative to each other, define "ambiguous" extensions of the word. Yet many semasic, even semantic, relations operate throughout the semasic field, especially at the periphery, where semasic transformations are involved. There is a dynamic relation among cores and peripheries that continuously produces abnormal discourse.[13] The view that every core is well-defined, altogether determinate, in an ordinary or ideal language, is an implausible view of the complexity of languages and semasic relations in and out of languages.

There are many semantic cores; there are also cores relative to every mode of judgment, and relative to many subordinate forms of judgment. Words are used to exhort and beseech, to persuade and impel, and some of the most effective rhetorical devices involve semasic relations quite different from propositional relations. There are, then, practical as well as propositional cores, for example, moral and political cores. And there may be metaphorical or figurative cores as well, responsive to the constraints of poetic discourse.

Generally speaking, poetic and rhetorical discourse function more at the peripheries of semasic fields than at the cores. This is especially true of poetic discourse, which exploits resonances throughout the semasic field. But to suppose that any semasic figure can inhabit the entire semasic field is unacceptable, largely equivalent to the view that the only meaning of a word could be its literal meaning, its extension.[14] What is required for meaning is semasic determinateness, and every semasic relation, to function semasically, within judgment, demands limits of some kind determined in part by its particular functions. Every such limit is indeterminate as well as determinate. It follows that meaning depends as much on semasic indeterminateness as determinateness. One of the fundamental differences between propositional and fabricative judgment, between science and art for example, is that the conditions of propositional assertion—precision, rigor, verifiability, communicability—constrict the relevant semasic relations to a relatively determinate core stable over time and person. The stability is nevertheless limited and temporary: scientific concepts undergo major transformations through time and from theory to theory, and every new hypothesis and theory is a function of semasic indeterminateness. Even scientific and technical concepts are conditioned and qualified by the dynamically variable and inexhaustible semasic fields in which they are situated.

Semasic relations vary with modalities of judgment and with time. These variations are represented by manifold semasic cores and by dynamic variation. Semasic relations are also proximately stable, over time and persons. This stability is represented by the limits and determinants of semasic fields and cores. The proximateness of the stability is doubly qualified, by the variability of semasic relations and by the inexhaustibility of any shared meaning. What is required for common understanding, among different persons or at different times by one person, need be no particular semasic connections, no particular extension for example. The presence of semasic cores that stabilize the common understanding of words by native inhabitants of a language does not entail or require that any core among different inhabitants be precisely the same in any definable respects. Similarly, the different languages of different cultural and social inhabitants do not entail that they cannot understand each other. Common understanding can be interpreted as calling for common cores, but the commonality of both understanding and semasis is a proximate commonality, in certain respects and among dynamically variable wider relations. Moreover, understanding depends on heterogeneity as much as on homogeneity, however local or proximate. Different understandings enrich any single understanding.

Even if we pursue an extensional analysis of literal or propositional meanings in the semantic cores, we find ourselves led to multiple cores and wider semasic relations in which every semantic core must be suspended if we are to be able to acquire understanding of it and to modify it. These demands are closely related, since understanding in any but a mirroring view is transformative in some respects, among and within semasic relations; it depends on heterogeneity. We cannot learn the meaning of any concept that contains an entirely determinate or unmodifiable propositional core; we cannot employ any concept without being able to modify its meaning.[15] None but open, partly indeterminate concepts can be acquired. This openness and indeterminateness is expressed here in terms of dynamically variable, partly overlapping, heterogeneous semasic fields. The principle, essential to hermeneutic theory, that mediation among horizons is always possible, that no horizon is closed, also entails a partly indeterminate semasic field for any semiate. Horizons must be permeable from within and without if understanding is possible. Concepts must be similarly permeable as well as modifiable if we can come to understand them. This overlapping and blurring of semasic relations is essential to every understanding of any semiate, both by the novice, first acquiring understanding, and by the expert, whose greater understanding is marked by the novel relations and limits he imposes on an established semasic field. We can acquire an understanding of novel concepts because no concept can be entirely new even insofar as it is heterogeneous. We acquire an understanding of any new semasic relation by modifying old relations, by establishing new connections. One of the greatest weaknesses of the traditional analytic-synthetic distinction is that it obscures the fact that every novel insight requires transformations in the wider semasic field if not within any particular semasic core.

It is essential that semasic fields and cores be inexhaustibly permeable, open to modification and transformation. Nevertheless, if we begin with the variability and overlapping of semasic fields, we are led by understanding and communication to the proximately stable cores that common understandings require. Nevertheless, common understandings cannot entail identical understandings. Semasic fields and cores are variable by individual and by social group. Put another way, commonality of understanding and commonality of core do not and cannot entail identity of core, or rather, returning to our generic understanding of the relation of similarity to difference, the cores are similar enough for common understanding despite and because of their differences and heterogeneities.

Semasic fields are not only socially and culturally variable, accommodating a modest reading of the Sapir-Whorf hypothesis,[16] but are person- and group-variable as well. For a given group, any semiate inhabits a semasic field, proximately stable over that group (though not synchronically stable, out of time). But for any member of that group, every semiate inhabits a uniquely personal range of fields and cores defined by personal experiences and associations. We may call these the "idiosemic" fields and cores. Idiosemic variation is not incompatible with commonality and agreement, though it characterizes and qualifies them, but coexists with them as one of the dimensions of semasis. Legislation at the semantic core cannot overcome the idiosemic variations that emerge as a consequence of the personal histories and social groups to which individuals who acquire technical concepts belong. Wittgenstein employs the notion of a language game to express the nature of constricted concepts. He seems to neglect the extent to which every technical language, or language game, belongs to many practices and is variable with many persons, many idiosemic fields. To recapitulate the above point, it is idiosemic variation, along with other semasic variations, that makes discoveries possible. If semasic agreement were complete and unqualified identity, we could never acquire novel concepts.

Semasic variation and semasic stability are complementary dimensions of semasis. The agreement required within any language for common understanding is limited by personal experiences and by the impossibility of defining any semasic core without complex wider resonances. Personal and social variations are found in languages, especially among regional styles and dialects. But they are also found in personal styles of expression and in group variations within a region—street talk as against pulpit talk. Far more important, however, are the contextual variations that make both communication and understanding possible and risky. The efforts required to make understanding secure—tone of voice, gesture, emphasis—make it insecure. Security and insecurity, stability and risk, are as intimately related in languages and other symbolic forms as are commonality and idiosemic variation, far less as antagonists than dimensions of an inexhaustible relation.

JUDGMENT

Whatever a person produces that involves selection and validation is a judgment. Whatever constitutes the milieu in which judgment transpires, determining the forms and conditions of validation, is a perspective. The perspective that constitutes the forms and conditions of meaning, of semiates in relation to judgment, is the semasic field. Judgment, perspective, and semasis are inseparable notions.

An important question is how we are to understand validation, or truth. It is not to be understood in terms that violate the principle of latitude. Every judgment maintains within itself a range of alternatives that do not vanish or cease to be relevant when it has been validated, when it has itself been judged. Latitude is essential not only to the capacity to err but to the alternatives that mark the selections inherent in judgment. The differences relevant to every similarity, the arbitrarinesses in every insight, are not only invalid alternatives, but include other valid alternatives. Any truth can be expressed in another way. Judgment entails latitude, the latitude inherent in alternatives for any validation. Nevertheless, the presence of alternatives is always accompanied by stable conditions.

There are two dimensions of judgment inherent in validation. One expresses the norms and determinations inherent in any epistemic activity. Every judgment needs to be distinguishable from other judgments in relevant respects, depends on relatively stable conditions of conception, perception, distinction, and discrimination, and is subject to norms of validation, to tests and evaluations. The other dimension expresses the latitude inherent in judgment, the relevance of alternatives and possibilities, of sources of error but also of inspiration. The first, related to necessity, may be called "compulsion." In the voice of language, we may call it "stillness," the irrelevance and unavailability of possibilities. We may call the second "latitude," related to what has traditionally been called "convention."[17] In the voice of language, we call it "polyphony," the relevance of alternatives in any situation, the play of language's music. Stillness and polyphony are ontological conditions of any local being. They express a functional, local interpretation of actuality and possibility.[18] They do not pertain uniquely to judgment and validation, but pertain

there in striking and unmistakable ways, expressing the inseparability of settledness and openness in judgment and truth. Stillness
and polyphony are dimensions of being and judgment. There
cannot be more stillness or less polyphony, only the particular
forms that are relevant in a particular situation.

The relevant principle is that every judgment is both settled and
open, limited and unlimited, in certain respects and ways, that
nothing in human life that may be considered judgment (and this
includes all but the most rudimentary and routine events), is
settled, without alternatives, or open, without settled conditions.
Judgments must be selected from relevant alternatives and must be
testable under some forms of necessity: evidence, argument, fit,
role in human life, or other forms of judgment. Latitude and
normativeness, polyphony and stillness, are dimensions of judgment, two complementary ways in which judgments function in
order to be epistemic.

A man stumbles over a stone, but may wave his arms about or
keep them at his side, may exclaim or fall silently. A woman is
nervous at having to deliver an important talk, but knows many
ways of responding to and controlling her anxieties: thinking
about them, seeking distractions, practicing at home, performing
in front of her friends. Diseases strike us without warning, but we
may both seek to avoid them and respond to them in different
ways. Judgment, here, is the condition of truth, and virtually
everything human beings do, whatever they perform, think, feel,
believe, construct, or combine, is a judgment, filled with stillness
and polyphony. Other creatures also judge. Judgment here is less
the mark of human being than of truth in its many heterogeneous
forms.

Language is clearly judgment—to some, perhaps mistakenly,
the paradigmatic form of judgment. In any case, the fact that every
label may be changed to another without destroying reference if
conforming to certain public norms is not a sign of the unique
latitude of language but, more generally, of the availability of
polyphonic alternatives in every judgment. Every proposition may
be uttered in another way, in another language or even within a
given language. There are no synonyms with identical semasic
fields or sentences that bear no significant differences.

Among the preeminent forms of multiplicity and latitude in
relation to language are the different modalities of judgment. We
have identified several: there may be many more produced by

division and combination. Query is the source of inexhaustibly manifold forms of validation and modes of judgment. But at the least, there are the modes of propositional, practical, and fabricative judgment. All are epistemic in their selectivity and concern for truth, though only some judgments are valid and only some are the result of query.

There are propositional judgments in linguistic form, but also propositional judgments in other forms, gestures of pointing, drawings and diagrams. Goodman offers compelling arguments to support a view of other forms of judgment as symbolic, in the sense described here, semasic and propositional.[19] Notational and representational systems, diagrams, drawings, all can be propositional, with syntactic and semantic properties. The question is whether languages possess unique symbolic or epistemic properties. Goodman suggests otherwise. His emphasis on reference entails that all knowledge is about what a symbol refers to. All knowledge is effectively referential and transitive, therefore propositional. Such an approach is valuable in expanding the range of propositional judgment to other forms of expression than languages but is limited in neglecting the epistemic nature of other modes of judgment.

The multiple functions of linguistic utterances that prohibit us from treating a language as any particular kind of object or instrument include the multiple modalities of judgment, with the provisos that every utterance may take on any modality of judgment, may be interpreted in terms of any mode of truth, that every mode is effectively pervasive throughout thought and experience, and that such pervasive modalities are nevertheless not to be identified with each other. They exceed and supplement each other. We inhabit language, as we inhabit thought and experience, not in the sense that we are enclosed in them, closed off from what includes them, but in the sense that they pervade our lives and constitute conditions for further life and judgment, in inexhaustibly manifold ways. Heterogeneity, an essential condition of locality, is manifested within languages in the multiply irreducible modes of judgment that every utterance serves, among the irreducible multiplicity of languages, and among the different modes of judgment and thought that pervasively overlap but are also pervasively different from each other.

Several things follow. One is that a propositional linguistic utterance cannot be propositional only. A second is that propositional judgment and query cannot be restricted to language, but are relevant throughout judgment. A part of the first principle is captured in speech-act theory in which utterances serve practice and accomplish tasks as much as they express propositions. We promise, insult, persuade, interest, and intimidate through linguistic utterances. Here, we must consider the distinction between a language and linguistic utterances very carefully, for only utterances accomplish tasks: a language does not do so. A speech-act theory is a theory of utterance, albeit a truncated theory. Thus, a third conclusion is that Language is a misleading notion based on a narrow sense of what is common among linguistic utterances. There is no linguistic competence that is distinguishable from performance: rather, there are multiple forms of performance, all the modes of judgment expressible in linguistic forms, and there are potentially inexhaustibly many such forms, such performances. A narrow view of Language results in abrogating the inexhaustibility of linguistic utterances, all the while ostensibly based on the inexhaustible creativity of language. This creativity is an inexhaustible creativity of judgment and of human experience manifested and realized in linguistic form, but not in language alone.

Every linguistic utterance is a judgment; many judgments are expressed in linguistic form, but many are not. Gesture, drawing, music, other semasic forms are quite as inexhaustible as language. But one of the attributes of inexhaustibility is that specificity is as relevant as pervasiveness, that each inexhaustible form is unique, though it may be as pervasive as others. What we can express through music and the plastic arts, even restricted to propositional judgment, is different from what we can express through language; what we can express in any language, even restricted to propositional judgment, is different from what we can express in any other language. This is one of the major reasons why we continually invent technical languages, jargons, both to stabilize the variations inevitably present in natural languages and to manifest the unavoidable differences among any languages, including technical languages.

In every semasic field there is at least one and usually many semantic cores expressing the pervasive capacity of every semiate to function propositionally. This follows from the pervasiveness of propositional judgment. It appears to follow also that there is no word without a "literal meaning," where we interpret this literal meaning as propositional or semantic in nature. Such an interpretation is plausible, but it is far from conclusive, for there are other semasic cores delimited by particular judgmental modalities. Using a list presented by Searle, but drawn from Austin, who suggests that there are over a thousand such expressions in English, the following all depend on the presence of a relevant semasic core, propositional or practical: stating, describing, asserting, warning, remarking, commenting, commanding, ordering, requesting, criticizing, apologizing, censuring, approving, welcoming, promising, objecting, demanding, arguing.[20]

In addition, there are practical semasic functions that do not appear to require explicit semasic cores, for example, arousing a crowd to action, to storm the Bastille. Such acts are sometimes called demagogic, as if to display their rational inadequacies. But this assumes two premises, both implausible: that there is a standard form of rationality from which political rhetoric departs, and that individuals are moved to action (or should be moved to action) by particular rational and expressive forms. Political rhetoric typically utilizes every means available, and we expect it to do so. We act not only based on what we believe and know, but on what we feel, what arouses our emotions. What we require is explicit acknowledgment that emotions are not simply servants of reason, but forms of thought, themselves capable of reason.[21] Political and moral persuasion utilize a wide range of semasic relations, and there is no obviously narrower core with a definite semasic function. This may be one of the important differences between propositional and practical linguistic functions: the former appears always to require a semantic core; the latter sometimes is effective without such a core, and functions largely at the periphery.

This differentiation of core and periphery is particularly relevant to art. Poetry certainly, and even prose, functions primarily at the semasic periphery, as does most everyday speech. "How are ya!" "What's up?" "Take care."[22] Metaphorical and figurative language frequently involve core interactions, but function largely at the periphery, sometimes a sound periphery, sometimes morphologically. We call this the "play" of language, as if only literal and propositional judgments were serious. But this play is deeply serious, since it involves the creative and inventive range of semasic relations that make a language effective in its different modalities. A language restricted to semasic cores, especially one in which only propositional cores or literal meanings were legitimate, would be deeply truncated both in expressibility and inventive capacities. We would either so restrict thought itself that it could no longer achieve its epistemic functions, or we would eliminate from language the most important properties of thought.

Language serves propositionally or semantically, practically, fabricatively, in art particularly, and "syndetically."[23] This latter synthetic function is found in its most complex form in philosophy, especially systematic philosophy, but also in other human works: literature, religion, and politics. Furthermore, with new forms of thought and understanding come either new semasic and linguistic functions or modifications of older forms. Thus, every language has its mythic and worshipful forms and functions. Psychoanalysis and marxism have brought new and complex semasic relations into language through emphasizing self-deception as repression on the one hand, as ideology on the other. Every new form of thought transforms the nature of language. This is the most obvious manifestation of the inexhaustibility of every language and of judgment.

The capacity of languages and thought to demand invention and to incorporate inventive products into themselves, as in psychoanalysis and structuralism, is both realized within and augmented by query. Judgment transformed into query is the realization of reason and expression of its inexhaustibility.

QUERY

Judgment is epistemic in the generic sense that every judgment involves selection and validation. But not every judgment is valid, nor does every judgment involve methodic interrogation and invention. The traditional distinction between knowledge and belief, largely based on foundational concerns, expresses an important principle: that knowledge is the achievement of valid results inseparable from continuing and unavoidable prospects of error. The foundational tradition may be interpreted as the attempt to answer the question of what transforms belief into knowledge in such a way as to avoid the possibility of error, at least of certain kinds of error. The rationalist response is that certain propositions are necessary to thought and being. The empiricist response is that certain sensory materials constitute the matter of thought, and although these materials are contingent, their constitutive role is necessary. In both cases, skepticism appears to be immediate and inescapable. Both traditions concede too much and too little to skepticism at the same time.

Skepticism is the position that error cannot be eliminated systematically or in principle, that every truth claimed, every belief known, is indistinguishable in form and origin from falsehood and error. Foundationalism seeks to reply to this position by establishing unimpugnable grounds of knowledge. In this sense, it seeks to overcome skepticism by eliminating error, a project that is impossible in principle. The expression of locality and inexhaustibility in epistemological terms is that there is no knowledge indistinguishable in principle from error, that distinctions in particular cases depend on contingent and particular evidence and argument. Another way of putting this is that error belongs to every stage of knowledge, including concluding stages. The hardest thing in the world is to avoid error, hard because there is no way of doing so, because every way is equally impugnable, because every precaution leaves us with prospects of further errors.

On the other hand, skepticism is implausible in supposing that this unavoidability of error somehow defeats understanding. That is, both skepticism and traditional forms of foundationalism presuppose that knowledge is adequate only to the extent that there is a general reply to the continuing presence of error. However, the fact that there is no general answer to the ongoing relevance of error, and consequently, of the continuing need for methods to detect and eliminate particular mistakes, does not and cannot make knowledge suspect.

There is no general solution to the problem of skepticism, and no intelligible sense in which there could be. Understanding in finite, local terms is the condition that relevant errors and criticisms have been replied to, not forever but in locally relevant terms. The inexhaustibility of the things that surround us is manifested in the inexhaustibility of every way of knowing them, inquiring into them, inexhaustible in the double sense that new and surprising properties are to be found in novel circumstances, and that everything known is proximate and limited, subject to its particular circumstances and contexts.

Skepticism does not need a solution because it is not a problem. We need only accept one of its major premises, that knowledge is not systematically distinguishable from error, and deny the other, that knowledge is legitimate only if so distinguishable. Instead, we have the results of the most thoroughly tested methods we have been able to devise for the criticism of proposed truths and for the development of new truths. In this sense inquiry is methodic, a sense entirely incompatible with the possibility of a systematically privileged Method. In the same sense, query, in all its modalities, is inventive, interrogative, and methodic. Methods here are local, inexhaustible, and heterogeneous.

Query possesses four properties: it is interrogative, critical and self-critical, inventive, and methodic. Knowledge is produced by unyielding criticism and self-criticism, by inexhaustible critical powers guided by the principle that what withstands criticism best is the only legitimate candidate for acceptance. To this we must add capacities for invention, that we are able to develop hypotheses, invent theories, construct alternatives, create new works, devise and adopt new policies, and so forth. The "so forth" is semasis, the unending play of judgment. Finally, methods of criticism and invention can be developed and directed at every judgment produced through query, including those self-critical methods themselves. Here methods are not foundational, but ways devised as a result of prior inquiries.[24] We may add, then, a fifth property of query, the reflexiveness required for complex forms of invention and interrogation, and a sixth, that such inexhaustible reflexiveness typically manifests itself in aporia. Finally, we must emphasize that the unavoidability of error, requiring unterminating criticism and reflection, and the related aporias, are not defects, but are sources of the inspirations that produce our greatest understandings.

The finiteness of judgments is expressed in their limits, not the skeptical limits of the impossibility of knowledge (effectively an unqualified, infinite impossibility), but the limits involved in interrogation, criticism, and invention. There are, moreover, still other limits profoundly important for semasis and query. There are different modes of judgment and different forms of criticism and invention. And among the forms of criticism required of propositional knowledge are forms that lie without, in other modes of judgment. The consequence is that inquiry is not and cannot be the only form of interrogative criticism and invention: not all such judgments are propositional. Every mode of query, including inquiry, requires criticism and interrogation from without as well as from within, in the other modes of judgment.

Are there internal marks in language of rational discourse? Are particular forms of language more rational than others, more epistemic than others? Certainly some forms of language are more effective than others in certain contexts and respects. And there are more or less normal or ordinary forms of propositional utterance. But every judgment can be interpreted as propositional as well as practical or fabricative. Similarly, many forms of linguistic utterance might be considered abnormal and ineffective in certain spheres of activity, but are propositional and valid in other spheres. Without such an understanding of multimodality in judgment, poetry and political exhortation would be unintelligible, not to mention everyday speech, slang, and informal chatter.

There are and can be no internal marks of rationality, for such internal signs would be forms of self-evidence and self-validation. Rationality resides not in such marks, not in the kinds of judgments we produce and interrogate, but in the interrogation itself, incessant and far-reaching. We interrogate judgments and their validation from within and from without, in all the ways we can interrogate them. If this is reason, it is neither particularly internal nor external, but more important, is ongoing and continuing, a dynamic process rather than a means or method. There could be no rationality without methods, but there is no method that is uniquely rational nor the highest or paradigmatic form of rationality.

Reason is ongoing interrogation and response, inexhaustibly and heterogeneously. It follows that reason does not lie in any particular methods nor in any particular origins, but in the continuing prospects of further interrogation. Query, then, is inexhaustible and unterminating, ongoing into the remote future and beyond. Epistemologically, this entails that certainty in knowledge is never achievable, that there is an inexhaustibility to all forms of knowledge that carries them forward to new interrogations and new forms of query, that every far-reaching truth is surrounded by aporia. Ontologically, this entails that nature is heterogeneous and inexhaustible, determinate and indeterminate, aporetic, open to new properties indefinitely, depending on its situations and locations.

Linguistically, this inexhaustibility entails both the pervasive indeterminateness of language and the determinateness inherent in every linguistic expression. Meanings are simultaneously definite and recapturable and indefinitely open and variable. In addition, the inexhaustibility of query entails an inexhaustible and unresolvable tension between language and utterance as well as between language and discourse. Language is always systematically more than any range of utterances, but they are pregnant with contextual and situated significations that language itself cannot embody. Language is thus more than utterance, and less; more than discourse, and far less. For discourse always includes more than language, or rather, language cannot be restricted to any range of constitutive elements given the open texture of discourse and query to which it contributes.

A language resembles a mode of judgment in its pervasiveness and validation, but it is not a mode of judgment. On the one hand, linguistic judgments do not include all forms of judgment, all utterances. There are gestures and drawings, diagrams and melodies. On the other hand, every subject matter, every judgment and everything in human experience, is open to linguistic expression. Every utterance may be given linguistic form. In this sense, a language has no intrinsic limits in subject matter, what language can be about, but only limits in what it expresses. More important, a language includes within itself every mode of judgment: propositional, practical, fabricative, and syndetic. Languages are not restricted by their capacity to describe, to influence, to create works, or to unify. In this sense, linguistic utterances are predominantly intermodal.

Language greatly resembles query in its intermodality and inventiveness, but is not always or merely query. The properties of query are not shared by every linguistic utterance: many are neither methodic, reflexive, nor inventive. Linguistic utterances may be truthful without query and may belong to query without being truthful. Rationality belongs to language and linguistic utterances as it belongs to any judgments and activities: language is as rational as it can be. What this means is that linguistic utterances may belong to query, that language is susceptible to whatever modes of truth and interrogation are appropriate to it, of improvement (as well as of corruption), but there is no ideal mode of truth appropriate to language or to any other judgmental form, and every form of judgment and query leads through self-criticism to other judgmental forms. Languages may be invented; established languages may be improved; linguistic utterances are situated among other forms of semasis and judgment. No such activities can produce an ideal language, for the notion of ideality in judgment or query is incoherent.

Judgment is always situated among perspectives, the conditions that enable an utterance to be interpreted and validated. Query is always situated among perspectives and judgments, the conditions that constitute the milieux within which reason can function interrogatively and validatively. Both interrogation and validation depend on specific conditions, historical and social, epistemic and interactive. There can be no understanding that proceeds from a neutral basis from which prior validation and judgment are absent. There can be no understanding that does not follow from a prior understanding, no perspective that does not require other perspectives, no human condition that is not itself humanly and judgmentally conditioned. Query, in its historicality, can have no beginning and no end. Every judgment and every query is situated among prior judgments and queries that comprise the materials out of which they are achieved.

We are addressing the other pole of the recognition that there is no understanding, no utterance devoid of difference, of indeterminateness. Identity is not understanding. Conversely, there is no being that is merely being and not something else, in this case, something knowable, experienceable. There are human events that are not judgments, because they involve no selections, no validation—subcellular events, for example—but no events that cannot be judgments, that would not be judgments under certain conditions. The boundaries between judgments and events, understandings and beings, rationality and judgment, are fluid, partly indeterminate. This is essential to their inexhaustibility.

There is evidence that the newborn infant enters the world with a developed system of complex neural pathways. Some of these disappear as others emerge in its interactions with its surroundings.[25] There is further evidence that the infant develops its understanding of itself as a self in a socially symbiotic interaction in which it is treated as a self.[26] Which comes first, being a person or being treated like a person? Which comes first, understanding or a prior understanding? These questions have no answers because they are not intelligible questions. Should we assume that the innate system of pathways is somehow not epistemic, but merely causal? Must we assume that such congenital conditions must be one or the other, innate or acquired, rationalist or empiricist, or does the truth involve rejecting these as the only alternatives?

We cannot understand anything without a prior understanding. This appears on the one hand to involve a situatedness that we may consider confinement, except that the second understanding is both dependent on and potentially novel, heterogeneous, with respect to the first. Similarly, a language is both a means of judgment and query and a pervasive constituent of the milieux in which judgment and query transpire. Shall we assume that, like understanding, there is no human condition that is not linguistic, that some form of language precedes all linguistic expression? It is not absurd to suppose that even the newborn infant possesses unrealized linguistic powers. Nor is it absurd to deny that linguistic powers are sharply differentiable from other human and non-human powers except in certain proximate ways.

The inventiveness that belongs to linguistic utterances suggests that languages cannot be so definite and structured in nature that they can be understood apart from the nature of human life and thought. They greatly influence life and thought, but they do not determine them either, not altogether. They influence even the physical development of the brain, for children who are kept from producing grammatical utterances never develop full left hemisphere functioning. Even so, they understand and can communicate, in some respects very well.[27] Languages contain within themselves the aporias that mark the diverse modalities of judgment and forms of query. They are a predominant expression of inexhaustibility in human experience. A language is perhaps the most prominent locale for rational utterance, but not all linguistic utterances are rational, not all linguistic utterances are inventive, and there are nonlinguistic utterances that are rational and belong to query. Linguistic utterances can be restricted to no single mode of judgment, no particular mode of truth, express no single form of rationality, incorporate all forms within themselves, but do not lose their nature as linguistic in doing so.

On the one hand, languages serve all the modes of judgment and query. On the other hand, languages possess their own determinate properties and characteristics beyond what is required by any mode of judgment or query. This is natural enough from the standpoint of the limits that constitute any local being including language. Locality is not only compatible with, it is the essential condition of inexhaustibility. But it is more important to emphasize that the nature of language affects (even in positive ways) the judgments of which we are capable. We are led to further knowledge by what we already know; we are led to other judgments by the judgments already established within languages. We think of knowledge as coded into language. Languages are a fundamental and pervasive means of acquiring and expressing knowledge, of judgment and query, but are also fundamental ways in which biological and social conditions of human life make their mark. We must therefore reject the glorious view of thought and language Aristotle expresses in his view of *nous*, "that it has no nature of its own."[28] Rather, we must understand, however aporetically, how the determinate forms of language contribute to the inexhaustible capacity of thought to grasp the nature of things, of judgments to be valid, and of query to interrogate and invent as required by its circumstances. Here languages are specifically and determinately among the conditions essential to truth and reason.

We may return to the semasic field theory to conclude that it bears the only structure known that can accommodate the capacities described for language, that propositional judgments and knowledge may be expressed within and carried on by means of linguistic utterances without being captured by propositional judgments. Languages can be propositional only by being nonpropositional. This aporia is a direct expression of the heterogeneity and indeterminateness that inexhaustible beings and truths require.

Every semasic field contains one or more propositional cores, and many other semasic cores as well. These cores express the diverse modalities of judgment. The pervasiveness of every mode of judgment, the inexhaustible interrogation of every semasic and epistemic relation through query, entails that every core's boundary be permeable relative to every other core and the full semasic field. Moreover, the latter itself blurs into other semasic fields, overlaps them at their peripheries. Interrogation and novelty, the fundamental conditions of query, open every semasic relation to other relations. Every concept requires the limits expressed by semasic cores; every limit is open to interrogation and transformation. No limit is altogether necessary, unqualified by context or location.

Languages here include literal meanings in order to fulfill their roles as mediums of propositional judgment. And they are extremely effective mediums for that form of judgment, though every linguistic utterance is a medium for other modes as well. That a language might be only literal is impossible, not only because natural languages serve multiple purposes, but because a wholly literal, extensional language could not be an instrument of discovery or interrogation, of thought. The inescapable presence in any mode of judgment of error, novelty, variation, of different forms of indeterminateness, is a conjunction of closely related conditions: the dependence of knowledge on query, on invention and interrogation.

Every language includes multiple semasic cores surrounded by a dynamically variable semasic field. Every such semasic field is composed of socially stable semasic relations, the consensual semasic field, and individually variable relations, idiosemic fields. The plurality and heterogeneity of these different fields and sub-fields is the source of all discoveries and invention as well as of mistakes in communication and understanding. Semasic stability is only a relative, qualified stability; variation is similarly qualified. The interplay of stable semasic relations with individual and subgroup variations is the dynamic arena in which languages accomplish their tasks along with every other domain of meaning. Again, languages can be propositional only in virtue of their nonpropositional semasic relations. Literal meaning depends on figurative meaning for the establishment or achievement of literal meaning. The diverse modalities of judgment and different forms of query impede the achievement of perfect semantic correspondence, but there is no such perfection and without the different modalities, there would be no semantic relation attainable. Impedance and achievement go together.

We have been writing as if languages were instrumental and had the purpose of attaining and expressing knowledge, possible only within complex milieux of other semasic relations and functions. This appears to be contrary to our earlier claim that a language is not an instrument, but is itself a milieu or environment, something we belong to. The point is that only in virtue of belonging to a language, as a milieu, can we use it to accomplish such tasks as understanding, expression, or communication. Languages are instrumental but not instruments, are employed while characterizing our experience. More accurately, we employ words and sentences, depending on semasic core relations, but inhabit a language. Two fundamental ways in which we inhabit a language beyond any instrumentality are thinking in a language and having social relations characterized by language.

NOTES

1. See Derrida, *On Grammatology*, pp. 10–13. Derrida also speaks of "phonocentrism."

2. Goodman, *Languages of Art*.
3. Ibid.; see also Goodman, *Ways of Worldmaking*.
4. See Peter Strawson, *Individuals* (London: Methuen, 1959).
5. The example is Wittgenstein's. See Hilary Putnam's discussion in "Analyticity and Apriority: Beyond Wittgenstein and Quine," in *Studies in Metaphysics*, edd. Peter A. French, Theodore E. Vehling, et al. Midwest Sudies in Philosophy 4 (Minneapolis: University of Minnesota Press, 1979). See also chap. 2, note 16.
6. Foucault discusses some of this in his discussion of "Signatures" in "The Prose of the World," *Order of Things*, chap. 2.
7. See Roy Harris, *The Language Myth* (London: Duckworth, 1981), for an extended discussion of this topic.
8. See chap. 2, note 71.
9. See Harris, *Language Myth*, for a sustained defense of this view of language.
10. Several historical and contemporary references may be cited here. One is Spinoza's absolutely infinite Substance with infinite attributes, each attribute expressing how Substance may be conceived by an ideal Intellect. The suggestion is that Substance may be conceived in infinite ways (inexhaustibly), and that each conception "is" Substance (under that conception), but is not identical with Substance, for it could not then be absolutely infinite. Here the inexhaustibility of Substance enables it to be conceivable but never exhaustively. A second is Quine's principle of the indeterminacy of translation, effectively that no ontology can be determined or presupposed outside the language in which it is expressed (Quine, *Ontological Relativity*). It is not necessary to interpret this thesis as so extreme that we have no way of determining an ontology from within a language, or understanding another culture's ontology, but that there is no unambiguous "reality" to which labels refer. A third related view is Goodman's notion of world-versions (Goodman, *Ways of Worldmaking*). See also the works cited in chap. 2, note 13.
11. See Margolis, *Persons and Minds*, for such an epistemic view of human capacities.
12. See my "Metaphor, Inexhaustibility, and the Semasic Field," *New Literary History*, 18 (1986–1987); 517–33; also *Inexhaustibility and Human Being*, pp. 88–148. For an important, related view of the multiplicity of semasic relationships that constitute human experience, see Bakhtin, with his view of *polyglossia* and *heteroglossia*: "Language—like the living concrete environment in which the consciousness of the verbal artist lives—is never unitary. It is unitary only as an abstract grammatical system of normative forms, taken in isolation from the concrete, ideological conceptualizations that fill it, and in isolation from the uninterrupted process of historical becoming that is a characteristic of all living language. Actual social life and historical becoming create

within an abstractly unitary national language a multitude of concrete worlds, a multitude of bounded verbal-ideological and social belief systems; within these various systems (identical in the abstract) are elements of language filled with various semantic and axiological content and each with its own different sound" (Mikhail M. Bakhtin, "Discourse in the Novel," *The Dialogic Imagination*, ed. Michael Holquist, trans. Caryl Emerson and Michael Holquist [Austin and London: University of Texas Press, 1981], p. 288).

13. The idea of abnormal discourse comes from T. S. Kuhn, *The Structure of Scientific Revolutions* (Chicago: The University of Chicago Press, 1962); it is developed by Rorty in *Philosophy and the Mirror of Nature*.

14. See Donald Davidson, "What Metaphors Mean," *Critical Inquiry* 5, No. 1 (Autumn 1978), 31–47.

15. This principle is inherent in Fodor's argument that no concept can be acquired (Jerry A. Fodor, *Representations* [Cambridge: The MIT Press, 1981]).

16. Edward Sapir, *Selected Writings of Edward Sapir*, ed. D. C. Mandelbaum (Berkeley: University of California, 1949); Benjamin Lee Whorf, *Language, Thought, and Reality*, ed. J. B. Carroll (New York: Wiley, 1959).

17. See Justus Buchler, *Toward a General Theory of Human Judgment* (New York: Columbia University Press, 1951). Also see my *Philosophical Mysteries* (Albany: State University of New York Press, 1981) and *Inexhaustibility and Human Being*. Especially see my *Ring of Representation*, chap. 1, for the sonant categories described here in chap. 2, note 62.

18. See my *Inexhaustibility and Human Being*, chap. 1.

19. "Symbolization, then, is to be judged fundamentally by how well it serves the cognitive purpose: by the delicacy of its discriminations and the aptness of its allusions; by the way it works in grasping, exploring, and informing the world; by how it analyzes, sorts, orders, and organizes; by how it participates in the making, manipulation, retention, and transformation of knowledge. Considerations of simplicity and subtlety, power and precision, scope and selectivity, familiarity and freshness, are all relevant and often contend with one another; their weighting is relative to our interests, our information, and our inquiry" (Goodman, *Languages of Art*, p. 258).

20. Searle, *Speech Acts*, p. 23. The list comes from John Austin, *How to Do Things with Words* (Oxford: Clarendon, 1962).

21. See my *Inexhaustibility and Human Being*, chap. 3.

22. See George Lakoff and Mark Johson, *Metaphors We Live By* (Chicago: The University of Chicago Press, 1980).

23. See my *Inexhaustibility and Human Being*, chap. 1.

24. This, of course, is Dewey's position. See his *Logic*, especially chaps. 1 and 2.

25. Konner, *Tangled Wing*, chap. 4.

26. Harré, *Social Being*.

27. Nadia communicated by drawing. The man who mistook his wife for a hat could do most things very well, to music. Genie's capacity for emotional interaction was truly extraordinary. See chap. 2, note 48; chap. 3, note 50.

28. Aristotle, *De anima*, in *The Basic Works of Aristotle*, ed. Richard McKeon (New York: Random House, 1941), 429a.

5

SOCIETY

Among the important characteristics of languages is that they inhabit social milieux, influencing and influenced by their social surroundings. We have expressed this sociality as a principle of language. The question here is how we are to understand its nature. For example, two recent developments in the theory of language emphasize the relation between language and society in important but highly restrictive ways. Speech-act theory concerns itself with how utterances can be socially effective, treating them as acts with implications and consequences. Communication theory directs its attention to how agents are persuaded by or understand the utterances of others. In this form, both views are limited to the microsphere involving agents and particular utterances while languages have a pervasive scope as cultural agents and representations.

Every utterance inhabits many public and private spaces; more important, so does every language. And it is important for us to keep this distinction between utterance and language in mind even if we insist that a language is embodied in potential utterances and has no other existence. One reason is that we think in language as well as speak and write, where thinking and feeling, even in linguistic form, are regarded as private. A second reason is that a language has powers that transcend the domain of even potential utterances. Again, we think in language as well as speak and write, even as thinking is not restricted to language. More important, a language is a primary form of culture and rationality. What we are, as cultural creatures, is embodied in our languages, uttered or not; what we think and how we reason are also embodied in our languages, beyond what we say or write. To be judging creatures, we interpret what befalls and surrounds us, constantly interpreting and reinterpreting, primarily in our native languages. Such interpretation is inseparable from language though it is not to be identified with utterance or speech. For other creatures judge and interpret, and we interpret and judge through music and painting as well as language. We may add that utterances play complex and heterogeneous roles in human life, many of which are only remotely related to their linguistic forms. By such roles, we are alluding to the multiplicity of modes of judgment.

Many of these considerations are related to the principle of autonomy. Emphasis upon the sociality and humanity of languages suggests that the situatedness of human affairs, including languages, implicates them in an inexhaustible range of relations; in those respects languages are not autonomous. More important, perhaps, language is not separable from discourse and from practice.[1] What people say, substance and form, inhabits complex social and intentional contexts involving multiple human relationships, emotional and intellectual, purposive and reactive. Our native language may not determine in all respects how we think, and certainly is itself determined by how we think and act, but thought and language are interrelated in inexhaustibly complex ways.

A firm principle of science is that we strive to establish the simplest natural principles by means of which we can explain complex phenomena and events. Yet we have understood human events and forms here as inexhaustibly complex and aporetic, as if no simple principles could underlie and pervade them. Nevertheless, simplicity and complexity are complementary, not antagonistic: phenomena are complex in certain respects, simple in others, and every respect is reversible, depending on context. That is all that is required for a science of language, provided we do not demand completeness. Even more, we have understood the surplus of meaning not to undermine technical sciences, but to bring about their efflorescence. Similarly, it seems plausible that if languages and discourse, sociality and politics, are all interrelated, linguistic structures cannot be autonomous, even as they must be supplementary. We should not suppose that autonomy here is unqualified. Rather, a qualified notion of linguistic autonomy is required in order to distinguish among languages, discourse, and other social institutions.

SOCIAL LOCATION

The principle that underlies inexhaustibility is that everything is multiply located, and that both its identity and its properties are functions of its locations. Yet equally, there is identity over variation in relations and locations, over time and through different contexts. Unqualified relativism suggests that every variation drastically changes the identity of the relevant relata; essentialism suggests that contingent variations are irrelevant to individual identity. The local alternative, entailing inexhaustibility, is that identities are contingent and a function of variations, but not in all ways and respects. Locality entails rejection of any unqualified identification of a being's identity with a class of its properties. Rather, identity, like every trait and condition, is a heterogeneous function of the diverse locations of a being among other beings.[2] We add to locality and inexhaustibility "functionality" or "ergonality": identity is a function of location, of the "work" done by an ingredient in that location. Identity, like locality, is multiple and inexhaustible.

That everything is inexhaustible in virtue of its multiple locations and conditions is the generic principle of inexhaustibility. It has the remarkable corollary that where inexhaustibility is manifest, as in most far-reaching human and natural locales, conditions and traits that would appear to have a relatively narrow purview stretch inexorably toward pervasiveness, but not toward universality or infinity,[3] a movement belonging to supplementarity. Such traits as consciousness, meaning, materiality, and language are at once local, specific, and particular, with narrow defining properties (syntax and morphology, for example), and also generic, pervasive, relevant over immensely varied conditions, expressing the creativity of language and the inexhaustibility of experience. This union of local specificity and pervasiveness is a direct expression of the aporias of inexhaustibility. We have seen it at work in the syntax and grammar of languages. We are now concerned with analogous heterogeneities on the social side of languages.

Every language is embedded in social institutions and cultural forms which in turn are represented in linguistic expressions, among their prominent realizations. One manifestation of this locality is that a language always has social functions, but the most striking manifestation is the entanglement of human being and human social life in discourses and languages.

Human beings, along with their thought and utterances, are complexly located in the social conditions of human life. A consequence of finiteness and multiple locatedness is that there is no social entanglement that is not multiple, no social context that is not effectively many contexts, therefore no social condition that is not heterogeneously divided, the source of specific forms of historical development and political circumstances, of novel points of view, and of important cultural transformations. It follows that there is no single form of reason, but many; no unified supporting or subjugating political order, but many; no single social environment, but many. An authoritarian regime seeks to consolidate the manifold forms of power into one, in vain, but it may nevertheless achieve sufficient hegemony that the variations that remain have little individual effectiveness. A pluralistic society seeks to disperse the forms of power among the different individuals and groups composing the society, again in vain, for power is inevitably both dispersed and focused wherever it is exercised.

These are political forms, the subject of the next chapter; analogous social forms are the following:

a. Every linguistic utterance inhabits manifold locales, social, individual, and semasic, though in each locale it has a definite, determinate function. This principle is expressed in part through the notion of semasic fields and subfields.

b. Every language inhabits manifold locales of individual and social activity, and is dispersed throughout multiple locales of application and instrumentality. It is primarily for this reason that a language cannot be regarded simply as an instrument or as serving any particular purposes and norms. Similarly, we have seen that no instrument is merely instrumental, but inhabits manifold spheres of application.

c. Every social environment is plural. Plurality here is heterogeneity, dispersion and fragmentation, consequences of the limits inherent in finiteness. Every social institution competes and interacts with other social institutions; every social code, however determinate in its particular locations, blurs at its peripheries and margins; every social purpose is fragmented into manifold social purposes. We cannot think of society simply as composed of multiple interests, for there are social entanglements that cannot be analyzed in terms of individual desires. But what classical theory tells us, if in overly simplified form, is that individual locales do not compose an overarching world locale.

The plurality of social conditions and entanglements has two sides, expressing the inexhaustible specificity of conditions that compose particular entanglements and the divisions from which alternatives and variations emerge. Every society and social institution is entangling and subjugating and exercises power covertly and overtly, but is also divided within itself institutionally, politically, and epistemically. Entanglement is not a uniform condition, but contains seeds of other entanglements. Classical dialectical theory, in Hegel and Marx, imposes a doctrinaire pattern on the inexhaustible variety of oppositions and variations. But the principle that any social and economic, rational and conscious, order is divided and entangled within itself, and that such divisions are the basis of new forms of order, is in gross terms true.

We have here one of the prominent applications and developments of the principle of inexhaustibility, entailing that every society is fragmented into many institutions, practices, and forms. It follows that there is no single purpose or structure for linguistic utterances that is a consequence of the social environments they inhabit. Normal conditions, essential to any formal account of either the structure or purposes of utterance, are dispersed and fragmented, plural conditions.

COMMUNICATION

"Of all affairs, communication is the most wonderful. That things should be able to pass from the plane of external pushing and pulling to that of revealing themselves to man, and thereby to themselves, and that the fruit of communication should be participation, sharing, is a wonder by the side of which transubstantiation pales."[4]

That things reveal themselves is indeed wonderful, as Dewey says, but the suggestion that they might not have done so seems unintelligible. Things might not have revealed themselves to human beings in the forms they do, but there could not be human beings or things that did not reveal themselves in some ways to each other. Things are present to one another, are embodied in each other, causally, influentially, and inexhaustibly. This is one of the most important ways in which the view of inexhaustibility here differs from its modern predecessors. Nature's inexhaustibility belongs to representation.[5]

If we distinguish semasis from being, as we must, then things must reveal or present themselves if they are present, and they cannot be otherwise where human beings are present. It does not follow that beings are ever present in unambiguous form, since every being is located in inexhaustibly diverse entanglements, or that every being will be humanly present, or present only in human form. Nevertheless, it follows that things inevitably reveal themselves as inexhaustible, as diverse plenitudes with heterogeneous identities. But in the specific sense in which things are present as meaningful to us, in which we judge them, then there is indeed something wonderful about our capacity to do so, though even here, to be able to wonder about that capacity is already to possess it. And things are wonderful in that they may be known.

But there is a profound difference between semasis and communication, between revelation and participation and sharing. In the passage above, Dewey seems not to distinguish them, in part because his view of semasis as means is inevitably public. We may provisionally identify society with publicness, individuality with privateness—we will presently reject that identification—with the consequence that, as Dewey and Mead argue from one side, Wittgenstein from another, every semiate has a public, social side, therefore a shared, communal side. In terms of the principle of stability, every semiate is stable over some public community of semasors. Every element of a language is in principle stable over some community.

Yet the public side of a language is only one of its sides, and every utterance, every linguistic element, every semiate, both remains stable over some shared community that inhabits the social spheres of the language and varies with heterogeneous understandings and interpretations. We may follow that side of Dewey (with Mead, Wittgenstein, and Vygotsky) that identifies communication with what is common and shared. But although sharing is essential to a language, it is no more essential than individual variation. For while we must share interpretations in order to understand each other, in order to communicate, we must vary in our interpretations in order to understand anything whatever, in order to assimilate meanings to our personal experiences. Again, publicness and privateness are not opposed but belong together, two sides composing a single semasic relation, in interaction composing inexhaustibility. Inexhaustibility adds heterogeneity and excess, supplementarity.

To communicate is to enable others to understand what we mean, what we understand. In this sense, communication presupposes a sharing of meaning and understanding. Yet if we examine this sharing more closely, we see that commonality is inseparable from heterogeneity, sharing inseparable from variation. Three considerations may be noted:

(a) *Semasis.* The semasic field comprises an inexhaustible wealth of subfields and peripheral relations. These subfields are intrinsic, not in the sense for example that the semantic core is prior to the full semasic field, but in the sense that a semasic field is a *differential* field, divided into subfields and complex relations. One way of putting this is that ambiguity or polysemasis is present in every semasic field. Another is that literal or semantic relations coexist in every semasic field with peripheral, figurative, and associative relations. A third is more relevant to our immediate concerns, that every semasic field, interpreted as a public, communal field, coexists with and is divided by a wealth of idiosemic fields, each relevant to the interpretations of different semasors. There can be no public field without these heterogeneous idiosemic variations, for semasic fields exist among individual interpretations.

What could establish a shared semasic field apart from or independent of idiosemic variations? One possibility is that there is a natural relation between signifier and signified, independent of linguistic practices. We have seen that no such natural relation could be devoid of arbitrariness, but this arbitrariness is not so much a defect inherent in a primordial relation as an expression of heterogeneity. It is in part because understandings are always in some ways individual, in some respects private, that there is arbitrariness in every semasic relation. This is a fundamental epistemic condition, with important applications to linguistic signs. It prohibits any stable semasic relation from becoming independent of the understandings of human persons. Thus, there can be no technical or scientific language, no epistemic or interpretive language, that is not variable with persons, groups, and contexts, and this variation is the major source of the development of new insights and new forms of understanding.

How are we able to understand each other when we speak and write idiosemically in different or even common languages? One kind of answer is that we are able to understand each other, in common, only in virtue of the many differences between us. One view of understanding sees its basis as repetition, though no repetition can be unqualified. The other view sees it as differentiation and variation, though no variation can be unqualified. One view of knowledge here seeks an unqualified commonality, un-qualified in that every variation is either relevant or damaging. The other view of knowledge is that it can be effective only insofar as it is possessed uniquely and differentially amid community. To the one, science is the field of shared conclusions. To the other, science is composed of multiple fields, including heterogeneous prospects of useful discovery.

Here commonality and variation are not antagonists but comple-ments. Similarly, the qualifications and conditions of all finite conditions do not subvert transcendence, but support it. What is required is that transcendence itself be local, therefore conditioned and qualified, transgressive. That is, every utterance bears the promise of novelty, of escape from repetition. But every realiza-tion of novelty is equally a representation of its tradition, for traditions can be represented and can develop in inexhaustibly manifold forms.

It may appear more appropriate to think of the public semasic field as derivative from private, idiosemic variations than the reverse. This is implausible. There is no escaping the principle of stability, that any meaning must be a public meaning. Any semasic field, however idiosemically variable, must be stable in some respects over different contexts and persons. There is no way around the public language argument, that any language must in principle be a public language. However, this is to repeat the point that nothing is intrinsically private, including inner experiences. Nor is anything intrinsically public. A semasic field that is alto-gether variable with context and person, one that is entirely stable over all contexts and circumstances, cannot be semasic.

(b) *Understanding*. To understand is to invent; to understand is to understand uniquely. We do not mean that every understanding is an individual understanding, by a person or subject, for there is knowledge in the community and environment. This distinction may not represent a kind of knowledge: what is known, like all semiates and experiences, has both a public and private side. But knowledge and understanding resemble an iceberg: far more is known implicitly, unarticulated, than is ever explicitly formulated.

The distinction between overt and implicit understanding cor-responds to the distinction between individual and public knowl-edge. In being possessed by no one, public knowledge is covert and diffuse; but that does not make it any less effective or pervasive. The peripheries of semasic fields are important and effective even when expressible in no explicit forms. We have viewed poetry (along with other forms of figurative language) as functioning at the peripheries of semasic fields more than at the cores. But functioning at these peripheries is effectively inexhaustible, as we discern wherever we try to fully express an effective metaphor.[6]

There is, then, knowledge (and correspondingly, semasis) that belongs to no one, distributed throughout public institutions and activities. But such knowledge is distributed, not communicated. Moreover, one of the intrinsic forms of such covert knowledge is its manifestation in overt, explicit forms. But explicit knowledge always has individual manifestations. And for individuals to possess knowledge, to understand, they must understand in some sense for themselves. Individual, idiosemic variations are a function of the complexity of understanding in its overt and covert forms, its communal and private manifestations.[7]

(c) *Complementarity*. We conclude, therefore, that neither the public nor private forms of understanding and semasis are primary and that such public and private forms are manifestations of knowledge and meaning. In the case of languages, the stability of the public form of the native or natural language is constantly transformed by the variations of expression that constitute individual and group variations of style. We do not speak our common languages in the same way, but differ by region, class, and individual. We cannot say that we do not speak the "same language," for that overlooks not only the stability of public forms but the importance and effectiveness of communication. Variation is an essential facet of semasic stability, both pervasive wherever there is semasis and a condition of its effectiveness.

Public and private, communal and individual, collective and idiosemic semasic fields, are not then alternative variations composing a part of the inexhaustible complexity of languages, but are dynamically interactive and complementary forms essential to each other, supplementing each other heterogeneously. There can be no altogether public language, however technical, that serves human understanding because understanding requires individual assimilation and therefore individual variation. There cannot be a wholly private language or semiate because semasis always has public forms of expression.

Put another way, one of the intrinsic and inescapable conditions of languages and other forms of semasis is that every semiate serves communication, but not communication alone. Or rather, in serving and achieving communication, our utterances also serve thought and individual expression, establish our identities, manifest our personalities, delineate conditions for the future, and more. Utterances and languages are inexhaustible, not in failing to achieve true communication, but in achieving communication among other purposes and functions. These functions are not competitive with communication, but belong to it intrinsically.

There appears to be a recurrent yearning among human beings for total and complete communication, closely akin to complete identity. The latter is impossible, not simply a defect of our finiteness, but a condition of the limits that define any identity. We can merge with another only by not owning an identity of our own, offering nothing to merge. Similarly, total communication is no communication, for what must be achieved is a shared understanding or semasic field, and there can be no understanding of anything, objects or semiates, that is not heterogeneously differentiated. Conversely, there can be no understanding that is not public. But the idea of total objectivity is similarly implausible. Objective knowledge is achieved by publicly reproducible methods undertaken by individual persons in their individual ways. As long as we can reproduce them publicly in the relevant ways, there can be publicly achievable results, but never in all ways. Likewise, we inhabit our common languages individually and differentially. These idiosemic variations are the dynamic source of variation in language through time and by context and conditions. But they are also the source of the stability that communication depends on and expresses.

Gadamer describes understanding in terms of a "fusion of horizons."[8] As long as we understand this fusion to preserve the limits of the relevant horizons, this figure is adequate. But the fusion is not a supersession, and the differences of the horizons are not so much to be overcome as the means whereby understanding is achieved. That is, understanding and communication doubly presuppose difference: in the need for understanding and as the medium of understanding and communication. Where someone does not understand what we say, we neither simply say it again nor are satisfied by having it repeated to us. Rather, we insist that true understanding involves personal expression. Paradoxically, but irresistibly, communication depends on difference. Others understand what we say and mean when they say and mean something else, not when they repeat our words.

PRACTICE

Utterances serve not one or even a few, but inexhaustibly many functions. A language is not simply one but also many, many instruments, environments, and spheres of activity. Utterances and languages are inexhaustible; like everything else they possess manifold identities, and are single, unitary, only in certain respects. The inexhaustibility of functions is not unique to languages, but is shared by them with other generic spheres of human activity: culture, society, consciousness, semasis, and thought. None of these is wider than the others without qualification, but expands throughout human experience. Yet none is equivalent to the others. This togetherness of pervasiveness and specificity is inherent within inexhaustibility. Languages are expressive, instrumental, communicative; utterances serve communication and thought, expression and understanding, action and contemplation, theory and practice.

Among the multiple functions of linguistic utterances is their capacity to serve human purposes, both to serve practice and to be practices themselves. Utterances not only express and communicate, tell and reveal, but accomplish and motivate, achieve purposes and influence events. Among their other functions, that is, utterances are speech acts. We may in this context consider Searle's analysis of a complete speech act of promising.

1. Normal input and output conditions obtain.
2. S expresses the proposition that p in the utterance of T.
3. In expressing that p, S predicates a future act A of S.
4. H would prefer S's doing A to his not doing A, and S believes H would prefer his doing A to his not doing A.
5. It is not obvious to both S and H that S will do A in the normal course of events.
6. S intends to do A.
7. S intends that the utterance of T will place him under an obligation to do A.
8. S intends (i-I) to produce in H the knowledge (K) that the utterance of T is to count as placing S under an obligation to do

A. S intends to produce K by means of the recognition of i-I, and he intends i-I to be recognized in virtue of (by means of) H's knowledge of the meaning of T. [Searle calls this the *essential condition*.]

9. The semantical rules of the dialect spoken by S and H are such that T is correctly uttered if and only if conditions 1–8 obtain.[9]

As Searle puts it, "The essential feature of a promise is that it is the undertaking of an obligation to perform a certain act."[10] We may assume that he means, as his detailed analysis indicates, that the undertaking is a public one, for one could undertake an obligation silently, and this would not normally be a promise. But the word "normally" is a danger sign, both here and in condition (1) above.

What question is begged in specifying "normal conditions," input and output? Most likely, it is the difficulty involved in understanding that a promise has been made in any but obvious circumstances. Someone says aloud to you, "I promise that I will help you move tomorrow," and intentionally or voluntarily accepts the obligation to help you move your belongings. In a culture in which such an utterance is normally followed by at best a sixty percent chance that the speaker will show up tomorrow, has a promise been made? Can what Searle calls a promise even be made in such a culture?

Suppose it is not clear whether a promise has been made? Where would the difficulties show themselves? It seems reasonable to take conditions (3)–(5) for granted as inherent in the nature of promising. Though we might dispute Searle's analysis in certain details, we are not concerned here with the notion of promising but with that of speech acts. And in this context, there are important questions concerning the other conditions. Are there "normal" conditions in a social-linguistic context that are stable enough to be passed over without reservations? There is a similar distinction in Rorty between normal and abnormal discourse. Yet is discourse ever normal, or is it not always undergoing modification, at least calling for modification? Is it not always heterogeneous? Rorty seems to assume that within a genre or stable paradigm, there exist stable rules for the interpretation of utterances. But such a view may be a vestige from the traditional position that there are stable rules of epistemological method. Rorty and Kuhn observe that stability is proximate, essentially epochal. If so, the more plausible position is that normal discourse is neither necessary to stable understanding of utterances (as Putnam persuasively argues), since people of different epochs or paradigms do understand each other—perhaps following Gadamer's view that understanding is a fusion of horizons—nor sharply distinguishable from "abnormal" discourse.[11]

As cultural practices change, promising changes also, not perhaps to the point where one practice is unintelligible from the standpoint of another, but enough so that neither the normal conditions cannot be said to obtain, nor can the intentions be understood straightforwardly (as in condition [6]). Searle takes for granted that since the promising occurs at a time before the promised action, the intention must be formed and complete before that action.[12] The reply is relevant to all intentional contexts, particularly where self-deception might be involved, but it is important in relation to works of art. An artist's intentions are neither independent of context nor dependent simply on historical circumstances. What we learn about other works of art defines the norms and expectations without which we cannot begin to understand a given work. Thus, not only does a work of art inhabit many cultures and periods, so do the intentions that compose its *telos*.[13] This is another way of expressing the unavoidable temporality belonging not only to works of art and any understanding, but to intentions and purposes as well. Similarly, the notion of artistic style includes within itself whatever the future brings to our understanding of other works and styles. This fragmented and circular temporality is one of the fundamental features of the inexhaustibility of works of art.[14] It is, however, equally fundamental to all practices, ordinary and technical.

Even relatively modest, everyday contexts of experience and expression have the same character. What people intend is frequently unclear, even to themselves, until later events have begun to unfold. The prospective nature of intentions clouds our understanding of our own activities. It also, under other circumstances, helps to clarify them. This complex state of affairs is natural if we recognize that we depend on intentions to explain the nature of our actions. We are caught in the dilemma that if intentions were entirely clear at the time they were effective, they could not explain the actions to which they were relevant, since an adequate explanation depends on information and understandings as well as conditions that have not yet been realized, while if intentions were explanatorily adequate, they would then include within themselves conditions that can neither be anticipated nor understood very far in advance.

Similar comments may be made about condition (9), as if we may reasonably expect a clear and invariant relation between the semantic rules of a language and a sincere utterance. This condition again betrays the assumption that there is a normal form of linguistic utterance relevant (in this case) to sincerity. It is implausible to suppose that there is a stable way in which sincerity is felt or manifested, over different cultures and times, or that there is a semantically stable form in which sincerity is expressed.

We have considered speech-act theory as a theory of language as communication, with the criticism that it neglects other features and functions of languages. What is required is a closer look at the way in which the principle of stability functions in this theory of language. Searle defines a very strong principle of stability to avoid what he calls "the speech act fallacy": "Any analysis of the meaning of a word (or morpheme) must be consistent with the fact that the same word (or morpheme) can mean the same thing in all the grammatically different kinds of sentences in which it can occur."[15] The question is how we are to interpret the notion of "sameness of meaning": in a qualified or unqualified way. But a closely related question is how we are to interpret the publicness of utterances and their meanings, whether the fact that linguistic utterances must have a public function entails that they have exactly or unqualifiedly the same meaning in every context and for every individual.

We have seen repeatedly that the public and private, common and individual, stable and variable features of judgments, linguistic and otherwise, are inseparable, that there is no utterance that does not have a stable, common meaning conjoined with variable interpretations. The relation here is complementary, so that we cannot disentangle the public and individually variable elements. Sincerity is not, in a complex, changing field of human life and experience, always the same either in terms of antecedent conditions, linguistic expressions, or inner feelings. Yet we can recognize it (for the most part) when we encounter it, though not to the point where we cannot be deceived.

The issue is whether, in order for human beings to communicate publicly and to understand each other, we must suppose that there is anything that is publicly stable other than the capacity to interpret utterances publicly, for example structural conditions and grammatical rules. In Wittgenstein's terms, there may be nothing other than that many things possess a common label that explains the application of that label. Rules do not provide that kind of explanation but repeat the story. Similarly, that language-speakers can make themselves understood, by gesture and tone of voice as well as by explicit linguistic utterances, does not entail that there is anything in common in different contexts of utterance, or even for speaker and hearer, other than the common under-standing. Common understandings may depend on nothing other than themselves. This does not mean that their existence is not an important achievement where attained and an important condition where socially established.

The continued relevance of conditions does not entail perma-nence. That every understanding depends on conditions does not entail that any of these be a priori or that any subconditions be stable over a wide range of contexts. That any word or morpheme, any sentence or expression, in a language must be able to mean the same in any context in which it appears does not entail that there is any other condition or criterion, any form or structure, that is the same over all these contexts.[16]

Two alternatives may therefore be considered. One is that where there is a common understanding, there is something else in common that defines the shared basis of community. This includes common intentions, meanings, syntax, or deep structure. The other alternative is that a common understanding, including a common meaning, is produced as necessary and however effec-tively in a dynamic context of semasic and epistemic interaction by various devices: gesture; tone of voice; variation in expression, emphasis, and tone color; and simplification and analogy. The immense variety of semasic resources utilized in judgment do not entail that common understandings are impossible; instead they are the basis of commonality.

More accurately, again, commonality and heterogeneity are not so much alternatives as complements in any utterance situation involving mutual understanding: there is common understanding only insofar as different individuals interpret this understanding differently, but not differently in every respect; similarly, individ-ual variations in interpretation are intelligible in a common context of communication only insofar as they entail community of understanding, tacit or explicit, but not an invariant community. This complementarity does not resolve its poles into identity, but takes each of the poles for granted as having a life of its own, as heterogeneous and supplemental.

Many traditional philosophic difficulties have responded to complementarity. The problem of other minds follows from the position that individuals relate to their minds and experiences uniquely, that no individual can experience another's experience as that individual experiences it. But this is true only under qualification: experience is both singular and common, shared and individual, public and private. We cannot share the experiences of another individual entirely, but we can share them in many ways: the objects and meanings of public experiences are largely shared. But sharing is compatible with variations. No language can be either wholly private or wholly public. We understand each other publicly and stably to the extent that we understand each other uniquely and differently. Or rather, we understand nothing unless we understand it both publicly and privately, commonly and variably.

Speech-act theory points out that linguistic utterances do important social and human work in addition to expressing thoughts and propositional knowledge. We act as well as think through language and utterance. In acting, we establish relationships, engender commitments, produce consequences. In all linguistic contexts, we succeed in our endeavors in any way we can, utilizing the resources of our languages, modifying and supplementing them where necessary. Perhaps the greatest weakness of speech-act theory, along with other one-sided views of our entanglements in languages, is its neglect of the heterogeneous inexhaustibility of such entanglements, unduly emphasizing linguistic and social situatedness. Whether or not we can think and understand without language, linguistic utterances serve thought and understanding as well as other human relationships. And because of the different functions that utterances must serve, their normal conditions include not only established forms and recurrent patterns but modification and variation.

Speech-act theory is a theory of language as communication, emphasizing shared purposes, understandings, and achievements. It locates linguistic utterances entirely in social contexts. Chomsky has criticized Searle for overlooking the capacity of utterance to serve thought; Searle has criticized Chomsky for neglecting the social, purposive functions of utterance.[17] We may say that each understands an important function of linguistic utterance but also weakens the power of that understanding, one through an implausible interpretation of structural or communal stability, the other by neglecting the inexhaustible complexity of the different functions of languages in interaction.

We conclude that the capacity of utterances to function in practice entails a technology of utterance, but one that includes within itself both the constraints of its own devices and an inexhaustible impulse to achieve human purposes, social and individual, however it is necessary to do so. Not everything or anything is possible, but that is not the issue. It is rather that the achievements of technology are always situated within established conditions while pregnant with both the obligation and capacity to respond to heterogeneity by heterogeneity. To a sophisticated technology, nothing is normal beyond the moment and the project; antecedent conditions define the project but never resolve it (unless we let them do so). In relation to languages, there are rules only insofar as there are linguistic practices, but the requirements of human practice call every rule into question.

ORNAMENTATION

Among its multiple functions, a language not only serves understanding and thought, communication, and action, but admits and partakes of ornamentation and embellishment, inexhaustibly enriching our lives and experiences. Ornamentation is, of course, not restricted to languages; rather, languages accommodate ornamentation insofar as it is pervasive throughout life and experience.

The forms of ornamentation are inexhaustible: ornamentation is one of the sources of inexhaustibility, of excess, supplementarity, and heterogeneity. Moreover, from such practices as promising, insulting, and avenging, it is clear that the most rudimentary forms of practice admit of diverse manifestations and inventions. Some forms of ornamentation are largely personal, though not in the sense that they are not prominently public; other forms are explicitly social in the sense that the ornamentation is directed toward others. Social ornamentation is not restricted to human beings, for birds and animals groom each other and preen, plume their feathers and strut their wares.

There are inexhaustibly manifold forms of ornamentation. Four, however, are of especial importance to linguistic utterance, and three of these are explicitly social. The three are (a) the public display of expressive utterances to establish and reinforce social esteem;[18] (b) "discursive formations";[19] and (c) those forms of play that involve other people. The fourth form of ornamentation is related to these three, especially the first two, but is not as explicitly social. We may think of it as (d) the expressive or ornamental forms of play that are part of the activity of thought and query. The togetherness of the public and private dimensions of experience entails that ornamental and expressive forms and practices that serve social requirements of utility and esteem also take on private and individual forms, manifested in the activity of thought.

(a) *Status and Esteem.* Harré defines his purpose, in *Social Being,* as exploring the "expressive order" in human social life concerned with status and reputation.[20] Goffman's work is largely concerned with the ways in which public verbal and gestural interchanges define both the kinds of individuals in a setting and the status they may succeed in establishing or maintaining in a public context. Thus, there are public gestures of dissociation that show the world that we are courteous in public but are not a member of a given (dishonorable or low-status) group.[21] And there are forms of talk that serve largely to define the status relationship of different members of a transiently public group—waiters and customers, professionals and clients, busriders, etc.[22] The useful distinction between discourse and language will govern much of the ensuing discussion. We may, following Goffman and Foucault, identify "discourse" with the public codes and linguistic manifestations that in speech and writing take on overtly social, public roles, and identify a "language" with the system of morphemes and phonemes that functions in relation to discourse. It is important, however, to emphasize that a language is not simply part of discourse. We will see that language and discourse cannot be separated, that a language includes both public-ornamental and formal-syntactical conditions. There is not, in this sense, something distinctive that is a language apart from and independent of the public forms and codes of discursive interaction. Speech-act theory expresses this social aspect of language, but lacks an emphasis on the difference between expressive discourse and discursive action and of the inseparability of public and private forms of expression. Our understanding of complementarity, as itself a complement of determinateness and indeterminateness, reciprocity and excess, allows us to understand the togetherness of language and discourse as maintaining both autonomy and heterogeneity.

How we understand the relation between the ornamental and other expressive functions of language is important. The issue is analogous to whether there is a satisfactory distinction between a language and the discourse that situates it. Such a distinction must presume either specific formal and structural conditions that define a language, blurred in discourse, or specific functions that are rendered more complex in social fields of interaction.

Our understanding is that the structural and functional characteristics of linguistic utterances are so entangled that there is no satisfactory way to disengage them. This is effectively the condition that any discourse on languages and utterances is itself entangled within the complexities of discourse, that there can be no "language of languages" in which we may speak of utterances singlemindedly. There is a political as well as a social or expressive form of this principle: the former, that there is no political discourse that is not embedded within and entangled among the political conditions that it would describe, or of which it would "speak the truth"; the latter, that there is no public discourse that is not effectively a social code defining status. Thus, every discourse is located within a system of rights as to who may speak and who may not, who is to be heard and who is not, who may listen and who may not. Put another way, every discourse serves expressive and ornamental functions in addition to its role in practice and thought; every discourse serves practical purposes and communication in addition to understanding and truth; every discourse functions epistemically in addition to its ornamental and practical functions. The characterization of each of these functions as served "in addition to" the others is an important interpretation of the surplus of meaning that characterizes semasic inexhaustibility. It is not, however, the autonomy of one function added to another, as if they could be distinguished and disentangled. The entanglement is thorough (if we cannot call it "complete"), but it does not overwhelm the distinctiveness of each of the functions.

We will have more to say about the entanglements of discourse and languages, but it is important to emphasize that "entanglement" and "complementarity" are not equivalent with holism. To the contrary, the inseparability of determinateness and indeterminateness that characterizes inexhaustibility requires an inexhaustible multiplicity of limits and conditions: limits for determinateness and the traversability of limits for indeterminateness. The belonging together of complementarity and supplementarity is a fundamental trait of finiteness, and finiteness depends on limits. The relatedness of all things together is more characteristically holism than is the complementary determinateness and indeterminateness of every pervasive trait of nature, which depends on limitation and permeability, on excess and heterogeneity. The inexhaustibility of discourse and language matches the inexhaustibility of human experience and thought, the inexhaustibility of judgment and semasis, and the locality and inexhaustibility of nature. Such inexhaustibility requires both an inexhaustible diversity of forms, distinct from each other, and the permeability and interaction of every form, with others, but not all others. This inexhaustible interaction and diversity is what we mean by entanglement and heterogeneity.

Some of this understanding is forcibly expressed by Foucault in characterizing the dispersion of power throughout relations involving discourse and desire.[23] He repeatedly emphasizes the specificity of the forms through which power is dispersed, the inexhaustible interrelatedness of discourse, desire, power, and truth, and the inexhaustible origins of power, conjoined with a continuing denial that power is thereby an abstract or generic condition, "everything." Power is everywhere and is inexhaustible but is not "everything." Like Chomsky in relation to linguistic structures, Foucault is concerned with emphasizing the specificity and density of discourse, but in historical and social terms.

(b) *Discourse and Power.* A second form of ornamentation, then, is given by the inexhaustible complexity of the relations among discourses, languages, knowledge, desire, and power. There is no discourse that is not expressive of a class structure or social codes typical of group status and reputation. There is instead a repertoire of discursive strategies that define status by expressing the kinds of individuals who are speaking as well as their authority to speak and what they may speak about. But such an authority is both political and social, and manifests an inexhaustible surplus in addition to status relationships and conditions of power. Authority is excessive and heterogeneous. Discourse is ornamental in the sense that beyond its practical and epistemic functions, it both defines and expresses the social status of speakers (and audiences) as well as their authority. The ornamentation is not to be thought of as without practical importance, but in the sense in which sovereigns manifest their authority by baubles of power, scepter and throne. Words are among the beads of authority. But such expressions of authority are to be distinguished from the ways in which utterances overtly characterize forms of activity and achieve purposes. The very notion of ornamentation, applied to relations of power, presupposes a view of power and discourse inexhaustibly dispersed among its multiple functions. Dispersion here is supplementarity and excess.

(c) *Play.* A more traditional sense of ornamentation is expressed in our understanding of the variety of forms of play with words and other forms of utterance. Some of these are social rituals defining one's role in particular groups or status in society at large. Others, however, are less serious and practical, varieties of entertainment. Jokes and stories are embellished by style and form; told well or poorly, they both establish reciters' status and exhibit their intelligence and cleverness. Moreover, these somewhat different characteristics, one social, the other more individual, are virtually inseparable. A good story told in public serves to define esteem and reputation, but the story is a discursive ornamentation, sometimes serious and sometimes not, sometimes a public form and sometimes the realization of inner experience.

Publicness and privateness are complementary forms; the serious and playful dimensions of ornamentation are also complementary. We include here both entertainment by discursive play with words, puns and other figurations, and more serious poetic discourses. In fact, no sharp lines can be drawn among these discourses. More important, however, is the fact that playful ornamentation, metaphors and other linguistic figures, is present both in everyday discourse—street talk, among intimates, throughout larger and smaller social groups—and in the most rarified of artistic and philosophic discourses. Rather than thinking of such ornamentation as atypical, we should realize that it characterizes an enormous variety of discursive situations.[24]

(d) *Private Play.* We conclude with the possibility that not all ornamental forms can be interpreted as social, even indirectly. There is an individual or private play inherent in the most public forms of expression and ornamentation that is required for them to serve their public functions. This play follows from the inseparability of public and private functions: where there is public ornamentation, there must also be individual embellishments, including those that never reach the light, repressed or forgotten, and those that do, in incipient forms. But there are in addition the idiosemic varieties of discursive ornamental practices, sometimes characterized in free association, dreams, or imagination. If we think in language, some of this thought will be ornamental, associative, a function of and modification of both public semasic fields and idiosemic fields. There is an inner life of language and thought, not in the sense that there are wholly private and inner semasic relations or meanings, but that every public semiate and semasic field undergoes heterogeneous variations wherever it functions. There is a play that is the result of the interaction of idiosemic variations and publicly consensual semasic relations, more serious and intentional when concerned with working through these differences to enrich our public sensibility, less serious and more individualized when coupled with distraction and superfluous relative to public and long-term purposes. It is in this dreamwork of private variation that the greatest inventions are initiated, as well as the emptiest forms of private whim.

There is a sense in which ornamentation expresses the surplus of meaning in all discourse and utterance. But there is also the sense that even ornamentation has practical and expressive functions, that the surplus of meaning here is not superfluity but a multiplicity of functions in interaction. Truth and realization of purposes are only some of the functions served by discourse and utterance. Ornamentation is, relative to these functions, superfluous. But within social life, it is functionally essential. When Derrida speaks of the "Parergon," the margins of the work, the ornaments, boundaries, and frame, he means to mark the necessity of the superfluous and, conversely, the arbitrariness of what is essential in the work.[25]

Discourse and utterance are inexhaustible in their functions, manifestly in the social functions they serve that are neither epistemic nor pragmatic. Here, among these functions, we find the deficiencies of all narrowly conceived theories of language. Instead, we must conclude that linguistic utterances participate in the inexhaustible functions of human experience, thereby themselves manifesting inexhaustibility. Our answer to the question of what language is depends on the question of what human experience and nature are, questions that we cannot answer without contributing to their definition.

COMPLEMENTARITY

It has become a commonplace in Anglo-American philosophy since Wittgenstein that languages are public, that the meanings of linguistic expressions must be stable over different persons if they can be said to understand each other. There is, here, a close relation between the principles of stability and of sociality, though the former includes stability over time for a single person and sociality is a manifestation not only of stability but of variation. This latter point is important, for it expresses a part of the complementarity that is inherent in inexhaustibility. For it has become an equal commonplace in recent Continental philosophy that meaning is variable, part of its finiteness, that in every stable form of meaning and expression there are arbitrary but compelling differences.[26] Both positions emphasize one side of the insight that the poles are less in opposition than complementary, where our understanding of complementarity emphasizes supplementarity and heterogeneity.

We find in Whitehead and Dewey a powerful emphasis on the complementarity of traditionally opposing terms, publicness and privateness, individuality and sociality. Whitehead is explicit, but perhaps does not carry the complementarity quite as far as necessary.[27] For he also holds that societies of actual entities can be understood only in terms of the experiences of their individual members, but not conversely. His emphasis on the primacy of actual entities makes it impossible for him to conclude that there could be no individual experience without societies.[28] Dewey does not define a principle of complementarity, but rather, argues repeatedly for the complementarity of traditional oppositions: freedom and determinism,[29] sociality and individuality,[30] means and ends.[31] Though he sometimes appears to argue, in his theory of pervasive qualities, that the complementarity presupposes an antecedent, undifferentiated unity, his deeper position is that all these distinctions are not so much independent factual determinations as oppositions located within thought, and thought is contextual and perspectival. Dewey shares this understanding with Whitehead and Nietzsche. The complementarity follows from the condition that intelligent thought is always purposive and selective, and that no purposes are unconditioned, valid without qualification. Thus, finiteness, qualification, locality, complementarity, and heterogeneity are profoundly interrelated notions. It is important to emphasize Dewey's view that experience is not intrinsically private, owned by an individual.[32] Experience is a double- barreled word, manifesting its complementarity.[33]

Such complementarities pervading nature and semasis are both the source and resolution of aporia. They comprise the fundamental meaning of ergonality, inherent in inexhaustibility. Several of them deserve specific attention in relation to language.

Sociality and Individuality

To suppose that a language serves thought is to hold as well that linguistic utterances must serve and be defined by both individual variations and common understandings. The public, communal side of thought is not the sharing of private thoughts, not only because insofar as they are private we cannot reveal their commonality, but because there are thoughts and knowledge that are not thought or known by individuals, but that inhabit a communal space. To think is to think in shareable terms by means of shareable materials about common objects. Yet sharing and commonality are not incompatible with individual variations and heterogeneity, but presuppose them. There is no individual thought that is not variable by person or condition; this is not merely a consequence of the inadequacy of private understandings but the source of both individual and shared discoveries. The argument, then, is that there can be no utterance, understanding, or experience that is not shared in part and individually variable in part, in such a way that the different parts, respects, or semasic fields cannot be separated, disentangled, except proximately; moreover, this commonality and variability profoundly contribute to each other.

Individuality and sociality are not exclusive and antagonistic properties of meanings and experiences but are rather supplementary dimensions of the locales, the fields, within which meanings and experiences are able to function. The very concept of utterance demands social and individual reciprocity. We may utter to ourselves, but what is uttered has a communal nature, is something that could be understood by others and derives from the communal sphere in which utterances transpire. Even distinguishing utterance from thought and practice fails to blunt the public or social requirements of its functions. A language is one of the social and communal forms that thought requires to be articulated and formulated.

But equally, articulation and formulation do not overcome individual variations among those who speak, think, and write. Linguistic utterances must have common forms to be public and shared, understandable to others, therefore common meanings, but the ways in which individuals understand such meanings, however common and public, are not and cannot be identical in all respects, because the individual variations are part of the ways in which understanding is realized. The contexts, the semasic fields, in which the judgments function determine their identity and relevance. And judgments function differently in different contexts, do different "work," their ergonality. Sociality and individuality, publicness and privateness, are complementary dimensions of understanding as well as meaning. We add the supplementality of these complements to emphasize their heterogeneity.

Public and Private

The sense of a public that we have been emphasizing is one involving anonymous manifestations, the sense in which something—event, experience, affirmation, utterance—belongs to no one in particular or to everyone. It is the sense of Dewey's view, in *Experience and Nature*, that experience is not necessarily owned.[34] Among the characteristics of so complex a field as human experience are some that are intelligible apart from particular individuals, that cannot even be intelligible if assigned to an individual, such as tradition, history, intelligibility itself. Other characteristics can be understood only relative to particular individuals. Moreover, of these two sets of characteristics, each requires the other for intelligibility, if not for any particular kind of intelligibility. This, in effect, is the togetherness of the public and private dimensions of experience. We have regarded this togetherness as a manifestation of the heterogeneity of nature and being. Dewey's view of experience is heterogeneous.

No language can be wholly private or wholly individual. A language serves communication as well as thought, presupposing the understanding by others of linguistic utterances. Similarly, linguistic utterances when uttered, like all judgments, enter public, anonymous spheres over which an individual has limited authority. Texts and works of art are read by others as they choose, interpreted by them as they wish, assimilated by them into their own spheres of experience, their own horizons. Every linguistic utterance in this sense is to be understood in both public and private respects by unique individuals who belong to social groups. Moreover, these respects, public and private, social and individual, are only proximately separable. It is as false that individuals can understand a linguistic utterance entirely in their own unique terms as that there can be a public understanding that is not permeated by individual variations.

The natural public sphere is that of other people, of society and social groups. The natural private sphere is that of individuals' inner experience. But relative to larger social and political spheres of agency, smaller domains of thought and practice like families and neighborhoods privately possess singular interpretive and linguistic codes, while within every person's inner experience are traits and conditions that belong to the world at large. This is the effective answer to both solipsism and unqualified relativism: that there can be no totally private, solipsistic experience, for it would not be experience, would not be anything at all; and there can be no relativism in which stability is not inherent in the presence of different spheres of thought and culture. Put another way, intelligibility presupposes both public, anonymous rational conditions and the personal assimilation and interpretation of any public judgments. Put a third way, intelligibility presupposes heterogeneity.

It follows that a language along with every linguistic utterance is private in certain of its interpretive relations and public in others, public and private together in the very possibility of interpretation and understanding. In this sense, "Language" marks less the universal in the particularity of linguistic utterances than the anonymous side of such utterances. What we have been rejecting, in refusing to speak of *Language* along with a multiplicity of languages, is the universal form of all languages as if such a form existed independent of or even within the diversity of languages. If the anonymous and idiosyncratic sides of both languages and semasis are inexhaustible, so too language resides within their public side. The complementarity entails that even this public side has a private nature, that it is not a permanent structure that defines language but the recurrent possibility of an anonymous understanding amid idiosyncratic variations both in utterance and assimilation.[35] Language is not what transcends all utterances as a permanent possibility of alternative expression, but is among the recurrent transgressions within heterogeneous utterances that enable them to function beyond personal idiosyncracies, to have a public side, but not one grounded on something lying outside or beyond.

Stability and Variation

Our discussion has led repeatedly to other complementary notions inherent in language and semasis, the togetherness of stability and variation, interiority and exteriority, simplicity and complexity. Like publicness and privateness, these inseparable pairs are more generic conditions of nature than of meaning and utterance, more, perhaps, than individuality and sociality. In a somewhat narrow sense, social groupings are distinctly human or at least organic, while aggregation is the corresponding ontological trait. But there can be no form of being that is not a togetherness of stability and variation, even if we refuse to interpret variation in exclusively temporal or historical terms.[36] We understand this togetherness to entail heterogeneity.

There are variations through time and historical developments; but there are also variations with location and context. Linguistic utterances change their meanings through time but also among different audiences—though not in all respects, since they are understood by those who inhabit other groups and who live at other times. Time is not the generic condition of variation but one of its pervasive exemplifications. The point is that there can be no stable conditions of judgment or being that are not subject to variation with conditions and contexts. The sense in which natural laws never fail to apply or universal structures obtain is not incompatible with but permeated by variation and novelty. Nature is uniform in its fundamental laws but inexhaustibly heterogeneous in its manifestations, not in any other sense uniform at all. One does not need exceptions to uniformity, but that uniformity is permeated by inexhaustibility.

Exteriority and Interiority

In a similarly generic sense, there is no being and no utterance that is altogether self-contained, either in the sense that it is wholly self-caused, self-intelligible, or altogether inclusive and comprehensive. Interiority and exteriority are reciprocal conditions of being and intelligibility. Nothing can be intelligible except from the outside, in some sense public; nothing can be intelligibly what it is except in virtue of its interiority. No linguistic utterance can be understood except in terms of other utterances; the value or meaning of a sign is a function of other signs, both positively and negatively in the sense that the differential alternatives depend on both established and potential signs.

Intelligibility of judgment or semasis is a complement of interiority and exteriority. This view is effectively a rejection of the entire tradition in which any being, Substance or God, may be thought to be either wholly self-caused or intelligible apart from anything else. And the sense of intelligibility here is stronger than that we human beings cannot understand something that is wholly self-caused, since we understand things in terms of their relations, but that nothing can be self-caused; self-causation is not a rational principle. It follows that intelligibility demands heterogeneity.

These complementarities are the most visible manifestations of the inexhaustible heterogeneity of nature, judgment, and truth, expressed through the notion of semasic fields and the manifold categories of linguistic utterances. Because of these complementary relations, no language can be understood as either an entity or an instrument. In this sense, a language is always characterized by a unique structure and grammar that is in constant tension with the requirement that utterances in that language serve to express whatever we know and understand, as well as facilitate human interaction and communication. The conclusion is that the social side of language is one of many heterogeneous poles that define linguistic utterances.

NOTES

1. This point is made repeatedly by Foucault, but it may be found also in speech-act theory.

2. I have called this locatedness and situatedness "ordinality." See my *Transition to an Ordinal Metaphysics*. I now call it "locality." See my *Inexhaustibility and Human Being*. See *Ring of Representation* for the triangle of locality, inexhaustibility, and ergonality, with the sonant categories of location and ingredience. See also chap. 1, note 62.

3. See my *Inexhaustibility and Human Being*.

4. Dewey, *Experience and Nature*, p. 166.

5. This is the burden of *Ring of Representation*.

6. See my "Metaphor, Inexhaustibility, and the Semasic Field."

7. I discuss this at length in *Learning and Discovery*.

8. Gadamer, *Truth and Method*, p. 273.

9. Searle, *Speech Acts*, pp. 57–61. (Text between each statement of condition has been silently elided; Searle's italics are here set as Roman.)

10. Ibid., p. 60.

11. Rorty, *Philosophy and the Mirror of Nature*; Kuhn, *The Structure of Scientific Revolutions*; Putnam, "Analyticity and Apriority."

12. See also E. D. Hirsch, *Validity in Interpretation* (New Haven: Yale University Press, 1967); and Searle, *Intentionality*, for a more complex, but still insufficiently complex, analysis.

13. Gadamer, *Truth and Method*, especially pp. 214–34.

14. See my *A Theory of Art: Inexhaustibility by Contrast* (Albany: State University of New York Press, 1982).

15. Searle, *Speech Acts*, p. 137. The speech-act fallacy is that the meaning of a linguistic expression is determined by the act in which it is employed.

16. It is useful here to recall Socrates' criticisms of writing in *Phaedrus*. We may conveniently identify "writing" with the stability of a common understanding. Socrates' criticisms of written words are that "they seem to talk to you as though they were intelligent, but if you ask them anything about what they say, from a desire to be instructed, they go on telling you just the same thing forever" (Plato, *Phaedrus*, 275e). One of the ironies of the history of philosophy is that this passage has been interpreted to support a theory of unchanging Forms, while the deficiency described is that written words (and presumably, knowledge of unchanging Forms) "go on telling you just the same thing forever." The deficiency is that understanding requires instruction and follows from interrogation, but written words can neither answer questions nor instruct, but simply repeat. We may, then, take Plato's criticism to be that any form of expression that simply repeats itself—*in any sense of "repetition"*—is similarly deficient. We are led to semasis.

17. For a discussion of these issues, see Noam Chomsky, *Reflections on Language* (London: Temple Smith, 1976).

18. See Harré, *Social Being*; Goffman, *Relations in Public*.

19. See Foucault, *Archaeology of Knowledge*.

20. "At the heart of the system of concepts I will be developing is the idea that the public and collective aspects of human life are to be treated as products generated by an interplay between a practical order, concerned with the production of the means of life, and an expressive order concerned with honour and reputation" (Harré, *Social Being*, p. 3). He thus summarizes his position: "In the expressive aspects of social activity we make a public showing of skills, attitudes, emotions, feelings and so on, providing, sometimes consciously, the evidence upon which our friends, colleagues, neighbors, rivals and enemies are to draw conclusions as to the kind of person we are. The expressive aspect will include both natural and conventional signs" (ibid., p. 21).

It is worth noting the movement from "an expressive order concerned with honour and reputation" to "conclusions as to the kind of person we are." The latter surely includes the former, but not conversely, for we are effectively "many kinds" of person, including the traits relevant to our status and reputation.

21. See Goffman, *Presentation of Self.*

22. See Goffman, *Forms of Talk.*

23. "The objective is to analyze a certain form of knowledge regarding sex, not in terms of repression or law, but in terms of power. . . . Power must be understood in the first instance as the multiplicity of force relations immanent in the sphere in which they operate and which constitute their own organization; as the process which, through ceaseless struggles and confrontations, transforms, strengthens, or reverses them; as the support which these force relations find in one another, thus forming a chain or system, or on the contrary, the disjunctions and contradictions which isolate them from one another; and lastly, as the strategies in which they take effect, whose general design or institutional crystallization is embodied in the state apparatus, in the formulation of the law, in the various social hegemonies. . . . Power is everywhere, not because it embraces everything, but because it comes from everywhere" (Foucault, *History of Sexuality*, pp. 92–93).

24. Lakoff and Johnson, *Metaphors We Live By*; see my "Metaphor, Inexhaustibility, and the Semasic Field."

25. Jacques Derrida, "Parergon," *The Truth in Painting* (Chicago: The University of Chicago Press, 1987).

26. Derrida, *On Grammatology* and *Speech and Phenomena*; Ricoeur, *Conflict of Interpretations.*

27. "The theory of prehensions is founded upon the doctrine that there are no concrete facts which are merely public, or merely private. The distinction between publicity and privacy is a distinction of reason, and is not a distinction between mutually exclusive concrete facts. The sole concrete facts, in terms of which actualities can be analysed, are prehensions; and every prehension has its public side and its private side" (Whitehead, *Process and Reality*, p. 290).

28. Ibid., Part II, chaps. 3, 4.

29. John Dewey, *Democracy in Education* (New York: Macmillan, 1916).

30. Dewey, *Human Nature and Conduct.*

31. Dewey, *Experience and Nature.*

32. "In first instance and intent, it is not exact nor relevant to say 'I experience' or 'I think.' 'It' experiences or is experienced, 'it' thinks or is thought, is a juster phrase. Experience, a serial course of affairs with their own characteristic properties and relationships, occurs, happens, and is what it is. Among and within those occurrences, not outside of

them nor underlying them, are those events which are denominated selves. . . . To say in a significant way, '*I* think, believe, desire, instead of barely *it* is thought, believed, desired,' is to accept and affirm a responsibility and to put forth a claim" (ibid., p. 232, 233).

33. Ibid., p. 8. See also William James, *Essays in Radical Empiricism* (New York: Longmans Green, 1912), p. 10.

34. See note 32, above. This view that experience is not owned by an individual entails its heterogeneity. James calls it a "blooming, buzzing confusion."

35. This may be what Gadamer has in mind in Part III of *Truth and Method*.

36. I call the general categories relevant here "unison" and "resonances." See my *Ring of Representation*; also chap. 1, note 62. In my earlier work, I used the terminology "prevalence" and "deviance." See my *Transition to an Ordinal Metaphysics*; Justus Buchler, *Metaphysics of Natural Complexes* (New York: Columbia University Press, 1966).

I might add that the representation of heterogeneity can have no preferred form. I regard none of my earlier efforts as privileged.

6

DISCOURSE

WE HAVE SPOKEN of a sense of publicness that is to be distinguished from sociality, a sense much closer to anonymity. This is the notion of the public spheres in which politics transpires as distinct from the private spheres of individual locales. Politics here is both collective and instrumental, a form of agency different, if inseparable, from the acts of individual agents. Arendt argues that the distinction between publicness and privateness, on which the notions of the state and politics traditionally rest, is both essential to the side of human life that involves civic responsibilities and has become blurred, virtually demolished, in contemporary life.[1]

This distinction, between a firmly entrenched public sphere of activities and responsibilities and multiple spheres of private affairs, is important. But the blurring may be due less to the corruption of modern life than to the distinction's theoretical weaknesses. The assumption that civic responsibilities are or were ever sharply distinct from personal or moral responsibilities is not plausible, though in a world in which geographical separation entailed both temporal and instrumental separation, it may have been practically effective. We may imagine that the collapse of the distinction between public and private spheres is due to the development of technological and bureaucratic devices that permit public institutions—governmental, corporate, and communicative—to invade private domains of authority. Nevertheless, modern technology may not so much produce this breakdown as call to our attention the permeability and fragility of the distinction between public and private powers.

The distinction is permeable because all limits are traversable, but especially because the distinction between public and private spheres, anonymous, generic spheres and individual, personal spheres, is complementary and entangled rather than opposing. Crudely put, civic life is constituted by individuals and households carrying on their normal activities while these activities are profoundly influenced by public events. The distinction is fragile because private spheres function as they do largely by public sufferance. This is the truth that contemporary life has made prominent. Although the inseparability of public and private spheres entails that wherever there are public powers, private spheres will function as well, the character of private spheres, the spheres in which private citizens are permitted to function privately and individually, are largely publicly determined. This is true even though there is no public sphere that is not divided by private undertakings. The complementarity is overshadowed in practice by the greater powers in public spheres. Public institutions define what can be accepted as private. In this sense, the prevailing distinction between private and public spheres belongs to the public sector.

However, it does not belong to the public sector always under explicit control. We revert here to the sense of publicness as anonymity, actions and influences effective over individual and social spheres generically. There is public determination of private activities in the regulation of practices by the market, but there is public determination of private activities by the existence of a market. There is public determination of private activities in the regulation of sexual activities by law, but there is public determination of private sexual activities by custom, practice, and discourse.

In this pervasive sense of public determination, the complementarity of private and public determinations is irresistible. No sphere of any complexity, particularly the diverse institutional practices that compose ordinary social life, can altogether determine the individual practices that compose them. Public life, in the nature of its diversity and of the heterogeneity of its practices, manifests its diversity in the relevance of individual spheres of private initiative. These may be controlled but they cannot be eliminated.

It is important to distinguish this anonymous publicness from sociality, the latter a form of collective being, the former the dispersed and anonymous influence of institutions and practices. Arendt treats the public as the sphere of work, of enduring appearances.[2] That the most visible forms of public influence are by and upon social collectives should not encourage us to equate the two. Questions of power and influence inherent in the public sphere always concern what is visible and what invisible in the workings of power, where social collectives are regarded as a prominent form of visibility.

It is the anonymous sense of publicness and this question of power that guide the approach in this chapter to politics and its relation to language, that is, to discourse, to the practical functions of language involving power and desire. There is an invisible side to the workings of power that is not encompassed within the social sides of discourse. We may reasonably interpret the question of sociality to be one of communication and interchange, the problem of understanding other people and the codes that are shared by the members of large or small social groups. There is an inexhaustible heterogeneity to such commonality, diverse social groups and the codes they employ, as well as diverse ornamental functions served by utterance. But there is also a covert side to utterance, expressed in what is excluded and prohibited rather than what is expected or required.[3] We are concerned here with what may be said and what may not, what is said and what is not, what is expressible in every discourse and what is not.

This question of expressibility is inseparable from several other important questions: what is true and what is false; what is real and what unreal; what we know and what we do not know; what we can know and what we cannot know; but also, what we desire and what is indifferent to us; what is permitted and what is not; what we may express and what we may not. These notions—knowledge, desire, power, and discourse—are inseparable.[4]

We are generalizing Foucault's view of the entanglements of discourse with power. He denies that he is seeking to define a general theory of the relations among power, knowledge, pleasure, and discourse, but only to define the *régime* that sustains the established discourse in our part of the world. Yet there is in his view of things a profound sense of the pervasive entanglements of discourse, power, knowledge, and pleasure as well as of the locality of all such conditions. These senses of entanglement and locality as they pertain to language in the context of human practices, dispersed and anonymous, are the subjects of the ensuing discussion.

POWER

What is power, and where is it located? Foucault answers that power is everywhere,[5] together with resistance.[6] He effectively offers a "metaphysics of power," though he does whatever he can to avoid the label. The reason for the denial lies in a particular understanding of the metaphysical enterprise, shared by many contemporary writers.[7] Foucault does not address himself explicitly to metaphysics in his analytics of power, but analogous themes recur throughout and in his other works.[8] The concepts at the center of his analysis, "discontinuity, rupture, threshold, limit, series, and transformation,"[9] exist in traditional (metaphysical) discourse only to be overcome. An important question is whether any discourse can concern itself with discontinuities and ruptures without promulgating other unities in terms of which to understand them, a question of the intelligibility of differences that has appeared throughout the present discussion in the form of aporia. Our entire project is devoted to a metaphysics of discontinuity, rupture, threshold, and limit, that is, of heterogeneity as aporia.

There is another way to express this question: how is difference manifested specifically in discourse?[10] Like Heidegger, Foucault understands the presence of difference in terms of absence. The themes of silence, the Forgotten, the unsaid, recur repeatedly.[11] For Foucault, discourse functions by exclusion as a site where power is effective. Difference may not be representable, but it inhabits the spaces and voids among representations. And it is as much on the surface, in this negative way, as the representations.[12] There are other questions as well, of the sites of discourse and their emergence. More important, however, is the principle that among the voids and absences that inhabit discourse and utterance are the exclusions that constitute the workings of power. Power works by exclusion and prohibition.[13] Among its effects are those Foucault describes as the "particular, fearsome, and even devilish features" of discourse.[14] Discourse, therefore language as well, is dangerous, perilous.[15]

Foucault distinguishes "discourse" from "language," "statements" from "propositions."[16] In this way, he can avoid the important but perhaps distracting question of whether the considerations that he takes to be essential to discourse—materiality, function, locatedness, danger—must also be regarded as essential to languages and linguistic utterances. The question is whether we are to understand the dangerousness of discourse (a) in the weaker sense that in addition to the formal elements of languages described by Saussure and Chomsky, there are complex entanglements of utterances in human events that have profoundly political, moral, and methodological consequences; or (b) in the stronger sense that consequently language itself is so located and immersed in political and other human entanglements that none of its features can be autonomous. This question is closely related to the analogous political question of whether any critical discourse can be freer of ideology than the discourses it criticizes. It is a question of heterogeneity.

It follows from a thoroughly local view of discourse that the distinction between discourse and language is provisional, a methodological distinction introduced to avoid the suggestion that more circumscribed theories of languages and utterances are somehow to be overcome in a more complete understanding of the inexhaustible entanglements of discourse. Discourse is language; linguistic utterance is discourse, including every theory of language. Nevertheless, just as there are formal conditions of legislation that can be understood to be relevant not so much "above and beyond," but alongside the historical developments that established them and the human purposes they serve, there are formal conditions of languages, syntactical and semantic, that are neither permanent and essential to linguistic utterances nor merely ephemeral conditions of a particular linguistic site, but entangled through and through with larger functional conditions, a *telos*, so to speak, serving human needs, the nature of the things they describe, and the ornamental features of human life. We are acknowledging what we have repeatedly called the "supplementarity" in locality and inexhaustibility, giving rise to the autonomy of semasic functions. Here supplementarity and complementarity give rise to discourse as language's heterogeneous excess.

With this understanding, we may return to the question of power in relation to utterances to conclude that if power is everywhere in the sense that it is dispersed through widely separated social institutions, practices, discourses, and understandings, then it is certainly dispersed throughout linguistic utterances and languages themselves. (Yet nevertheless, it is not everything; it cannot be equated with understanding, practice, or sociality, with judgment or semasis in general. These represent the limits of language.) Not only is who may say what important for understanding an utterance, but who has the right to speak and who must listen are both productive of and consequences of relations of power. This point bears emphasis. It is not simply that discourse displays marks of the oppressed and their oppressors, but that discourse is a major site where that distinction is effective.

If power is such that it has no specific locus, then it has no specific essence. In this sense, the dispersion and entanglements of power characterize it more essentially than its more traditional expressions of dominance and subordination. In the sense in which discourse is dangerous, in its ponderousness and materiality, power is dangerous because it is not located only where some are oppressors and others are oppressed, but everywhere, entangled with everything. Put another way, power is a name for material entanglements, for dispersed relevance, not for a particular constellation of forces. Foucault himself distinguishes power from Power, the former everywhere and dispersed, the latter the traditional implementation of power: " 'Power,' insofar as it is permanent, repetitious, inert, and self-reproducing, is simply the overall effect that emerges from all these mobilities, the concatenation that rests on each of them and seeks in turn to arrest the movement."[17] To note that among the entanglements of utterances are relations of power is not only to note that utterances function politically—the specific and narrow sense that those who govern both persuade and motivate through language—but also that utterances function in terms of the general relations of human authority and influence. Foucault extends and develops Nietzsche's view of the relation between truth and power:

> "Truth" is linked in a circular relation with systems of power which produce and sustain it, and to effects of power which it induces and which extend it. A "régime" of truth. . . .
> The political question, to sum up, is not error, illusion, alienated consciousness or ideology; it is truth itself. Hence the importance of Nietzsche.[18]

Power represents relevance, manifested in dispersed and entangled spheres of influence, crystallizing into structures of domination. It appears as locality, inexhaustibly multiple spheres of location, dispersed and entangled. Identity and truth are functions of multiple location.

In every discipline, not only formal ones but social practice, governance, and all forms of exchange, some have authority over others in the sense that the former are to be listened to by the latter. And within such imbalances, we find not only relations of authority, but relations of knowledge and understanding. Moreover, what the authorities know defines what human beings "ought to know," and this is defined by norms of expectation and of desire. Power, knowledge, and desire are inseparably entangled. This is the materiality of discourse, perilous both because of its arbitrariness and because it threatens every human relationship with dominance and authority, with being other than it is.

Having gone so far, we must conclude that there is no linguistic utterance that can be understood, in any of the senses of that term, without considering who has spoken (sometimes a group), the speakers' standing and authority, what they know and to what group they belong, and what their purposes are in speaking, covert and overt. Even the act of writing conveys and depends upon the establishment of its own authority, for otherwise no one would read what has been written. Thus, speaking or writing, on any subject whatever, presuppose the establishment of authority in relation to an audience.[19]

Can there be a neutral relation between audience and speaker in which the former listens respectfully but voluntarily and the latter merely offers opinions without coercion? Can there be a sense of rational dialogue that avoids the perils and dangers of material forms of tangible authority? In the social practices that compose discourse, such a notion of dialogue represents an ideal that, admirable as it may be, blinds us to its practical limitations. Publishers, reviewers, peer institutions in the disciplines constitute the authorities who define by extension further authority. That such power is dispersed is less a form of abolition than a strengthening of its effects by decentralization. If we cannot locate the sites of power, then we cannot oppose it directly.

Moreover, the ideal of rational dialogue can function ideally only where sites of power constitute it as a practice. And in this sense, reason cannot escape power but must conform to its imperatives. Plato expresses this eloquently in his conception of the philosopher as the lover of wisdom who will rule the state. To know the truth of power is not to escape it. To be able to speak of power is not to avoid it.

In this sense, to understand an utterance, linguistic or not, is already to be situated among relations that call that understanding into question as arbitrary and oppressive. This is not true merely of discourse as against language, but of any utterances including the most ordinary linguistic and nonlinguistic forms. The neutralization of language is oppressive by design and neglect. The terror we may feel at the dangers of discourse is expressed in part in the image of Oedipus, who blinds himself upon discovering the perils of the quest for truth and suffering the horror of learning that knowledge (as well as ignorance) has tangible consequences, that there is no practically neutral form of understanding or expression. Language's alleged neutrality works oppressively against women and members of minority groups. Irigaray expresses this understanding repeatedly, the sweeping ways in the Western tradition in which women pay the price for language's rationality.[20] Lyotard expresses the political force of language as the *différend*: the silencing of heterogeneity.[21]

It may be worth considering a synthesis within the aporias of our account of inexhaustibility and language. We may say that Foucault emphasizes the ponderousness and materiality, the tangibility and specificity, of the finiteness of local situations while Gadamer and Dewey emphasize their permeability and openness to other situations. Both views are important, if we emphasize their limits and the ways in which they speak of limits: it is the nature of locality to involve both specificities of entanglements and openness to otherness, each complementary with the other, but also supplementary, excessive. In virtue of this excess, it is extraordinarily tempting to emphasize one of these poles over the other, since our intellectual tradition has tended to identify objectivity with universality and contingency with skepticism.

What is left out of such a polarization is the positive side of finiteness and locality. The specificities of our contingent situations are indeed limiting conditions, even confining, but they are also sources of the very insights that promote invention and the enrichment of human experience. The continuing presence of otherness, of heterogeneity, is both a continuing threat—call it "danger"—and the source of the differences that all understandings and truths require. Within the entanglements of human practices are the practices that become traditions, establish norms of understanding and communication, and project themselves into the future, not to overcome the risks of change but to enrich ongoing tradition. The entanglements of human practices express the inexhaustible plenitude of nature.

Thus, every finite situation is open to other finite situations, and their mediation comprises the establishment of a particular tradition. Only within such a tradition can understanding possess standing. But are there not radical shifts in traditions, from normal to abnormal discourse? Not without establishing another tradition, even many traditions. Traditions are not alternatives as much as centers of intelligibility and practice. They, like every finite locus of human activity are neither closed nor radically differentiated from other traditions. They nevertheless impose structure, delimit possibilities, and, overtly or covertly, institute oppression. Dispersed power coalesces into régimes.

Every tradition is divided within itself by alternative interpretations and understandings, different perspectives, and variable norms, however authoritarian or conforming it may be. Conformation in no human practice can be complete and undivided. Heterogeneity pervades human life and nature. But the dividedness of practices and traditions into subpractices and subtraditions is the source inseparably of both openness and variation and of misunderstanding and the clash of different points of view. Insight and confusion are less opposed than so intimately conjoined as to be virtually indistinguishable, recognizable only through time, by their results.

With Gadamer, we recognize that understanding is the overcoming of or mediation among differences in conditions and points of view, a mediation that cannot eliminate differences. With Foucault, we recognize that these conditions and points of view possess tangibility and specificity, that they are indeed the differential material conditions of human life. With Irigaray, we recognize that differential material conditions institute oppression. These specificities in practices, especially the multiplicity of different practices, express two dimensions of locatedness: the specificities of entanglements and the prospects of mediation among any divided practices.

RULES AND PRACTICES

We have discussed some difficulties with the view that rules can explain language, where the paradigm was rules of a game. There is another paradigm of rules, derived from power, that plays a pervasive role in our understanding of discourse. This notion may not be susceptible to the criticism that rules distort our understanding of language and other human institutions and activities.

Foucault indifferently speaks of rules and of codes, formations, conditions, procedures, and practices. We may suppose that for him the notion of rule has no particular efficacy, despite belonging to an ongoing practice. Put another way, we may suppose that in attempting to analyze the sites of power and discursive formations in human practices, Foucault is indifferent to any particular terminology that would suggest a privileged site and a privileged analysis.[22] Such a discourse may be able to speak of rules, as well as codes, practices, and formations, without the distortions that lie behind our criticisms of rules, in particular, that they suggest too restrictive a view of the conditions that compose human traditions and experiences.

We have the following very different kinds of rules in *The History of Sexuality*:

1. Rule of immanence
2. Rule of continual variations
3. Rule of double conditioning
4. Rule of the tactical polyvalence of discourses

But also, the "insistence of the rule," situated among several other conditions:

a. The negative relation
b. The insistence of the rule
c. The cycle of prohibition
d. The logic of censorship
e. The uniformity of the apparatus[23]

The rules here constitute the workings of power. They compose a particular discourse centered on desire, sexuality, that enforces a particular system of relations of power, but also, a system of knowledge and of truth. Truth, here, belongs to power and to rule.

We have, in relation to language, discussed the notion of rules derived from games. Foucault draws upon another paradigm: that of rule and authority. Among his concerns is to argue that modern power is not typically located in a sphere of rule or sovereignty, but is dispersed throughout different social sites, including the disciplines of knowledge and the manipulation of desires.[24] Another concern is that power, and therefore the social spheres in which it is situated and dispersed, functions by exclusion, negatively, but also positively, constituting material and discursive formations.[25] The entanglements of discourse with power produce what Foucault calls its "ponderous, awesome materiality."[26] This materiality is the way in which discourse inhabits social practices, constitutes institutions, both constrains human life and threatens it with departures. Rules here are the forms whereby power is exercised. Yet the very same materiality includes resistances to power and a multiplicity of discourses. There is no discourse that is not thoroughly divided within itself, the locus of power and of the only forms of reason and critique that we will ever know. In the sense in which a tradition is complex and fluid, changing over time and in virtue of its future, a discourse includes within itself many of the resistances that define its heterogeneities.[27] Discourse here is tangled and dense, not unitary or homogeneous.

To the extent, then, that there are rules in this sense of control, there are dispersed workings of power, resistances, and forms, that entangle every discourse with contingencies and variations. In this sense of form of life, practice, or discursive formation, human activities are entangled in a nebulous mass of practices and sub-practices, some of which may be governed by definite rules in the sense defined by the paradigm of games, but others of which include the resistances and variations that contradict the basis of governance by rules.

Like the notion of "normal discourse," a practice defined by rules in the sense of a game presupposes a strong sense of normality. We have seen that the practices in which human activities are located are also typically abnormal, heterogeneous, pregnant with both the possibility and the reality of departures and variations. These are not to be described as "departures from rules." The gestures, emphases, rhetorical flourishes, tonal variations, atypical forms of linguistic utterance that are employed in everyday discourse are not departures from the normal rules of language but ways of making oneself understood. Understanding often requires recurrent patterns, but equally often requires variation. Understanding is not merely a form of the Same, but requires heterogeneity. What we know in common we understand in different, sometimes incommunicable ways. The notion of rules masks this heterogeneity behind an opaque notion of normality. The notion of rules in language and social practices serves to define the norms of a practice on the one hand and the authority inherent in such practices on the other. Both of these functions are very important, for there are no practices without norms or without relations of power. What must be added is that every norm and rule, all conditions of power, is dispersed and divided, promoting alternative expectations and resistances. Power is both opposed and supported by resistances; norms both establish normalcy and promote heterogeneous departures from it. The negativities in rules are essential to their positivities.[28]

Discursive Entanglements

In his foreword to the English edition of *The Order of Things*, in 1970, Foucault makes the following "request to the English-speaking reader": "In France, certain half-witted 'commentators' persist in labelling me a 'structuralist.' I have been unable to get it into their tiny minds that I have used none of the methods, concepts, or key terms that characterize structural analysis."[29] This seems clear enough, as do his remarks at the conclusion of *The Archaeology of Knowledge*, in 1969: "You must admit that I never once used the word 'structure' in *The Order of Things*. But let us leave off our polemics about 'structuralism'; they hardly survive in areas now deserted by serious workers; this particular controversy, which might have been so fruitful, is now acted out only by mimes and tumblers."[30] Yet he is constantly classified *with*, if not *in*, structuralism, and states in *The Discourse on Language*: "And now, let those who are weak on vocabulary, let those with little comprehension of theory call all this—if its appeal is stronger than its meaning for them—structuralism."[31]

Foucault wrote his most important books during the height of French structuralism, and any serious form of analysis that was not directly hostile to structuralism was likely to be classified as belonging to it. But the more important issue at stake is that of entanglement in discourse. What does it mean to be so entangled, and what are its consequences?

One answer is that if we are always located within discourse and practice, then there is no unbiased form of knowledge, for locatedness is intrinsically biased. Now objectivity contrasts with subjectivity, while discursive entanglements do not entail subjectivity but collectivity: our individual activities and expressions are located within and circumscribed by collective, public, institutional spaces. Bias contrasts with balance, but we need not be unbalanced by our circumstances and expectations: what we can think of and say is a reflection of our situations, but both positively and negatively. Discourse here functions both to regulate and to make possible. Locality is no more bias than endowment.

Foucault describes himself as a man with "no face," though not the first to write anonymously.[32] The irony is that to write about Foucault is to seek his face and to grant him a center. But this raises the question we are considering, of how to carry on discourse given the entanglements in which we are located. Foucault suggests that a decentered, anonymous discourse is possible. This is anything but obvious, and certainly aporetic. But it is an aporia that we may assume he is entirely aware of and responsive to.

Before examining Foucault's explicit responses to aporia, it is worth considering some other views on the possibility of articulating the entanglements of discursive practices. One alternative is Wittgenstein's famous line, "What we cannot speak about we must consign to silence."[33] Every discourse is situated among human practices and historical developments that establish the conditions of its intelligibility. We cannot then speak of the conditions of discursive intelligibility except from within a discourse. There is no disentangled discourse or form of knowledge.

Several other positions may be considered. At the risk of oversimplification, we may consider the following schematic summary of some established alternatives.

1. There is a relation that constitutes the foundation of all discourse, lying either in the nature of the things discourse addresses or in the nature of the intelligibility of discourse.

2. There is an ideal form of discourse against which every actual discourse may be measured.

These alternatives define possibilities of disentanglement, that we may either become cognizant somehow of the object of all epistemic discourse or define objectively superior methodological principles for the most effective epistemic discourse. Locality entails that every discourse is enmeshed in historical conditions, networks of power, manifestations of desire, and practices of expression. If we cannot disentangle our thoughts and expressions from such conditions—we may identify this impossibility with the pervasiveness of finiteness and the absence of any unconditioned transcendence—the alternatives appear to be as follows:

3. If we cannot *speak* of the essence of discourse, we may at least experience it.[34]

4. If we cannot experience the essence of discourse, nevertheless we may confront it, even "think" it, in the infinite play of differences.[35]

5. If we cannot escape from the entanglements of discourse, nevertheless, we should not suppose that entanglement is entrapment.[36]

6. If there are established conventions within normal discourse, every discourse is potentially abnormal. Where a discourse becomes abnormal, we continue the conversation and seek to establish new normal forms, but there is no privileged account of the nature of discourse, normal or abnormal.[37]

There is no way to disentangle ourselves from our finite, local conditions, either in thought or in language. The more alert we become to human conditions, the more we understand how historical conditions shape the forms of thought and expression. (1) and (2) must then be rejected. The question is what follows.

(3) and (4) are not plausible if they would reconstitute a privileged, generic realm of discursive conditions. One of the most important features of discursive entanglements is that they are specific, not generic or abstract. There is a "specific reality of discourse" that is typically avoided by any theory of transcendent ideality.[38] We have repeatedly discussed this specificity in relation to grammar.

Gadamer's view of language is crudely expressed in (5): we are not "trapped" in language because language is what makes it possible to overcome our conditions. Discourse has two sides, not just one, a side in which entanglement is specific and determinate, the particular circumstances of our historical and temporal locations, the other in which, through discourse, we are able to understand alien points of view and other particular circumstances. Every discourse is, with every human locale, both closed and open, definite and permeable, normal and abnormal. Every discourse is entangled amid the inexhaustible conditions and activities of human practices. We are both confined by such entanglements and enabled by them to move beyond them. And it is precisely this double character that we may emphasize as inherent in the nature of discursive entanglements.

It is worth emphasizing the political form of the issue before us: how may we establish a basis for political norms if we are always enmeshed in ideology.[39] How are we able to engage in a political discourse that presupposes an understanding of alternative ideals and norms? How are we to escape from the finite contingencies of historical events so as to criticize them, especially where the future of humanity is at stake? The premise of the present discussion is that there is no such escape, but as Gadamer points out, there is no absolute entrapment either.[40] What is again involved is the nature of locality.

We have noted Foucault's claim that he "writes in order to have no face." He is an author who recognizes the pitfalls in being an author, in particular, that he is "the unifying principle in a particular group of writings or statements, lying at the origins of their significance," although "all around us, there are sayings and texts whose meaning or effectiveness has nothing to do with any author to whom they might be attributed."[41] His is a discourse that is "trying to operate a decentring that leaves no privilege to any centre."[42] But how can a discourse be so decentered? How can an author write without being an author?

We are concerned with exploring some of the ways Foucault "decenters" his discourse in order to determine whether it is possible to do so. But it is important to observe that he does not in fact "have" a discourse. Even to suppose he does assigns him the status of an author. Rather, Foucault's writings are themselves located ("entangled") in discursive formations. We may imagine a later Foucault, writing in the twenty-fifth century, describing the "postmodern discourse" of the twentieth century, a discourse in which discourse itself became an object. Here all the writings we have referred to, with many others, compose the discourse.[43] In this sense, Foucault's writings, along with other contemporary writings, are seeking to establish their own discourse.[44] This "future thought" is a future discourse in which contemporary writings can participate only through historical development.

Briefly, we may note a few of the ways in *The Archaeology of Knowledge* in which Foucault "decenters" his discourse, a decentering that is overtly a centering. Foucault must identify his position in relation to the tradition in which he is located, the "discourse" of which he is inevitably a part. Thus, he tells us how his archaeology is similar to but different from the history of ideas, tells us how he may appear to use structuralist methods but is not a structuralist: "It may well be that this transformation, the problems that it raises, the tools that it uses, the concepts that emerge from it, and the results that it obtains are not entirely foreign to what is called structural analysis. But this kind of analysis is not specifically used."[45] He describes "a group of statements not as the closed, plethoric totality of a meaning, but as an incomplete, fragmented figure," but suggests that this "is to establish what I am quite willing to call a *positivity*."[46] More important, every such affinity, with structuralism, positivism, a priorism, is carefully qualified. "This explains the *de facto* privilege that I have accorded to those discourses that, to put it very schematically, define the 'sciences of man.' But it is only a provisional privilege."[47] He is "careful to accept as valid none of the unities that would normally present themselves" but is quite explicit in his recognition that he inevitably presents other unities.[48] He introduces schematic lists that appear indistinguishable from structuralism: surfaces of emergence, authorities of delimitation, grids of specification. But "such a description is still in itself inadequate."[49] And he accompanies these accounts with such comments as: "The conditions for the appearance of an object of discourse . . . are many and imposing,"[50] or the first aspect of the law of rarity: "It is based on the principle that *everything* is never said."[51]

Perhaps the most striking example is Foucault's claim that "positivity plays the role of what might be called a *historical a priori*" but "what I mean by the term is an *a priori* that is not a condition of validity for judgments, but a condition of reality for statements."[52] We have a historical *a priori* that is not an *a priori*, structuralist devices but not structuralism, an author who is not an author. These are ironic claims, but it is a particular kind of irony, and that is precisely the point of this discussion. Foucault's ironic discussion culminates in a wonderful passage describing "our diagnosis . . . [which] establishes that we are difference, that our reason is the difference of discourses, our history the difference of times, our selves the difference of masks. That difference, far from being the forgotten and recovered origin, is this dispersion that we are and make."[53] The historical a priori and the "archive" establish "our" identity as heterogeneous masks.

It is not possible to write and not to write, to write and not be a writer (except in some special sense of "a writer,") to write for a public and not be read by that public in its ways rather than as one wishes (and besides, one's wishes are also public). It is not possible to write at a particular time and not belong to the discourses of that time, even in opposition to them. Or rather, to take a critical stance against the entrenched voices of one's time is still to belong to one's time and to be among those voices, but in a divided, aporetic way.

This is why irony has always been the preferred form in which a distanced theoretical voice speaks, in Plato and Kierkegaard for example, but in Foucault as well. Irony's doubling preserves the doubling of the critical voice, the novelty of a perspective that nevertheless belongs by affinity among the points of view to which it is most opposed. The theoretical point is that every discourse, every voice, every point of view is divided, aporetic.

Every tradition contains its opposition within itself. To think that any political or ideological circumstances can altogether compel our assent, in an undivided way, is closely akin to skepticism's view that since there is no absolute assurance, there is no understanding whatsoever. Rather, politics always contains within itself forms of dissent. These are, of course, "acceptable" forms, or rather, forms of dissent are classified into those that are acceptable and those that are not. But even this classification is divided, since every tradition undergoes changes and comes to include what it once regarded with repugnance. (The reverse is also frequently the case.)

Foucault locates his archaeology where it must be located, among the questions and discourses, theoretical and material, of his time: "among so many other, already constituted, discourses."[54] He is acutely sensitive to the reflexiveness in his situation: every discourse may disappear, but only as a discourse, by interrogation and revelation, can it serve the historical purpose of inspiring new discourses. Thus, in saying that his discourse is "an attempt to reveal discursive practices in their complexity and density,"[55] Foucault must acknowledge both the complexity and density of his own discursive conditions and the possibility, even likelihood, that such revelations comprise conditions for their own disappearance.

We could have said "conditions for their supersession," but that is the point at issue: discursive entanglements establish conditions for other discursive entanglements that supersede them without transcending their local entanglement. There is no means, from within or without, of disentangling a discourse from its history or its materiality. This is the "awesome, ponderous materiality" of the "risky world of discourse."[56] But this inexhaustible entanglement is not entrapment, not least because without it there would be no hope of change, in practice or in thought.[57] The materiality of discourse, its *specific* entanglements, give it whatever influence it can have, practical *and* theoretical, even scientific. If we respect and admire such specific materialities, then we must seek new means for disclosing them and realizing them in new discourses that will supersede the conditions they unearth (but may not eliminate any conditions in particular). We seek to disclose ideology without confidence that we will eliminate it.[58]

To reject any form of absolute transcendence, to emphasize discursive entanglements, is to accept locality and finiteness. But locality is not equivalent with entrapment, and its acceptance does not entail despair, for although these entanglements are specific, they also embody whatever forms of ideality and positivity exist: local ideals and goals. What must be rejected is any presumption that it all makes sense, somehow, or that it fails to make sense altogether. There are irresistible aporias, oppositions and conflicts, limits and conditions, to all thought, discourse, and life that express their finiteness and locality. " 'Discourse is not life; its time is not your time; in it, you will not be reconciled to death; you may have killed God beneath the weight of all that you have said; but don't imagine that, with all that you are saying, you will make a man that will live longer than he.' "[59] It takes a strenuous and extraordinary form of writing to acknowledge its own specific entanglements without employing a voice that speaks to and for eternity.

PRAXIS

We may think of politics as the art of practical judgment in relation to what escapes all other forms of power yet is irresistible and intimidating in its ramifications.[60] It is that form of judgment that directly confronts the terrifying side of finiteness, that local events have inexhaustibly far-reaching ramifications. Foucault identifies this condition with the powers and dangers, the ponderous, awesome materiality of discourse. We will now explore the political implications, especially for language, of such a view of discourse and power.

It seems to follow from our emphasis on discursive entanglements that every political program is but a manifestation of the conditions in which it is entangled. We have responded to this conclusion that historical conditions are neither monolithic nor uniform, though they may be politically daunting, but are always both internally and externally divided, exceeding any limits. The "but," the "only," of the position described imposes absolute closure on permeable limits, denies both complementarity and supplementarity. Inexhaustible and local limits limit multifariously and heterogeneously. Inexhaustibility is this aporia of being and human being, nature and truth. Every truth escapes the limits it requires to be a truth, whether universal or local. When Foucault speaks of the "régime of truth," he marks another local excess of truth, to be constituted by social procedures, by power, monolithically (in the modern régime), and heterogeneously. The truth of truth is its untruth, and conversely.[61] If there is no disentangled truth, there is no altogether entangled falsehood, containing no means within itself to extricate itself from bias. Similarly, although the ponderous materiality of discourse is the source of its perils, that same materiality is essential to any effective political program.[62]

Foucault discusses two ways in which his writings, or a practical program based on them, might be politically effective: by leading to new forms of discourse and by functioning in local centers of resistance. The former is so important, so fundamental to the position he develops and to the view of politics we are exploring here, that it may be taken to embody our entire answer to the question of political practice. No discourse can do anything more than, other than, engender other discourses; no political program can do anything more than, other than, bring about other political entanglements, other relationships and dispersions of power. Why should we suppose that there are power relations that somehow transcend the complexities, normative and factual, of power relations? Why should we suppose that there are forms of discourse that speak to and for eternity? In return, however, why should we suppose that speaking at a particular site speaks to that site alone? Discourse speaks, or works, multiply, heterogeneously, and excessively.

This understanding presupposes a strong commitment to the finiteness of history, to the principle that every discourse, scientific, philosophic, or otherwise, belongs to history both in the conditions that make its conceptual relations possible and in the ponderous materiality of discursive events. Similarly, every political action or ideal belongs to history in the double sense that every action and norm is initiated from within established political conditions of authority and practice and that every political purpose is realized within practical conditions. This historical entanglement applies equally to political "realism" and "idealism," for both actual conditions and ideal norms are equally historically located.

What we are emphasizing in addition is that being located historically is not one-dimensional, not simply captivity and entrapment. If we cannot escape ideology, it does not follow that every thought is false, but that ideology includes within it a division between truth and falsity. If we cannot escape from history—and why should we hope to—this does not entail confinement to prevailing political conditions, for history also includes the divisions and oppositions that provide openness to the future. Specific historical determinants—slavery, torture, ignorance—produce particular limitations in their time and place, but also produce resistances that bring about their own specific transformations. Equally truthfully, and perhaps far more important, the most far-reaching achievements of which we are capable produce untold misery—toxic wastes, destruction of habitats, urban crowding. There is no generic captivity or falsity, only the particular illusions that belong to particular discursive and political formations.

In the context of questions concerning a political program, Foucault rejects all talk of the "whole of society."[63] He rejects every totality or notion of a whole, along with views that assign a content to "man," who is also an invention of the modern period.[64] Man is but a figure occurring between two modes of language. What kind of political program can such a refusal entail?

What we understand of ourselves, Man, and of language, Discourse, are intimately related, and as one is called into question, the other is also. Can we suppose there is a unity on the horizon? To the contrary, such a dream is part of the very epistemic and political system that it would replace. It is one strain of Enlightenment thought that supposes that all understanding will comprise a unity, human power over nature, comparable to the suggestion that all power will be absorbed into Humanity's sovereignty over itself.

If we deny that there is a predetermined future, in any of the many senses of that predetermination—destiny, natural law, or ideality—then what have we left? If there is no ideal norm of liberation, how can there be any thought of liberation? The irony is that this "any thought of liberation" is a thought without a subject, *any* and all liberation. It belongs neither to humanity nor to any individuals, but belongs collectively to the totality.

We have given such a totality up as part of the framework of thought that characterizes the modern period. Is there no room for political action? The answer is that we have not changed the nature of political practice in the least: it has always been local and can only be local, for every action along with every formation is specific and situated. Again, we are arguing that specificity and situatedness are themselves situated, local, entailing excess and supplementarity, inexhaustibility.

If we oppose the collective authority of a total state, we cannot advocate a total society of another kind. If we oppose the covert forms of inhumanity that pervade a capitalist society, we cannot advocate other covert forms of manipulation and influence. Rather, it is the collectivity and the covertness that must be opposed, but they can be opposed only locally. It follows that political effectiveness must be local and regional as well as self-critical and interrogative.

Is this not virtually quiescence? If power is dispersed, shall we say, "metaphysically," where are the levers that agents must be able to move? But politically we are in Archimedes' position, having no place to stand to move the world. Rather, we stand where we stand, entangled amidst discursive events and practices, including every movement toward liberation. But the conclusion is not that liberation, along with truth, disappears in this entanglement, but that truth and freedom reside within the entanglements. There is no other place they can be located.

The question to which we are led is how an effective political program can be understood in terms of the discursive entanglements that constitute the workings of power. We embark upon this controversial discussion because the answer may tell us something important about both politics and language. Language is political because power is everywhere; language is a political instrument, to the extent that it is an instrument at all, but also a medium in which injustice and oppression both appear and are fought. It is not simply an instrument, then, but serves and pervades every human function, individual and collective, a locus at which human activities transpire.

We have suggested that Foucault's view of power may be called "metaphysical." Yet metaphysics is no more "one thing," pervaded by unjustifiable assumptions concerning essences and totalities, than is language, being, or power. Foucault's view is that the nature, form, and unity of power have been systematically misunderstood.[65] Power is everywhere, comes from everywhere, is produced at every point, but is not equivalent with the totality. The metaphysics of power includes the denial that power is everything, for nothing can be everything: totalization is part of the regime of power. The multiplicity of force relations includes struggles and confrontations, disjunctions and contradictions. There are elements here of both Nietzsche's will to power and of Marx's view of ideology, but the interaction of the two involves a cancellation. The will to power is "metaphysical" in the sense that it is "everywhere," subject to the critique that the specificities of productive relations vanish in so generic a perspective. Ideology is likewise pervasive, entirely in the interests of a particular class conflict and particular forms of oppression, subject to the critique that even this view of the class structure is ideological.

Foucault's metaphysics of power is a consequence of the outright rejection of every utopian form of thought as a relic of infinite transcendence. There are ideological deceptions and oppressive relations, but there are no generic alternatives in the sense that we may oppose to ideological deception a free and untainted truth, to oppressive relations a free and untrammeled individual sovereignty. Indeed, these latter assumptions are part of the ideology. Yet to be part of the ideology is not to be "false" any more than to be "true" is to be non-ideological. All of these are entangled among the discursive relations that constitute the contrasts, that therefore cannot escape those relations.

Such a metaphysics of power has been criticized by some political theorists as leaving no room for understanding oppression or opposing it by radical action.[66] If all reasons and proposals are entangled within the discourses that they simultaneously criticize and influence, how are we to understand them? If we imagine new codes and categories, are we imagining them exterior to the conditions they would replace or from within, located in those very conditions?

What is overlooked is that within the metaphysics of power there is a metaphysics of resistance.[67] And it affords the possibility of effective practice, even revolution, but only in particular circumstances:

Just as the network of power relations ends by forming a dense web that passes through apparatuses and institutions, without being exactly localized in them, so too the swarm of points of resistance traverses social stratifications and individual unities. And it is doubtless the strategic codification of these points of resistance that makes a revolution possible, somewhat similar to the way in which the state relies on the institutional integration of power relationships.[68]

In this metaphysics of power, we are asked to understand that power works covertly as well as overtly, in innumerable relationships as well as in overt domination. But equally, since resistance is the other face of power, resistance works pervasively, covertly and at innumerable sites. Political developments are, then, the result not only of explicit groups and leaders, but of innumerable events and influences.

Is this a social determinism? In the sense that we are to take social relations seriously, the answer must be affirmative, that is, social conditions do influence the future. However, to the sense that there are no alternatives to a given social milieu, that we are "trapped" within, unable to "escape," we have given an explicitly negative reply: that both resistance and the imagination of alternatives belong as much "within" the power networks as the forces they are designed to oppose. If there is a social determinism, it includes the alternatives and possibilities engendered by its own divisions.

What, then, is the possibility of an effective political program in terms of a metaphysics of power, particularly one that seeks to change our political circumstances? And what are the implications of the entanglements of power for our understanding of discourse and language? One possibility is that we can envisage such very different social codes and structures that we may justify political actions as founded on a vision of an ideal social order. This is utopian, not least because the ideals belong to the repressive social order. We cannot imagine ideals that do not belong to history. The alternative is that such ideals belong to their historical circumstances, as much to the power networks they oppose as the force relations themselves. However, the relation of belonging here is neither entrapment nor oppression, but goes together with "departing," with heterogeneity. The ideals are sites at which resistance occurs, but it occupies many other sites as well. Revolutionary movements tend to identify a particular social site, for example the intellectuals or the proletariat, with the locus of resistance and liberation. Social change is a complex phenomenon like the phenomenon that it opposes. It follows that proposing alternative codes and categories is a local form of resistance, not a global one, for there is no global resistance or movement. There is no "better world" to be won.

Why does Foucault not imagine the results of organized resistance? Why does he not develop new and superior forms of justice? Our reading suggests that to demand that he do so, instead of what he does, is to de-radicalize his position, where we mean by "radical" the understanding required for major changes in social practice. What Foucault does is not to give answers, new forms of life, new and better practices, but to raise new and different questions about our present and past forms of life. The answers, he suggests, belong to the system under interrogation. The questions reveal the underside of that system, its covert workings. In this sense, Foucault's approach is radical in its critical perspectives.[69]

Can there be practical political questions, paving the way to future thought, if we cannot give the answers, at least plausible or possible ones? But of the two responses, which is the more significant, the one that would repeat the approach to power and to political action that has been part of the tradition under attack or the one that would avoid older forms as much as possible, even to the extreme of posing questions without answers?

There is, however, a kind of answer, that we must give up all thoughts of totalities and unqualified transcendence, even those involving a better world and the rejection of the past. Totality belongs to the tradition we are calling into question: the entire state, a better world, a harmonious arrangement of interests. There is no such harmony or union, only local conflicts and oppositions where they occur. Where they occur is power, but also resistance. And this resistance, local and specific to the particular dispersions of power in the neighborhood, is the only resistance that an effective political program can support.

This notion of "locality" is itself local, relative to particular circumstances of power and resistance. It may be national in scale or pertain to a community or neighborhood. Foucault suggests that the university offers a site for local resistance. So may certain organizations and institutions. These sites of resistance are where the monolithic and dispersed workings of power are halted. But they may work by opposition or by compromise, by terror or by reconciliation. Cooptation is not just submission but is also a form of resistance. More accurately, both cooptation and revolution belong to their milieux inevitably, in both support and opposition.

There is no totality, neither of truth nor of the human condition. There are dispersed discursive sites and foci of local action. If there is no totality, and if any totality belongs to the system of power, then an effective political response must be local. We may conclude by considering the implications of this view for a theory of political discourse.

If we reject all totalities, including both a comprehensive political strategy and a comprehensive scientific political discourse, then there appear to be only two alternatives (though our understanding of supplementarity strongly suggests that wherever there are "only two" alternatives we have taken something for granted that should be called into question): (a) we are so entangled in historical and discursive conditions that we can find no grounds for alternative norms; (b) our entanglements include resistances and oppositions. In the latter sense, political transformations are not totalistic but dispersed, along with power, and fragmented. If power has no unique site, then resistance has no unique site either. Instead, both occur here and there.

What this means is that a political discourse is a fragmented, dispersed discourse. But this does not mean that it is without power or ineffective. Rather, it possesses whatever effectiveness can be relevant to such complex networks of power. Political developments here are complex and dispersed, confronting oppositions at every turn but finding resistances there as well. Resistance occurs wherever there is discourse, in the divided and critical nature, the opposing side, of every established discourse.

Major social and political transformations are possible only in virtue of the dispersion of power and resistances throughout a dense web of points of influence. This means that there is no particular discourse, no particular language or science, no particular focus of activity, at which ideas function; instead they function here and there, dispersed along with power, defining pathways through which resistances can be effective.

A discourse is effective when it constitutes itself as a discourse, in contrast with words and ideas, events and material relations, that are both dispersed and mutually unsupportive. A discourse is effective when it is constituted at multiple sites by multiple resonances and influences, reinforcement and support, that is, when it becomes a discourse. There is no uniform condition whereby a multiplicity of sites of resistance compose a discourse or a program, but there are many conditions that can nullify the effectiveness of the most persuasive tongues. Discourse and language produce transformations not by the vehemence of their opposition to entrenched powers nor by the clarity of their vision of an ideal society, though both may be helpful, but through the multiplicity of relations that together constitute new practical conditions and new forms of discourse.

What has all this to do with languages and linguistic utterances? Little, perhaps, from a standpoint in which form and communication are predominant; everything from a standpoint in which efficacy and resistance are paramount. We have been examining the view that a language exercises multiple semasic functions, and that it serves these functions in whatever ways are necessary. The form and structure of language, its specificities and determinants, characterize and repeat, but do not impede these heterogeneous functions of discourse. And among such functions are those of power and resistance. Languages manifest and influence social and political differences in multiply semasic ways, including grammatical and other structural properties. Wherever there are utterances, there languages intersect with discourses, ideas with power and resistance.

One of the conclusions of this discussion is that a political discourse is not in some intrinsic or ideal way sharply differentiated from other discourses. All are dispersed and fragmented. What makes a discourse politically important is less what is said than how, but "how" here refers to the multiplicity of force relations that compose the discourse.

DISCURSIVE DIFFERENTIATIONS

Our aim in this chapter has been to explore the complexity and richness of the entanglements of language as discourse with power and desire, that is, within the complex locales of human life. Discourse, here, is intelligible only in terms of inexhaustible entanglements, a condition that is not merely generic or abstract, but that possesses a profound, inexhaustible, density and locality. That is, discourse is entangled among the specificities as well as the generalities of human experience.

There are relevant poles that compose density. On the one hand, every discourse is implicated within strategies of power and influence; on the other hand, every strategy of power and desire is weighed down by the specificities of forms of writing and speech. This is the materiality of discourse, but similar poles inhabit the relations among knowledge, power, and desire. Every form of knowledge is influenced both by the forms of discourse and the specific strategies of control that inhabit the epoch that defines the relevant forms of knowledge. Conversely, every discourse is profoundly influenced both by the disciplines of knowledge and the relations of power that together compose the epistemic epoch.

We are speaking of the specificity and density of human entanglements, observing that when we acknowledge their locality and historicity, we affirm not only their generic conditions but the particular and dense events and circumstances of human locations, a metaphysical more than a discursive fact. The metaphysical fact, however generally, resists generality with density and particularity. This is what we mean by locality, together with inexhaustibility.

To say that we confront a metaphysics of power, then, is not to depart from the densities and specificities of the workings of power into their generic and universal forms, but to reaffirm that power always works specifically and materially. Another way of putting this is that power always works by differentiation, negativity, and absence, heterogeneously. And in this recognition, we see the core of the understanding of languages that is lost in our worship of their universality as Language.

When Saussure emphasizes that languages function by differentiation, he ignores some very important differences in his definition of both *langage* and *langue*, differences among languages and semasic forms. We have understood semasis to be intelligible only as inexhaustible heterogeneity, including differences among manifold semasic forms and manifold languages. Semasic intelligibility requires a multitude of languages and expressive forms, differences in how different persons express common understandings, in how different cultures assimilate their experiences into linguistic expression, and in how what is expressed in linguistic form may be supplemented by nonlinguistic expressions and conversely. We add to Saussure's understanding of differentiation all these other inexhaustible differences, pertaining to languages as they pertain to experience.

So generic a condition as differentiation is, however strangely, not abstract but functions densely and specifically among the forms of power and desire. Put another way, language here is not conceived so abstractly as to become detached from the specific contexts of human experience in which desire and power function. There is no adequate distinction between discourse and language, as if we may understand the latter as either the syntactic or morphological realization of the former, existing abstractly apart from human activities. To the contrary, a language is but a common sphere in which dense and material utterances function.

Even here, to understand that languages exist only in specific utterances is to understand both too much and too little at once. It is not that there is nothing common among utterances that is the language, but that what is common may have no larger form of being than within the context of shared utterances and understandings. Far more important, however, and this is the point of this discussion—utterances are not intelligible as either expressive strings or even actions alone, but are implicated in all the human activities that have dense and material conditions. We have equated utterance in this extended sense with judgment. The intelligibility of judgments resides in their local specificities, including absences and exclusions, not just in generic conditions of validation. Put another way, there is no generic validation or truth: every validation of a judgment is densely specific, implicated and entangled in inexhaustible local conditions.

What we understand, then, as a language apart from the discursive and judgmental entanglements that every language and utterance inhabit is either an abstract condition of formal utterances, an atrophied, lifeless form that does not possess semasic depths, or must be the common sphere of semasic conditions that we inhabit when we share semiates and semasic expressions. These common conditions compose a semasic field, and it is filled with idiosemic variations, individual contributions, differentiations and abnormalities, heterogeneities. Far more important, a common semasic field is unintelligible without heterogeneous differentiations. Similarly, linguistic utterances are to be understood in common only in virtue of the density and materiality of the alternatives that surround them.

When we speak or write, we exercise power and are exercised by the powers of others. Utterance is not simply the exercise of power, though it is always its manifestation and its creature, for in utterance we manifest the powers of others, other speakers and audiences and of history in its materiality. What we are capable of saying and expressing, therefore of knowing and influencing, belongs densely and specifically to history as its creature, thereby manifesting the powers of conditions and events. Moreover, the large-scale forms that power takes, in Foucault's analysis, become the large-scale forms of expressiveness and language. The languages we are speaking of here form the discourses that individuals at different levels and scales of authority inhabit. Ministers, priests, journalists, politicians, university professors, all those who carry influence and power, but also husbands and wives, children and neighbors, wherever power is situated or influence occurs, all have their linguistic forms: words that are used instead of others, syntactic forms and elliptical departures. All are understood contextually, and within such an understanding are the forms of social interaction that embody desire and power.

A language has manifold functions, works in multiple ways; among these are functions it is not designed to serve, but serves nevertheless, since it is a site at which both understanding and power work. In this sense, every language is divided into many sublanguages, and discourses into subdiscourses, where social interaction and power exercise their influences. Traditional theory of language tends to disregard many of these differentiations, in part as if by taking heed of them we might lose the object of our theory, language itself. To the contrary, we have seen here that the theory, the science, of language impoverishes itself to the extent that it requires so abstract an object that the densities and specificities of linguistic judgments are lost.

To what extent is such an impoverishment another conceptual error? Or should we consider the possibility that we have another site at which power is exercised? There are manifold practices and manifold agents here for whom power is relevant: those who would establish a discipline in which they are authorities; those who would establish the acceptable forms of expression to which others must be subservient. But the most insidious, and closest to the kinds of power we have been discussing, are the forms that would establish a community of language where strong differentiation is required.

Battles over language, then, among linguistic nationalists but also over regional and class differences in the schools, are often passionate and bloody because language is a site at which power and truth manifestly meet. The issue is always one of power: establishing the terms in which understanding is to be permissible. The natural arena in which such a struggle is to be fought is that of language: which language, and under what terms? Politically, the issue is one of qualified pluralism: that is, given pluralism, for there is no society that is not pluralistic in important ways, which qualifications are permissible, and how are such qualifications to be promulgated? This is a question of language.

More important than taking sides is recognizing the nature of these debates, which treat power and language as if power must be established in relation to language. In these terms, power is exercised not only by explicit forms of control, but by hidden disappearances and denials. And the most effective of such denials belong to languages and to discourse, the reason why these are so perilous. Languages are perilous because within their multiplicity and differentiations, large and small, are to be found the widest range of human differences, and of other differences as well. Here we return to the notion of difference to add to Saussure that languages function in virtue of differences not simply by closure in the system of signs, but because all differences come to function in languages.

This remarkable truth is not a consequence of differentiation being unique to languages, for difference is a generic condition. Nevertheless, generic conditions both inhabit and manifest themselves in languages, for that is where we both encounter them and understand them. Differences, like power, are dispersed and inexhaustible. But they are to be both understood and ameliorated, leading into languages. In this generic and remarkable sense, language, discourse, power, and desire are the forms in which we simultaneously encounter, understand, and obscure heterogeneity and differentiation. That we always understand such differentiation in generic terms, a metaphysics of power and desire, therefore of language and semasis, is but one of the extraordinary consequences of the differentiation that is inexhaustibility. Put another way, that there are such generic forms is part of the density and specificity that we find to be inescapable in inexhaustibly local entanglements.

NOTES

1. Hannah Arendt, *The Life of the Mind* (New York: Harcourt, Brace Jovanovich, 1978).

2. Hannah Arendt, *The Human Condition* (Chicago: The University of Chicago Press, 1958).

3. "We know perfectly well that we are not free to say just anything, that we cannot simply speak of anything, when we like or where we like; not just anyone, finally, may speak of just anything" (Foucault, "The Discourse on Language," p. 216).

4. "The essential thing is . . . the existence in our era of a discourse in which sex, the revelation of truth, the overturning of global laws, the proclamation of a new day to come, and the promise of a certain felicity are linked together." (Foucault, *History of Sexuality*, p. 7).

"Why has sexuality been so widely discussed, and what has been said about it? What were the effects of power generated by what was said? What are the links between these discourses, these effects of power, and the pleasures that were invested by them? What knowledge (*savoir*) was formed as a result of this linkage? The object, in short, is to define the regime of power-knowledge-pleasure that sustains the discourse on human sexuality in our part of the world" (ibid., p. 11).

5. "Power is everywhere; not because it embraces everything, but because it comes from everywhere. And 'Power,' insofar as it is permanent, repetitious, inert, and self-reproducing, is simply the over-all effect that emerges from all these mobilities, the concatenation that rests on each of them and seeks in turn to arrest their movement. . . . Power is not an institution, and not a structure; neither is it a certain strength we are endowed with; it is the name that one attributes to a complex strategical situation in a particular society" (Foucault, *History of Sexuality*, p. 93).

6. "Where there is power, there is resistance, and yet, or rather consequently, this resistance is never in a position of exteriority in relation to power" (ibid., p. 95).

7. "What characterizes metaphysical thinking which grounds the ground for beings is the fact that metaphysical thinking departs from what is present in its presence, and thus represents it in terms of its ground as something grounded" (Martin Heidegger, "The End of Philosophy and the Task of Thinking," *On Time and Being*, trans. J. Stambaugh [New York: Harper & Row, 1972], p. 56). It is tempting to interpret Heidegger's position as the claim that there is a deeper and more accurate form of thought and understanding than metaphysics, one that does not "depart" from what is present. Yet far more important is his view that presence includes absence, nearness includes farness, revealing includes concealing, and identity includes difference, a view close to (and perhaps far from) the view set forth here of complementarity.

8. We may consider, for example, his contrast of his "archaeological" method with the history of ideas: "The history of ideas usually credits the discourse that it analyses with coherence. . . . it regards it as its duty

to find, at a deeper level, a principle of cohesion that organizes the discourse and restores to it its hidden unity. The history of ideas recognizes, therefore, two levels of contradiction: that of appearance, which is resolved in the profound unity of discourse; and that of foundation, which gives rise to discourse itself. For archaeological analysis, contradictions are neither appearances to be overcome, nor secret principles to be uncovered. They are objects to be described for themselves" (Foucault, *Archaeology of Knowledge*, pp. 149, 151).

He speaks of metaphysics in *The Order of Things*: "Where there had formerly been a correlation between a *metaphysics* of representation and of the infinite and an *analysis* of living beings, of man's desires, and of the words of his language, we find being constituted an *analytic* of finitude and human existence, and in opposition to it (though in correlative opposition) a perpetual tendency to constitute a *metaphysics* of life, labour, and language" (p. 317).

But perhaps the most telling example, close to our understanding of inexhaustibility, can be found in "Theatrum Philosophicum," where Foucault says: "The univocity of being, its singleness of expression, is paradoxically the principal condition which permits difference to escape the domination of identity, which frees it from the law of the Same as a simple opposition within conceptual elements. Being can express itself in the same way, because difference is no longer submitted to the prior reduction of categories; because it is not distributed inside a diversity that can always be perceived; because it is not organized in a conceptual hierarchy of species and genus. Being is that which is always said of difference; it is the *Recurrence* of difference" ("Theatrum Philosophicum," *Language, Counter-Memory, Practice*, p. 192). We read this as metaphysical, a local, inexhaustible, heterogeneous metaphysics.

9. Foucault, *Archaeology of Knowledge*, p. 21.

10. Foucault's reply is in terms of the *law of rarity*: "*everything* is never said. . . . The discursive formation is not therefore a developing totality . . . it is a distribution of gaps, voids, absences, limits, divisions. . . . There is no sub-text. And therefore no plethora" (*Archaeology of Knowledge*, pp. 118–19).

11. See Lyotard and Levinas. Foucault himself speaks of the Unthought, in *The Order of Things*, chap. 9. We have noted Irigaray's exhortation to "overthrow syntax" (See chap. 3, note 40).

12. "Who is speaking? Who, among the totality of speaking individuals, is accorded the right to use this sort of language (*langage*)? Who is qualified to do so? Who derives from it his own special quality, his prestige, and from whom, in return, does he receive if not the assurance, at least the presumption that what he said is true? . . ." (*Archaeology of Knowledge*, p. 50).

13. Foucault calls the effects of such negativities "positivities" (ibid., p. 125).

14. Foucault, "Discourse on Language," p. 215.

15. "What is so perilous, then, in the fact that people speak, and that their speech proliferates? Where is the danger in that? . . . I am supposing that in every society the production of discourse is at once controlled, selected, organised and redistributed according to a certain number of procedures, whose role is to avert its powers and its dangers, to cope with chance events, to evade its ponderous, awesome materiality" (ibid., p. 216).

16. Foucault, *Archaeology of Knowledge*, esp. Part III.

17. Foucault, *History of Sexuality*, p. 93.

18. Foucault, "Truth and Power," *Language, Counter-Memory, Practice*, p. 133.

19. Authority is the subject of my *Injustice and Restitution: The Ordinance of Time* (Albany: State University of New York Press, 1992).

20. One sweeping expression is, "We can assume that any theory of the subject has always been appropriated by the 'masculine' " (Irigaray, *Speculum of the Other Woman*, p. 133), leading to her demand to overthrow syntax to establish a "feminine" subject. A far more sweeping expression, despite its links to psychoanalysis, is that "Freud brought to light something that had been operative all along though it remained implicit, hidden, unknown: *the sexual indifference that underlies the truth of any science, the logic of every discourse*" (Luce Irigaray, "The Power of Discourse and the Subordination of the Feminine," *This Sex Which Is not One*, p. 69).

Language, here, functions politically, as do all forms of discourse and representation, semasis, all forms of truth. Contemporary feminists have shown the concrete manifestations of such power on women and others who have suffered a double oppression, that of being injured, harmed, and abused, frequently physically, and of being refused standing to speak of their wrongs.

21. "I would like to call a *differend* [*différend*] the case where the plaintiff is divested of the means to argue and becomes for that reason a victim" (Lyotard, *Differend*, p. 9). In the extreme, the differend belongs to the world, reality, nature, as heterogeneity. "*La réalité comporte le différend*" (translated as "Reality entails the differend"). "This is what a wrong [*tort*] would be: a damage [*dommage*] accompanied by the loss of the means to prove the damage. This is the case if the victim is deprived of life, or of all his or her liberties, or of the freedom to make his or her ideas or opinions public, or simply of the right to testify to the damage, or even more simply if the testifying phrase is itself deprived of authority" (ibid., p. 5). "The title of this book suggests (through the generic value of the definite article) that a universal rule of judgment between heterogeneous genres is lacking in general" (ibid., p. xi).

22. He tells us that "for the moment, and as far ahead as I can see, my

discourse, far from determining the locus in which it speaks, is avoiding the ground on which it could find support. It is a discourse about discourses: but it is not trying to find in them a hidden law, a concealed origin that it only remains to free; . . . it is trying to operate a decentring that leaves no privilege to any centre" (Foucault, *Archaeology of Knowledge*, p. 205).

23. Foucault, *History of Sexuality*, pp. 98–100. He describes this insistence of the rule as follows: "Power is essentially what dictates its law to sex. Which means first of all that sex is placed by power in a binary system: licit and illicit, permitted and forbidden. Secondly, power prescribes an 'order' for sex that operates at the same time as a form of intelligibility. . . . And finally, power acts by laying down the rule: power's hold on sex is maintained through language, or rather through the act of discourse that creates, from the very fact that it is articulated, a rule of law. It speaks, and that is the rule. The pure form of power resides in the function of the legislator; and its mode of action with regard to sex is of a juridico-discursive character" (Foucault, *History of Sexuality*, p. 83).

24. Foucault, *Archaeology of Knowledge*, p. 119.

25. "The discursive formation is not therefore a developing totality, with its own dynamism or inertia, carrying with it, in an unformulated discourse, what it does not say, what it has not yet said, or what contradicts it at that moment; it is not a rich, difficult germination, it is a distribution of gaps, voids, absences, limits, divisions" (ibid.).

26. "[I]n every society the production of discourse is at once controlled, selected, organised and redistributed according to a certain number of procedures, whose role is to avert its powers and its dangers, to cope with chance events, to evade its ponderous, awesome materiality" (Foucault, *Discourse on Language*, p. 216).

27. "The horizon of archaeology, therefore, is not *a* science, *a* rationality, *a* mentality, *a* culture; it is a tangle of interpositivities whose limits and points of intersection cannot be fixed in a single operation" (Foucault, *Archaeology of Knowledge*, p. 159). "Instead of considering that discourse is made up of a series of homogeneous events (individual formulations), archaeology distinguishes several possible levels of events within the very density of discourse" (ibid., p. 171).

28. These considerations have led me to reinterpret Hobbes' famous but apparently perverse claim: "Fear and liberty are consistent; as when a man throweth his goods into the sea for *fear* the ship should sink, he doth it nevertheless very willingly, and may refuse to do it if he will; it is therefore the action of one that was *free*; so a man sometimes pays his debt, only for fear of imprisonment, which because nobody hindered him from detaining, was the action of a man at *liberty*. And generally all actions which men do in commonwealths, for fear of the law, are actions

which the doers had liberty to omit" (*Leviathan* [Indianapolis: Bobbs-Merrill, 1958], chap. 21, p. 171). The references to liberty and fear are somewhat misleading: Hobbes' insight is that the state functions within, is "entangled" in, many practices and subpractices. Within such practices, even the most stringent threats presume disobedience.

29. Foucault, *Order of Things*, p. xiv.

30. Foucault, *Archaeology of Knowledge*, pp. 200–201.

31. Foucault, *Discourse on Language*, p. 234.

32. "Do you think that I would keep so persistently to my task, if I were not preparing . . . a labyrinth into which I can venture, in which I can move my discourse, opening up underground passages, forcing it to go far from itself, finding overhangs that reduce and deform its itinerary, in which I can lose myself and appear to eyes that I will never have to meet again. . . . Do not ask who I am and do not ask me to remain the same" (Foucault, *Archaeology of Knowledge*, p. 17).

"My discourse, far from determining the locus in which it speaks, is avoiding the ground on which it could find support. . . . it is trying to operate a decentring that leaves no privilege to any centre" (ibid., p. 205).

33. Wittgenstein, *Tractatus Logico-Philosophicus*, p. 151.

34. Heidegger entirely agrees that language is entangled within itself. "We speak and speak about language. What we speak of, language, is always ahead of us. . . . Accordingly, when we speak of language we remain entangled in a speaking that is persistently inadequate" (*On the Way to Language*, p. 75). But he appears to hold that we may nevertheless have an experience with language from within language. "What is left for us to do is to point out ways that bring us face to face with a possibility of undergoing an experience with language. Such ways have long existed. But they are seldom used in such a manner that the possible experience with language is itself given voice and put into language. In experiences which we undergo *with* language, language itself brings itself to language" (ibid., p. 59).

35. "*The (pure) trace is differance.* It does not depend on any sensible plenitude, audible or visible, phonic or graphic. It is, on the contrary, the condition of such a plenitude" (Derrida, *On Grammatology*, p. 62).

"The trace is not a presence but is rather the simulacrum of a presence that dislocates, displaces, and refers beyond itself. The trace has, properly speaking, no place, for effacement belongs to the very structure of the trace. Effacement must always be able to overtake the trace; otherwise it would not be a trace but an indestructible and monumental substance. In addition, and from the start, effacement constitutes it as a trace—effacement establishes the trace in a change of place and makes it disappear in its appearing, makes it issue forth from itself in its very position" (Derrida, "Differance," *Speech and Phenomena*, p. 156).

36. "I would say that the basic misunderstanding concerning the linguistic character of our understanding is one of language, as if language were an existing whole composed of words and phrases, concepts, points of view and opinions. In reality, language is the single word whose virtuality opens up the infinity of discourse, of discourse with others, and of the freedom of 'speaking oneself' and of 'allowing oneself to be spoken.' Language is not its elaborate conventionalism, nor the burden of pre-schematization with which it loads us, but the generative and creative power unceasingly to make this whole fluid" (Gadamer, *Truth and Method*, pp. 497–98).

37. "Normal discourse is that which is conducted within an agreed-upon set of conventions about what counts as a relevant contribution, what counts as answering a question, what counts as having a good argument for that answer or a good criticism of it. Abnormal discourse is what happens when someone joins in the discourse who is ignorant of these conventions or who sets them aside. . . . The product of abnormal discourse can be anything from nonsense to intellectual revolution, and there is no discipline which describes it, any more than there is a discipline devoted to the study of the unpredictable, or of 'creativity.' But hermeneutics is the study of an abnormal discourse from the point of view of some normal discourse—the attempt to make sense of what is going on at a stage where we are still too unsure about it to describe it" (Rorty, *Philosophy and the Mirror of Nature*, pp. 320–21).

38. Foucault, *Archaeology of Knowledge*, p. 227.

39. Habermas' early statement of the issue, remaining largely unchanged since, is as follows: "If philosophical ethics and political theory can know nothing more than what is anyhow contained in the everyday norm consciousness of different populations, and if it cannot even know this in a different way, it cannot then rationally distinguish legitimate from illegitimate domination. Illegitimate domination also meets with consent, else it would not be able to last. . . . If, on the other hand, philosophical ethics and political theory are supposed to disclose the moral core of the general consciousness and to *reconstruct* it as a normative concept of the moral, then they must specify criteria and provide reasons; they must, that is, produce theoretical knowledge" (Habermas, *Communication and the Evolution of Society*, pp. 202–203).

His solution: "In adopting a theoretical attitude, in engaging in discourse—or for that matter in any communicative action whatsoever—we have always (already) made, at least implicitly, certain presuppositions, under which alone consensus is possible: the presupposition, for instance, that true propositions are preferable to false ones, and that right (i.e., justifiable) norms are preferable to wrong ones" (ibid., p. 177).

Habermas' premise, stated in discussing psychoanalysis, is that the assumption of repression (and similarly, of ideology) "presupposes unconstrained, pathologically undistorted communication" (ibid., p. 70). He appears, then, to accept some form of (2) above as a solution, that there are norms of discourse that are so presupposed, in every discourse, that they may be regarded as disentangled from the finite contingencies and circumstances of historical events. Such a view belies any thorough understanding of historical and discursive entanglements.

40. I have taken the liberty of converting Gadamer's claim that there is "absolutely" no entrapment to the claim that no entrapment is "absolute," for I take specific entanglements to entail contingent determinations in our discourses and understandings, but not to be able to confine any discourse absolutely.

41. Foucault, *Discourse on Language*, p. 221.

42. Foucault, *Archaeology of Knowledge*, p. 205.

43. Two interesting attempts to define the "discourse" of the latter half of the twentieth century are in Richard Bernstein, *Beyond Objectivism and Relativism* (Philadelphia: University of Pennsylvania Press, 1983); and Jean-François Lyotard, *The Postmodern Condition: A Report on Knowledge*, trans. Geoff Bennington and Brian Massumi (Minneapolis: University of Minnesota Press, 1984).

44. As Foucault says at the end of *The Order of Things*, posing questions concerning the "figure of man": "they are at most questions to which it is not possible to reply; they must be left in suspense, where they pose themselves, only with the knowledge that the possibility of posing them may well open the way to a future thought" (p. 386).

45. Foucault, *Archaeology of Knowledge*, p. 15.

46. Ibid., p. 125.

47. Ibid., p. 30.

48. Ibid., p. 125.

49. Ibid., p. 42.

50. Ibid., p. 44.

51. Ibid., p. 118.

52. Ibid., p. 127.

53. Ibid., p. 131.

54. In other words: "it is not in order to give it a definitive place in an unmoving constellation . . . but in order to reveal . . . a specific domain. A domain that has not so far been made the object of any analysis" (ibid., p. 207). However, it is "a domain that has no means of guaranteeing . . . that it will remain stable and autonomous. . . . I accept that my discourse may disappear with the figure that has borne it so far" (ibid., pp. 207–208).

55. Ibid., p. 209.

56. Foucault, *Discourse on Language*, pp. 216, 215.

57. "What political status can you give to discourse if you see in it merely a thin transparency that shines for an instant at the limit of things

and thoughts? Has not the practice of revolutionary discourse and scientific discourse in Europe over the past two hundred years freed you from this idea that words are wind, an external whisper, a beating of wings that one has difficulty in hearing in the serious matter of history?" (Foucault, *Archaeology of Knowledge*, p. 209).

58. "By correcting itself, by rectifying its errors, by clarifying its formulations, discourse does not necessarily undo its relations with ideology" (ibid.).

59. Ibid., p. 211.

60. See my *Inexhaustibility and Human Being*, chap. 6.

61. This is very close to Heidegger's language, for example, in "The Origin of the Work of Art," where he says: "Truth is un-truth, insofar as there belongs to it the reservoir of the not-yet-uncovered, the un-uncovered, in the sense of concealment" (Heidegger, "The Origin of the Work of Art," *Poetry, Language, Thought*, trans. Albert Hofstadter [New York: Harper & Row, 1971], p. 60). See also my *Ring of Representation*, chap. 6, where I take up the reciprocity of truth and untruth as the far-reaching supplementarity of inexhaustibility. Heidegger does not fulfill the reciprocity of untruth as truth, a thought essential to our understanding of nature's semasis.

62. See note 57, above.

63. "I believe . . . that this particular idea of the 'whole of society' derives from a utopian context. This idea arose in the Western world, within this highly individualized historical development that culminates in capitalism. To speak of the 'whole of society' apart from the only form it has ever taken is to transform our past into a dream" (Foucault, *Language, Counter-Memory, Practice*, pp. 232–33).

64. "For the entire modern *episteme*—that which was formed towards the end of the eighteenth century and still serves as the positive ground of our knowledge, that which constituted man's particular mode of being and the possibility of knowing him empirically—that entire *episteme* was bound up with the disappearance of Discourse and its featureless reign, with the shift of language towards objectivity, and with its reappearance in multiple form. If this same language is now emerging with greater and greater insistence in a unity that we ought to think but cannot as yet do so, is this not the sign that the whole of this configuration is now about to topple, and that man is in the process of perishing as the being of language continues to shine every brighter upon our horizon?" (Foucault, *Order of Things*, pp. 385–86).

65. "By power, I do not mean 'Power' as a group of institutions and mechanisms that ensure the subservience of the citizens of a given state. By power, I do not mean, either, a mode of subjugation which, in contrast to violence, has the form of the rule. Finally, I do not have in mind a general system of domination exerted by one group over another,

a system whose effects, through successive derivations, pervade the entire social body. The analysis, made in terms of power, must not assume that the sovereignty of the state, the form of the law, or the over-all unity of a domination are given at the outset; rather, these are only the terminal forms power takes. It seems to me that power must be understood in the first instance as the multiplicity of force relations immanent in the sphere in which they operate and which constitute their own organization; as the process which, through ceaseless struggles and confrontations, transforms, strengthens, or reverses them; as the support which these force relations find in one another, thus forming a chain or a system, or on the contrary, the disjunctions and contradictions which isolate them from one another; and lastly, as the strategies in which they take effect, whose general design or institutional crystallization is embodied in the state apparatus, in the formulation of the law, in the various social hegemonies. . . . The omnipresence of power: not because it has the privilege of consolidating everything under its invincible unity, but because it is produced from one moment to the next, at every point, or rather in every relation from one point to another. Power is everywhere; not because it embraces everything, but because it comes from everywhere. And 'Power,' insofar as it is permanent, repetitious, inert, and self-reproducing, is simply the over-all effect that emerges from all these mobilities, the concatenation that rests on each of them and seeks in turn to arrest their movement. . . . Power is not an institution, and not a structure; neither is it a certain strength we are endowed with; it is the name that one attributes to a complex strategical situation in a particular society" (Foucault, *History of Sexuality*, pp. 92–93).

66. "One can't even be downcast, angry, grim, indignant, sullen, or embittered *with reason* unless one inhabits some social setting and adopts, however tentatively and critically, its codes and categories. Or unless, and this is much harder, one constructs a new setting and proposes new codes and categories. Foucault refuses to do either of these things, and that refusal, which makes his genealogies so powerful and so relentless, is also the catastrophic weakness of his political theory" (Michael Walzer, "The Politics of Michel Foucault," *Dissent*, [Fall 1983], 490).

67. Foucault elaborates his metaphysics of power in five propositions: "(1) Power is not something that is acquired, seized, or shared, something that one holds on to or allows to slip away; power is exercised from innumerable points, in the interplay of nonegalitarian and mobile relations. (2) Relations of power are not in a position of exteriority with respect to other types of relationships . . . but are immanent in the latter. . . . (3) Power comes from below; that is, there is no binary and all-encompassing opposition between rulers and ruled at the root of power relations. . . . (4) Power relations are both intentional and nonsubjective.

. . . (5) Where there is power, there is resistance, and yet, or rather consequently, this resistance is never in a position of exteriority with respect to power" (*History of Sexuality*, pp. 94–95).

The first three of these compose what I call a "metaphysics of power": power is everywhere, exercised from innumerable points, immanent in other types of relationships, and grounded in no fundamental relationship of oppression. How then are we to carry out a political program where we must gain control of the levers of power?

But we must not neglect the final two propositions, in particular that wherever there is power there is resistance. Foucault goes on to say: "Should it be said that one is always 'inside' power, there is no 'escaping' it, there is no absolute outside where it is concerned, because one is subject to the law in any case? Or that, history being the ruse of reason, power is the ruse of history, always emerging the winner? This would be to misunderstand the strictly relational character of power relationships. Their existence depends on a multiplicity of points of resistance: these play the role of adversary, target, support, or handle in power relations. These points of resistance are present everywhere in the power network. Hence there is no single locus of great Refusal, no soul of revolt, source of all rebellions, or pure law of the revolutionary. Instead there is a plurality of resistances, each of them a special case: resistances that are possible, necessary, improbable; others that are spontaneous, savage, solitary, concerted, rampant, or violent; still others that are quick to compromise, interested, or sacrificial; by definition, they can only exist in the strategic field of power relations. . . . Resistances . . . are the odd term in relations of power; they are inscribed in the latter as an irreducible opposite" (Foucault, *History of Sexuality*, pp. 95–96).

68. Ibid., p. 96.

69. "Of course, these are not affirmations; they are at most questions to which it is not possible to reply; they must be left in suspense, where they pose themselves, only with the knowledge that the possibility of posing them may well open the way to future thought" (Foucault, *Order of Things*, p. 386).

7

LANGUAGE AND LIMITS

THE CENTRAL THEMES of the understanding of language set forth here are the entanglements of language and other forms of semasis and judgment in human experience and nature, our participation in language and discourse, and the inexhaustibility of languages, thought, and nature. The purpose of this final chapter is to develop the notions of locality and inexhaustibility in relation to languages and judgment. But it would be appropriate first to consider entanglement in languages, if only by way of review and summary, before considering a general theory to express the complexity of such entanglements.

INEXHAUSTIBILITY

The twenty-six principles and other predominant features of the analysis of language presented in our discussion to this point can be summarized in two major principles that together express the fundamental and pervasive inexhaustibility of languages and semasis: the principles of entanglement and of surplus. In combination they express the togetherness of locality and inexhaustibility. Since the notion of inexhaustibility appears to ring primarily of openness and surplus, it is essential that we emphasize the specific entanglements of discourse and language, indeed of all human affairs. We have explored such entanglements in the context of the sociality and politicality of discourse. But even such a discussion barely begins to explicate the kinds of entanglements that compose the local spheres of human experience. Discourse and language are thoroughly entangled among the determining features of human life and experience, historically and prospectively. Temporality is important here, though it generically exemplifies our two major principles, the two sides of inexhaustibility: the determinate influences of the past upon all forms of understanding and practice, and the possibilities of transformation in any of them, given their heterogeneity and temporality. We are speaking of finiteness as locality, the joint entanglement in finite conditions and limitations, and the transgression that pertains to every limit, to be broached or overcome, transformed into other local conditions, a finite transcendence. We are speaking of the limits of limits, of heterogeneity, transgression, and excess. All of these pertain to the limits of language.

The principle of entanglement includes the inexhaustible density of discourse, its awesome and ponderous materiality. The principle that we are always immersed in languages would be trivial if it were not accompanied by the understanding that immersedness involves events entangled in irresistible and ponderous materiality. Here Foucault's emphasis on discourse is important, though we should note his distinction between archaeologies and genealogies, as if the former notion, emphasizing discursive formations, needs to be supplemented by a more situated sense of the formations and events that characterize human history and experience in other than discursive ways. Thus, there are material productive relations, exchange relations, and labor and institutional relations, not all of which are forms of discourse, though all are manifested in discourse and influence discursive formations.[1] The panoply of locales in which human beings are located and entangled suggests the inexhaustible plenitude of nature in which human beings are also always located. We join the thought of social and semasic entanglement with the material inexhaustibility of nature.

The point of introducing the materiality of discursive formations is to emphasize the entanglements of linguistic discourses and the materiality of the local historical events in which they are situated. Here we must supplement the notion of immersedness with that of surplus to avoid too narrow a sense of equivalence. That there might be no human relationship that did not involve discursive expressions, that the pervasive feature of human material relations might always involve representations and forms of expression—for example, exchange relations in economic milieux—does not entail equivalence between discourse and the material systems in which it plays its semasic roles. Such an assumption of equivalence would be a denial of surplus. Finite entanglements are not incompatible with surplus of meaning or of being. Similarly, there is no human relationship that does not involve us in natural events, with natural things. We emphasize the uniqueness of human social and linguistic practices while emphasizing the permeability and mutual supplementarity of natural and human boundaries. Where the natural and human meet, in this sense of limit and unlimit, is where we find heterogeneity.

It is Foucault's achievement to have shown quite irresistibly overall, though we may dispute some of the details, that many if not all of the institutional forms of discourse related to what we claim to know and to understand, therefore involving truth and rationality, are inextricably entangled among material forces of power and desire. Power is everywhere, not in the sense that it is everything, but that it comes from everywhere, is entangled in everything. This qualification is closely akin to the recurrent difficulty we find in expressing supplementarity: desire is everywhere also, as is reason, but neither is everything, not only in the sense that reason demands its contrasting term, madness or unreason, as power and desire appear not to, but more profoundly in the sense that each expresses not only an entanglement with the other, but also a surplus relative to it. The "everywhere" expresses inexhaustibility, supplementarity and heterogeneity.

Our subject is an inexhaustible, local finiteness. The principles of power and desire clash with the specificity of events and of material conditions. If everything is but a manifestation of the will to power, then the tangible specificity of events and individuals evaporates into an indeterminate overarching project. If everything is but an expression of the pursuit of libidinal pleasure, alienated from itself by repression and rejection, then either specific individual forms of life evaporate into blind larger forces or else history bears responsibility for specification as the general forces and forms cannot. But although history reveals the specificity of individual events, it cannot produce that specificity unless other conditions support individuality within the finiteness of human events. The great forms of recollection that close *The Phenomenology of Spirit* play out the tension between historical forms and historical density and specificity.[2]

The temptation as we acknowledge entanglement in historical and natural events is to let ourselves become susceptible to generic forms at the expense of specificity and individuality. Yet the notion of entanglement is abused in succumbing to this temptation, for entanglement is the natural consequence of finiteness, and finiteness here means specificity, though not specificity alone. To say, for example, that thought is entangled in language, after Sapir and Whorf, might be to maintain that we can think only what our particular language permits us to say. Yet the conclusion is overstated if it suggests that we can never say or think what has not already been said or thought. Here entanglement is incompatible with creativity and heterogeneity in language and thought. It follows that entanglement must convey the force of both the specificity of languages and the capacity of languages and thought to go beyond any of their particular specificities. The inexhaustible plenitude of nature multiply calls forth the inexhaustibility of languages, for they are deeply and inextricably entangled in nature. We understand inexhaustibility here to represent heterogeneity and excess.

The conclusion is that human beings are entangled, in thought and action, in the specific forms and structures of the languages and discourses they inhabit, but that these forms and structures cannot determine, specifically, whatever is thought or said, practiced or achieved. Specificity is part of finiteness, as inherent in limitation as transgression, but every limit is itself limited, transcendable and transcended, though never absolutely, never infinitely. Material and discursive entanglements are a natural consequence of this double nature of finiteness, since the multiplicity of local entanglements makes such transcendences possible while entanglement itself is specific and determinate, exceeding every abstract possibility. Thus, the surplus of meaning is part of every meaning intrinsically, insofar as such meaning is finite; and the arbitrariness of signification and meaning is not so much a feature of meaning as of the surplus inherent in every local being.

This chapter is the generic expression and summary of the discussion of the preceding chapters, the attempt to integrate the complex ramifications of languages and discourse that we have unfolded in relation to the ideas of locality, inexhaustibility, and ergonality. One of the subsidiary purposes of this theoretical formulation is to respond to the critique that metaphysics is and must be either foundational or totalizing. Our argument is that discursive entanglements are finite, where finiteness means not only locality but also inexhaustibility and multiple locality, and are compatible with neither foundations nor totalities. The generic expression of this position is through our emphasis on the togetherness of indeterminateness with determinateness: everything finite is indeterminate in certain ways and determinate in others.

Moreover, determinateness and indeterminateness are inseparable functional conditions of finiteness, since whatever is determinate in some ways is indeterminate in others and conversely. We have interpreted the indeterminateness in local being as supplementarity, excess. It gives itself to us in the arbitrariness of language. Thus, the principle of entanglement at first blush expresses the finite determinants of human situations, the principle of surplus the openness inherent in any local human situations. This interpretation, however, is misleading insofar as the multiplicity of entanglements both presupposes and gives rise to indeterminateness in human situations while the surplus inherent in finite situations is sometimes more determining rather than less, a specific surplus rather than unintelligible variation.

To enforce these qualifications in preparation for more general discussion, we may briefly review and re-characterize the twenty-six principles of semasis and language in connection with inexhaustibility and its major expressions: entanglement and surplus; determinateness and indeterminateness; complementarity and supplementarity.

a. Autonomy. A language is, in some respects at least, independent of any of its functions—epistemic, social, expressive, or semasic. This understanding is a direct expression of supplementarity and inexhaustibility, though possibly one of its less expected ramifications. The point is that every local condition is in certain respects indeterminate relative to any functions we may assign to it. We have described this multiple, local functioning as "ergonality," the heterogeneous work that local conditions do in different locations. Local ingredients work or function in multiply heterogeneous locations. In the case of languages, structure and form are conditions of all linguistic expressions. These very specific conditions of natural languages both determine and introduce alternatives into what may be expressed and how, but also give them the character they require to produce such figurative forms as poetry and story. The most inventive forms of linguistic expression depend most heavily on what is most determined by tradition and social conformation. The most structured and repetitive forms of expression work by departure and variation. In this sense, the functions of a language cannot altogether determine its structures and forms; yet languages change under functional and expressive pressures. It follows that the independence of a language, structural or functional, is part of the surplus that expresses its finiteness within the generic and social functions that a language must serve. Another way of putting this is that no language can be merely an instrument, not only because we are more deeply entangled in it than in other tools, but because it embodies something of our understanding of ourselves and our surroundings. Yet we must add that instruments are finite and excessive, multiply entangled in human locales.

   b. Stability
   c. Structure
   d. Composition
   e. Mechanism
   f. Synchronicity
   g. Generation
   h. Rules

We have rejected the position that languages are governed by rules. Yet it is surely true that while a full historically developing natural language may not be, subsidiary components of such a language, such as technical languages or language games, are governed by definite rules. Each of these principles conforms to the analysis of autonomy under (a): to the extent that a language is well-defined and determinate, it is composed of specific elements in definite combinations. There is a formal structure to natural languages and procedures whereby complex strings of elements are constructed out of more elementary strings in a specific and definite way. Yet every language repeatedly breaks the structures that give it its identity, both in colloquial and informal speech and in carefully contrived writing, poetic or rhetorical.

Such formal specificity may be regarded both as the definite and entangled side of languages, in this case biological or historical, relative to which functional considerations may entail variation—to facilitate communication or to produce novel understandings—and as the supplementary side in relation to the work of linguistic utterances, since they are confined by formal constraints that are stronger than any functional considerations can entail. In this context, the thesis that syntactic structures carry the weight of semantic considerations, at least at the deep structural level, is the only theoretical means whereby surplus can be eliminated. Even here, the elimination is only at the level of deep structure, since surface variations are immense. We have expressed strong reservations concerning such positions.

Languages and other forms of semasis are only subsidiarily rule-governed, to the extent that there is a greater latitude in all utterances than can be expressed in terms of rules and that discourses along with other entangled human social practices are divided within and against themselves, while the concept of rules, dependent on the notion of perfectibility, cannot carry the weight of such conflicts. There can be a (game-like) rule only if it can be adopted and followed, perfectly and correctly. But social practices and forms of expression are not so perfectible: rather, acceptability is a form of social stratification more than of prohibition.

The principle of stability is more generic than can be gathered from its association here with mechanism and synchronicity. There can be no communication without stability. However, in this respect, stability is entirely functional, while it is clear that there is both more stability than required by social functions—as in grammatical distinctions by social class—and less insofar as there can be communication and understanding even where every rule has been broken, where stability largely becomes unintelligible.

i. Arbitrariness. We have understood the arbitrary relation between signifier and signified to be an expression of far more generic relations, the surplus in all semasis, the heterogeneity in all relations, the supplementarity of truth. We will explore the possibility that meaning is not more arbitrary than being.

j. Choice
k. Context
s. Intentionality
t. Sociality
v. Personality
w. Surplus
x. Inexhaustability

The presence of human individuals in situations of utterance inevitably entails that there will be individual variations, by intention, choice, and personality. Yet this personal side of semasis and utterance is a surplus only relative to the social, public side of languages, for individual variations may be entirely determinate in terms of individual histories. The point is that the public and private dimensions of semasis are both generic and inseparable. Thus, individual utterances are entangled in social and historical conditions, but may transcend these conditions where necessary, and will inevitably do so in virtue of supplementarity; also, social influences both shape individual utterances and transcend individual intentions. Entanglement and surplus, the dimensions of inexhaustibility, belong together in any situations and relative to any utterances.

l. Episteme A
m. Competence
n. Ideality
o. Tacitness
p. Innateness
q. Episteme B
r. Intensionality

Languages are both something known and means of understanding. All of the entanglements and surpluses of human life and of nature must therefore be involved in languages, inexhaustibly. Once we emphasize finiteness in knowing, and relinquish unqualified determinations, then in every epistemic expression there is a surplus both of what has not been said and of what cannot be said in the terms involved. Relative to every explicit expression of understanding there is understanding known but unexpressed. Every expression and understanding is a function of how it is known and expressed, a consequence of the principle that there is no neutral form of understanding or expression. Every understanding strives for ideality and loses specificity in abstraction, yet without idealization, there can be no understanding whatever. Every truth is therefore finite in the sense that it can be known and expressed only in terms made possible by tradition and history, yet every truth transcends any particular finite conditions, both in its relevance to other such conditions and in its ideality.

u. Politics
y. Expressibility

The most vivid entanglements of languages and discourses are manifested in the social and political side of semasic utterances and in the interpretability that every facet of human life both affords and demands. Whatever is meant can be expressed; whatever is intelligible can be meant. But meaning is then as complexly entangled as intelligibility, and there are inexhaustibly diverse and heterogeneous forms of intelligibility, a natural consequence of finiteness. Again, finiteness is not entrapment or closure, for there is also surplus, and finiteness is not simply openness, for there are both finite limits and definite conditions. Without such limits, there would be unconditioned, infinite openness.

z. Semasis. The conclusion, then, is that there are inexhaustibly diverse and manifold forms of semasis, of judgments and of judgments upon those judgments, which are differentiated but also interrelated. A specific form of semasis is language, though language is so generic that it can incorporate within itself any semasic form, if obliquely. The notion of semasic fields, containing both idiosemic and consensual subfields, but involving cores and peripheries, carries as much of the force of entanglements and surpluses as we may desire into the theory of language and semasis. We must understand the larger social or political determinants of such semasic fields to grasp the "awesome materiality" or "ponderousness" of human circumstances.

What we need to do, the burden of this final chapter, is to transmute the concept of semasic fields into the heterogeneous realms of nature and experience, spheres of relevance, in which all factors of human life and nature can be understood to work, in some cases ponderously and materially. It is essential, that is, to take entanglement seriously before we can work with the surpluses. It is essential to understand the complementary interrelationship of determinateness and indeterminateness in such entanglements before we can understand how heterogeneity pertains to surplus of meaning and openness in inexhaustibility.

LOCALITY

The first condition of our understanding here, metaphysically and linguistically, is that every being and every meaning is finite, local. This sense of finiteness, and the corresponding sense of the infinite, is not incompatible with an infinite succession of integers, with the continuum of real numbers, or with the infinite class of well-formed strings in any natural language. The distinction is between what is unconditioned, whatever it may be—being or knowing—and what is thoroughly conditioned, locally entangled. Locality, finiteness, is conditionedness, immersedness in situations that define conditions for what is located within it. We reject any unqualified state or condition, ontological or epistemological. Our difficulty with a mirror theory of language is not that words fail to correspond to things but that the mirroring or correspondence is either trivial if qualified or unintelligible if unqualified. Even

where all-inclusive absolutes are rejected, unqualified and unconditioned states recur at other levels. That is the immense and
virtually irresistible appeal of epistemological foundationalism that
Richard Rorty has called the mirror theory of knowledge.[3] We
have explored the idea of an all-inclusive locality that represents its
own locality, its own conditions. That gives us inexhaustibility.

What is it to know something? Do we, in such knowledge,
overcome the conditions and limits of finite human historical
circumstances? Can the languages we speak and write lift themselves out of their social and cultural conditions? If not, and if all
knowledge and semasis is historically conditioned, then perhaps
there may be no secure norms of conduct or reason. Alternatively,
all such norms may themselves be conditioned and qualified by
their historical and human circumstances. That does not make
them any less normative, any less influential.

How are we able to understand each other when we speak and
write in different or even common languages? One kind of answer
is that such understanding presupposes a shared propositional or
semasic ground, but, by the nature of the argument, an unqualified
ground. Another kind of answer is that we understand each other
insofar as, not because, we share common surroundings and
circumstances, including traditions and humanity, but what is
shared may be only that part of what we understand that is
common. Still another, related answer is that we may be able to
understand each other, in common, only in virtue of the manifold
differences between us. One view of understanding is repetition,
though no repetition can be unqualified. The other view is that we
understand by differentiation and variation, though no variation
can be unqualified. One view of knowledge here seeks an unqualified commonality, unqualified in that every variation is either
relevant or damaging. The other view is that knowledge can be
effective only insofar as it is possessed uniquely and differentially.
To the one, science is the field of shared conclusions. To the other,
science is composed of manifold fields including divergent prospects of useful discovery, and divergences without usefulness, still
important to truth.

Here commonality and variation are not antagonists but comple-
ments, where the complementarity entails heterogeneity. Similarly, the qualifications and conditions of local conditions do not
subvert transcendence, but are means for it, the local limits of
transgression. We add that transgression itself is finite, therefore

local, conditioned and qualified. That is, every utterance and the promise of novelty, of escape from repetition, bears the threat of unintelligibility. But every novelty is a repetition, a representation of its tradition, for traditions can be represented and can develop in inexhaustibly manifold forms, some of which transgress the limits we take to represent intelligibility.

The point, then, is that to be finite, every being must inhabit definite but multiple local spheres of relevance and must itself be a sphere of relevance.[4] Locality entails participation in definite spheres of relevance, inexhaustibly many such spheres. We are defining here the generic form of the principles of entanglement and surplus: every being is entangled in many locales and possesses definiteness in virtue of its particular locations while it exceeds any such location in virtue of its multiple location. Analogously, to be finite, every semiate must inhabit a definite and local sphere of semasic relations, its semasic field. But although definite, with definite traits and limits, every such field is inexhaustible—inexhaustibly multiple and heterogeneous—in its relations and ramifications. The definiteness of a sphere of relevance is by no means incompatible with its inexhaustibility or heterogeneity. Rather, definiteness and indefiniteness belong together, and their mutual relations are the basis of inexhaustibility. A semiate possesses meaning in virtue of the work it does in a particular location, but every location is inexhaustible, effectively many locations. This multiplicity is heterogeneity.

The fundamental and generic principle here is that everything is finite, conditioned and qualified, including its conditions and qualifications. Everything participates in, is ingredient in, particular locations with particular and definite relations, is ingredient in inexhaustibly many such locations, each with definite relations but together indeterminate in manifold ways; finally, each being is itself a sphere of relevance, a locale, in which other ingredients are located. The togetherness of determinateness and indeterminateness is a direct consequence of multiple locatedness. Before pursuing the linguistic ramifications of such an ontology, the principles that define finite entanglements are worth explicating.

a. To be finite, a being must be limited in definite ways. Limitation here is locality, manifested in definite entanglements and relations. Each local being is what it is in virtue of belonging to a particular location, working there, but every local being is multiply located. Locality, inexhaustibility, and ergonality express locatedness, multiple locatedness, and multiple identity in virtue of the heterogeneity of locations.

b. To be local, finite, limits cannot be absolute, unqualified, altogether determinate and immutable, for they would then not be finite but would be unqualified. Specific entanglements in any sphere of relevance are always accompanied by entanglements in inexhaustibly other locations. Following an ancient principle, limit and unlimit are inseparable, related complementarily, with each the other's supplement. Locality and inexhaustibility express this inseparability of limit and unlimit.

c. Locality is the belonging together of determinateness and indeterminateness that composes inexhaustibility. Inexhaustibility here is not simply openness and indeterminateness, as if that were beyond determination, but the indeterminations that are a consequence of multiplicities of local determinations.

d. It follows that locality involves transcendence, a conditioned and qualified, finite transcendence.

e. It follows also that every limit may be surmounted if not overcome or superseded. More powerfully, limits are relevant only as they involve differences, unlimits, heterogeneities, excesses.

These principles define finiteness as locality, inexhaustibility, and ergonality.[5] Our understanding does not depart from other contemporary views of finiteness so much as it enriches them with complementarity and supplementarity, reinterprets them in terms of locality and inexhaustibility. It follows that to the extent that finiteness involves specific limits and locations, it is a form of "entrapment," not in the sense of enslavement in contrast with liberation, since finite freedom is a function of specific conditions, but in the sense that particular circumstances determine what human beings are capable of thinking and doing, determine human and natural identities and possibilities. Nevertheless, to be located in particular circumstances is not to be confined to them if this means that there remains no openness to new possibilities and variations, for all circumstances, however definite, are heterogeneous, divided within themselves and without. That is, finiteness entails both the specificity and multiplicity of locations. A consequence of such multiple locatedness is heterogeneity, the continuing presence of unthought and alternative possibilities and of new forms of relevance.

Another way of putting this is that the specificities of participation in a tradition and historical circumstances are both conditions and qualifications of all forms of understanding and action and themselves qualified by the possibilities they unleash. Specificity here is irresistible but qualified, the locality of locality. This double locality is excess. Specificity exceeds the fluidity of language, even as languages allow us to say whatever we wish to say. Similarly, alternative possibilities, always present as a consequence of the multiple relevances and locations of any being, are no less determinate, no less a function of specific conditions, than the actual determining influences in human cultural life. Only certain possibilities are relevant in given circumstances, but these may contain possibilities of change, allowing other, equally specific possibilities, as certain options are realized. Excess and heterogeneity belong to every specificity.

To suppose that finiteness entails skepticism is to overemphasize one side of finiteness, its specificities, without a sense of their finite transcendences, their inexhaustibility. Similarly, to suppose that finiteness entails formlessness and infinite freedom is to overlook the specific determinants of our human conditions, individual and social. Both views are effectively a rejection of finiteness, a reversion to infiniteness in the name of the finite.

That finite human beings can know only what circumstances make possible, can realize only finite truths, that historical, social, and biological conditions are important limits of all forms of knowledge, that languages also are historical creatures, emergent through human activities and relationships, does not and cannot entail skepticism except in a trivial sense that repeats the principle that knowledge is finite, local, heterogeneous, and inexhaustible. To think that if all human activities are finite knowledge is impossible presupposes that what is impossible is infinite, unconditioned in certain ways. Does it follow, because human beings at different times, or in different cultures, begin from different premises or inhabit different languages, that what one claims to know the others cannot even begin to understand, that cultural and linguistic differences produce incommensurability? Does heterogeneity entail unintelligibility? Only to the extent that specific differences are regarded as effectively absolute. Heterogeneity, then, opens possibilities of understanding. Even so, it also entails that specific differences are specific, and are differences. These may be barriers to understanding, but never without conditions. The barriers themselves are finite.

The knowledge that is deemed impossible by the skeptic is absolute. But there are finite forms of understanding that may be finitely distinguished from caprice and error—if such a distinction is our finite goal. Latent within skepticism is a demand for unqualified grounds. The skeptic emphasizes the specificity of the finite conditions in which all human beings and their knowledge are situated: for example, the finiteness of all perception. The skeptic neglects the fact that the conditions of perception are inexhaustible, that they are variable with theoretical and cultural conditions—if not absolutely or altogether—and that such variabilities are means to understanding. We develop instruments whereby we correct the distortions of ordinary perception; we look for relatively stable forms of perception among complex variations. Finally, without the specific determinants of perception, which we may not share in common, we would not be able to perceive anything.

Knowledge is a function of the local and determinate circumstances of human activities coupled with the inexhaustible but equally local possibilities inherent in every human situation of variation and heterogeneity. There are new discoveries to be made in every established sphere of knowledge, and new forms of knowledge in every established taxonomy of disciplinary forms. The skeptic demands an infinite and unqualified knowledge relative to which finite epistemic forms must fail. But there is ample transcendence, local transcendence, in the inexhaustibility of local human activities that accommodates inexhaustibly manifold but still local epistemic forms and variations. Within specific determinants and conditions, there is an inexhaustible surplus of possibility and meaning that finite understanding can build upon.

A form of relativism is sometimes offered in reply to skepticism. Different people and people from different cultures know what they know, locally and relative to their circumstances. This view emphasizes the specificities of circumstances and their influences, interpreting these as limitations, but neglects the limitations of these limits, the qualifications of every circumstance. And among these qualifications are the fact that members of different cultures communicate and understand each other, if finitely and limitedly. Such a relativism makes finite differences of location and circumstance effectively absolute. It neglects the last of the principles above, that every finite limit is to be surmounted. That is, every local limit is local, and cannot be made absolute.

It follows that a language, like every semasic field and activity, is both finite and transcendent, more accurately, it is supplementary because finiteness includes local transcendence. We are speaking of the creativity of languages but also of the specificity of linguistic forms, grammatical, phonological, and morphological; of the autonomy of languages, manifested in their specific structures, and of their inexhaustible utility. Languages are inexhaustible, entangled throughout human concerns and circumstances but permeated by creative surpluses. But so is every significant semasic form, every art—painting, music, dance, and so forth—along with every form of practice, political or social. And so is every being, not least because it belongs to these inexhaustibly entangled spheres.

Is a language more inexhaustible than a rock or stone? Inexhaustibility does not admit of degrees, but of kinds. Rocks and stones are inexhaustible in that they possess properties that, in new circumstances, will surprise us, will transgress the limits of our understandings. But the most striking of these circumstances reside in human experience, a human future with its multiple semasic forms. Stones are inexhaustible in their inexhaustible physical properties; but their most obvious inexhaustibility resides in our uses of them in our practices and their roles in our contrivances.

There is nothing in our surroundings that we cannot employ, however indirectly, or embody in our contrivances and work. Any semasic form possesses this inexhaustible power, and any language possesses it clearly, both in its poetic manifestations and propositionally. But no language can be more inexhaustible than any visible semasic form, painting or sculpture, music or dance. Each form possesses its unique specificities and determinatenesses, part of its inexhaustibility and entanglements, but also the source of its excesses. Reflexiveness, though it is the most apparent manifestation of inexhaustibility, is not its only source or manifestation.

The parsimonious spirit seeks to explain the complex forms of human life and experience in terms of less complex forms. The approach has enormous benefits in scientific understanding, but it pays too great a price. It suggests that these less complex forms are not inexhaustible. The explanatory results show that everything, intelligible in certain contexts, is inexhaustible, takes on novel properties in new surroundings, manifests specific determinants in any surrounding. It follows that everything is inexhaustible because it is a hybrid of specificity and surplus.

A language is, from the point of view of such an analysis, unique not in its inexhaustibility, shared by everything we encounter, nor in its semasis and reflexiveness, shared by every semasic form. Rather, every language possesses those specific determinants, historical and structural, that demarcate it uniquely while its functional properties are shared with some other forms or conditions in human experience. Sophisticated and reflexive linguistic expressions are inseparable from other forms of semasis and expression, a manifestation of the principle that we find a way to say what we mean, somehow. Language is not unique to human beings because animals are capable of more or less rudimentary linguistic achievements—whatever these may be—just as animals are capable of more or less rudimentary understandings and judgments. Yet on the whole, given human social practices, languages and other semasic forms compose the center of human creative achievements, the paramount manifestations of inexhaustibility. The point is that such inexhaustibility is not so much different from the rest of human experience and other activities and events as a consequence of the interplay of affinities and variations.

Every human language is unique in certain of its structural features, deep or surface. But every such language also functionally serves human purposes along with other forms of semasis and judgment. This complex interplay of typical function, structural uniqueness, and functional novelty is a direct expression of inexhaustibility.

HETEROGENEITY

Heterogeneity belongs to languages both because it is found everywhere, as multiple locality, and because languages mark such differences where they are to be found—not every difference, for that would be impossible, but the repeated presence of heterogeneity, its obtrusiveness and irresistibility. Still, other semasic forms also represent differences, and language is not unique in this respect. Rather, it is the locale historically where natural and human heterogeneity is both manifested and denied. In both Chomsky and Heidegger, as different as they may be in most respects, Language represents The Human.[6] This may be the most important feature language possesses in the Western philosophical tradition.

Yet even this characteristic is not unique to language, and could not be. There are many reasons for this, having to do with the manifold affinities as well as differences among languages and other semasic forms. The major point is that a language is not unique in its larger functions, but in its small: in its grammar but not its semasis, its lexicon but not its truthfulness. Every language is inexhaustible, but so is every being and every semasic work and medium. The growing literature on animal rights emphasizes that animals feel pain. This emphasis on a criterion of concern, like the criterion of grammar, deemphasizes the inexhaustibility of animals, who feel, respond, care, protect, think, and dream, and more. There is also the rest of nature, with its inexhaustibility. In this sense, inexhaustibility is an ethical condition.[7]

Is language the medium of thought? Yes and no: yes in that in our time, stable thoughts require linguistic expression; no in that linguistic utterances are surrounded by a penumbra of other semasic relations, other forms of thought, other material relations. Is language the medium of understanding? Yes and no: yes in that whatever we understand can be expressed in linguistic form; no in that such an understanding is frequently a translation of an insight achieved in another semasic medium. Is language closer to nature and being than other human conditions? Yes and no: yes in that metaphysics, where being and nature are represented, is singularly linguistic, and that our changing relationship to nature is manifested in the creativity of languages; no in that nothing can be closer to nature and being than anything else, for this closeness does not admit of degrees. Nature appears in heterogeneous ways.

If there is no Language and no Being (or Nature), but only languages and beings, then there is finiteness, locality, but a finiteness equivalent with inexhaustibility, that is, with limitation and transgression, with heterogeneity. There are multiple languages and natural things, and different scales to measure the relations among them. If so, then the locality of any inexhaustible being, an ingredient in a given location, entails its multiple location, its ingredience in multiple locations. This multiple locatedness, this heterogeneity, expresses a certain pervasiveness or inclusiveness. We have informally called it "entanglement." Locality, here, includes a certain inclusiveness, an entanglement and dispersion of relevance, and the locality of any language entails a certain pervasiveness relative to other semasic forms and to truth. Locality entails a plurality of overlapping and frequently unrelated locales, a plurality of entanglements.

The most striking aspect of Foucault's view of the discourse of modernity and the Enlightenment is the suggestion that there are large-scale formations, not necessarily but frequently discursive, that mark our modern sensibility. With the qualifications that such formations must always belong to particular historical locations, that there may be no universal, permanent large-scale formations, that there is no necessary a priori, but only contingent, empirical a prioris—that is, particular conditions that make particular formations and discourses possible—then we have here a theoretical expression of the formations and discourses that express and manifest particular, contingent, and heterogeneous relations of human beings to nature.

Many forms of modern thought, especially since Nietzsche, advocate the abolition of metaphysics. From the point of view of locality and inexhaustibility, every such view of metaphysics imposes absolute limits on it. We are sketching an idea of metaphysics, of nature, and of language that dwells upon the contingencies of historical locations and the specificities of particular formations. One of the consequences of such an understanding of the historicality of representation is that the framing of the questions of difference and of the abolition of metaphysics themselves belong to modern sensibilities. Foucault suggests that they are the natural culmination of modernity. Taking up this suggestion, we may hypothesize that by characterizing the singular forms of modern sensibilities, we come as close as we can to understanding the forms of modern thought, and these are the only forms available to us if there are no absolutely universal forms. We are concerned with understanding nature and semasis from within our historical circumstances, modern and perhaps postmodern, but where the locality of belonging to historical circumstances is excessive, multiple, heterogeneous, and inexhaustible. The "post" in the postmodern, poststructuralist, and postcolonial may express this understanding of the heterogeneity of historical locality.

The point of this discussion is that our understanding of language is among the most important and typical of the forms of modern thought, whether or not we distinguish sharply between languages and discourses. Among those who have followed the transcendental turn, language has replaced subjective consciousness as the primary domain of thought and understanding. Here finite transcendence is eloquently expressed in the role of language as mediator between nature and the contingencies of human locatedness.

Among those who have not followed the transcendental turn quite so closely, language or discourse manifests the inexhaustible limits of human forms of life, social and historical. We find, then, that language plays the double role of universal mediator of all forms of expression and the direct manifestation of local historical conditions. We may express both of these poles in terms of the poles of temporality: the openness of the future and the conditions of the past are the determinants of the present.

It is important to emphasize that language is not alone among the forms of modern sensibility, the pervasive domains in which our understanding of ourselves is expressed. Heidegger speaks not only of Being and Language, but of Truth and Technology. Foucault's categories are more specifically modern: power and desire along with discourse, but also madness, punishment, and sexuality. Each of these contains within itself the Story of Humanity—more accurately, a particular and incomplete story of how we understand ourselves and what we take ourselves to be. And each, if more obliquely, contains within itself the story of nature and the world, told from the standpoint of humanity.

These are pervasive stories, pervasive forms of understanding, pervasive perspectives on nature and human experience, pervasive affairs of human locatedness. They are crystallized inevitably in the general question of how we are to understand our humanity and in the more particular question of whether a human science is possible. But the latter question is in certain respects absurd, since as Foucault also points out, it is essential to a modern sensibility that we seek to understand ourselves and our humanity in scientific terms. Human sciences are possible, but they are not exhaustive, even of themselves. Human sciences are possible, as is any science, in virtue of the inexhaustible openness of semasis and query, so that we can learn whatever we desire to know, but not whatever there is to know, for that is an unqualified, unintelligible notion.

The question of a human science such as linguistics is a repetition of the question of these manifold stories and forms of discourse, which is itself a repetition of the question of the inexhaustible plenitude of beings, understandings, and truths. The forms that characterize a sensibility must be multiple because of the inexhaustibility of experiences and things. That is, the discursive formations are each pervasive, even comprehensive, permeating human life and nature, yet each is different from the others and unique to itself, and many must coexist together in any epoch characterizing a sensibility. Thus, the sites at which modern practice recognizes itself are generally those of power, desire, and truth, but specifically, the sites of madness as the other face of rationality, punishment as the other face of normality, sexuality as the explicit form of desire containing the otherness of male and female. These are Foucault's sites: I would add the site at which science is distinguished from non-Science, nature from Nature, perhaps the most insistent debate of contemporary thought.

There are multiple discursive formations that characterize any actual humanness, in any period, expressing the heterogeneity of relations among power, desire, and truth. This heterogeneity is an overt expression of inexhaustibility. Similarly, language and discourse are among the heterogeneous sites at which humanity expresses its relation to itself, along with technology, sexuality, history, even metaphysics. If we give up metaphysics as too all-seeing, we replace its revelation of nature and being with multiple relations that are no less pervasive, but that manifest the pervasiveness of science or speaking.

The contemporary emphasis on language, then, is not a revelation of new understandings of the nature of language or thought, or even of humanity, but the formation of a particular kind of humanity, with particular relations to nature. It is more a novel affair of human experience framed in language than an insight into a permanent condition of human being. This is Foucault's point. It is particularly evident in the attempt to define a science of language. For the very possibility of a science of language presupposes language on the one hand, for there could be no science as we know it without language, and a particular view of language on the other. Yet it is a view, as Foucault points out, that is effectively contradictory, and doubles itself, since the language that science can provide as object cannot be the language that science employs.

We repeatedly return, then, to the inexhaustible plenitude of discursive formations—linguistic but also practical and cultural, epistemic and even metaphysical—that together express the force of our understanding of our local sensibilities. The many stories that we tell of ourselves and of natural affairs overlap but frequently vary greatly in perspective and point of view, though not so much in scale or pervasiveness. We may say that language is the domain in which humanness is achieved only if we also recognize that a language is a practice and that practice, with its heterogeneities, profoundly affects linguistic utterances. For technology and sexuality are as central and important to humanness as language, and each of these is important to the others. So, for that matter, are visibility, sonance, and our natural surroundings. Even more important, perhaps, is how important technology and language, sexuality and visibility, are to our surroundings, to nature and to natural locales. Every medium of every art has the same pervasive particularity, as do other major forms of human expression. The overlapping among them and their manifold differences are the most visible manifestation of the inexhaustibility that characterizes human experience.

Language, then, is marked by differences both because everything is marked by differences and because of the pervasiveness of language along with other equally pervasive but differentially unique human realizations. Language is neither instrument nor vehicle of truth alone, but heterogeneous in its inexhaustibility throughout human experience and natural conditions, serving many functions and inhabiting every milieu. We inhabit a language, belong to it, more than we employ it or tell the truth by means of it, though both are linguistic achievements. We relate to animals and our surroundings by means of language, by participating in language, but not through language alone. In the relations between language and nature, between linguistic expression and any truth, there are the heterogeneities of inexhaustibility, along with differences involving relations among languages and other forms of semasis and practice. In this sense, the principle that anything can be expressed in language carries the full force of inexhaustibility, provided that we emphasize that it can also be expressed in any other medium, and that these different expressions are not identical in "what" they say. What is at stake is the way in which inexhaustibility is related to identity, itself a profoundly inexhaustible question. What is at stake as well is the inexhaustible possibility of new locales, human and otherwise, in our time a possibility of language, always a work involving languages.

SECULARIZATION AND SANCTIFICATION

A language is a wonderful thing, yet it is not after all everything, nor even the most important and wonderful of human achievements and capabilities. A language is something we can study and understand, yet it is not an object amenable to exhaustive analysis, both because it is inexhaustible and because it manifests and reveals inexhaustibility.

The temptation, marked by the alternatives just described, is either to sanctify language as the heart of human being, infinitely permeable and open, or to secularize it to the point where it is but one thing among other things. Neither alternative is satisfactory. Yet what is important in each alternative, without its deficiencies, may be expressed by the principle that language is inexhaustible, both because every being is inexhaustible, and language is a being among others, and because language, with other forms of semasis, reveals inexhaustibility. It does so in poetry primarily and in other inexhaustibly heterogeneous forms of thought and practice that are realized in language. It does so in virtue of and because of its inexhaustible multiplicity. There is no universal language, no perfect language, because all forms of thought—and these are legion—require and employ language, but also because language is not a universal medium, despite its pervasiveness: it is both too specific to participate in all forms of thought indifferently and too generic to fulfill all needs and provide all the requirements of human life and experience.

Language is inexhaustible in abetting any and all forms of thought and expression, but also in not fulfilling every such form in every way. The modes of judgment and query, of representation and semasis, are inexhaustible themselves, so that no particular form of expression or practice could fulfill them, exhaust them. But more to the point, a language is a medium with specific characteristics. We may think of them as constraints, provided they are not taken to interfere with the inexhaustible pervasiveness of such a medium. The formal structures of a language both enable it to function as effectively as it does, and constrain it so that it can achieve only what is possible in its terms. It must, then, be supplemented by other forms and mediums of expression, some without articulative structures, others more sinuous and flexible, others more precise in certain ways and less precise in others, though none can be very precise when we are dealing with the pervasive expressive forms in which we manifest our judgments.

There is language, and every language serves us well, but there are also gesture and dance, display and visual art, not to mention bodily orientation, tone of voice, music, and spatial and temporal environmental forms. All the forms of human practice are expressive, if not primarily expressive, and are certainly profoundly judgmental. We are what we say and how, but also what we see, display, and make visible, also our practices and our forms of power and desire, entangled together.

In this sense, every art, every form of representation, is both inexhaustible and manifests inexhaustibility, none more than others, each in its own ways and to different purposes, with different results, utilizing different forms, requiring different modes of interpretation. In this sense, every language, along with every other expressive form, is inexhaustible and displays inexhaustibility. In the same sense as well, every form of practice, including but not restricted to the larger forms of politics, national and state forms of power, is inexhaustible and displays inexhaustibility.

This inexhaustible multiplicity of the manifestations of inexhaustibility is the most powerful demystification possible of any particular form in which inexhaustibility is manifested. Given one, we could abandon it for inexhaustibly many others; any might be absent or very different, yet human experience might be no less inexhaustible, though very different. The demystification, however, the secularization of language, cannot turn it into a mere object, even a mere inexhaustible object, along with every other, for language is a primary medium, vehicle, or form of judgment, complexly entangled among the other mediums of judgment and experience.

The secularization of language that permits a science of linguistics to emerge is a function of inexhaustibility. Since every being along with language is inexhaustible, inexhaustibility is not incompatible with science. It is only incompatible with too positive and foundational a view of science. That language is not only inexhaustible but reveals inexhaustibility puts it in the company of other forms of judgment and expression, specific and dense in its particular ways, thereby suggesting that a science of language, or of thought, understanding, practice, or history among others, must itself be inexhaustible, thereby entering the company of what it would seek to bring under its surveillance. But this reflexivity belongs to language and thought, and is then not a singular problem for science.

The very same secularization, dependent as it is on inexhaustibility, therefore includes within it the sanctification of that inexhaustibility. Language is both secular and sacred, not because it is unique in these respects but because inexhaustibility conveys to every being the poles of heterogeneity that our opposing categories call to our attention. Everything is what it is, both determinate and indeterminate, in inexhaustibly manifold and complementary ways, therefore both mysterious and accessible.

Yet language as a medium of expression shares with other such mediums and representations the reflexiveness that makes inexhaustibility a subject as well as a condition. Put another way, determinateness and indeterminateness not only pertain to languages and other symbolic forms, but are expressed and realized there, brought to our attention and displayed. This makes language as well as music and painting neither more complex nor inexhaustible—these do not admit of degrees—nor more mysterious or sacred. It does locate inexhaustibility within these expressive forms, with their mysteries and indeterminatenesses, irresistibly and unavoidably. We mark within the mysteriousness of heterogeneity something of the sacredness of inexhaustibility.

The inexhaustibility of languages and their capacity to manifest inexhaustibility, in poetry and among a multiplicity of disciplines and semasic forms, supports the emphasis on language in our time. The inexhaustibility of other semasic and representational forms, the inexhaustibility of every being and of every human practice, reveals the limitations of too great an emphasis on language. Just as language cannot be the avenue to nature's inexhaustibility, for there is no such privileged way and language has its limits, language is not unique in its intimacy with inexhaustibility. It follows that the contemporary emphasis on language is justified by the inexhaustibility of languages while it also reveals the inadequacies of so strong an emphasis on language in the absence of an adequate linguistic expression of inexhaustibility.

The inexhaustibility of languages demystifies them insofar as their mysteriousness is shared by all natural things and by all forms of representation. Inexhaustibility is everywhere. This same inexhaustibility is also the source of the heterogeneity of human experience and its relationship to nature. In this respect, insofar as language, with the other forms of semasis and query, is a medium in which we both encounter inexhaustibility and contribute to it, language represents what is sacred in our rational and spiritual means, providing us with whatever forms are required by the exigencies of truth. Among these forms are the excesses and heterogeneities of inexhaustibility.

More important perhaps than any attempt to represent the specific uniquenesses of languages is recognition of how pervasively human experience is linguistic, but not linguistic alone. In this sense, there is no determination that is not differentiated by the inexhaustible locales and ingredients that inhabit human experience. And it bears repeating that languages are among the locales that give greatest richness to human life and thought. In this final vein, we may conclude that the greatest truth of any language is that it is a microcosm of the plenitude of human experience and of inexhaustible natural conditions.

NOTES

1. "Archaeology also reveals relations between discursive formations and non-discursive domains (institutions, political events, economic practices and processes)" (Foucault, *Archaeology of Knowledge*, p. 162). Also: "A genealogy should be seen as a kind of attempt to emancipate historical knowledges from [hierarchical, scientific] subjection, to render them, that is, capable of opposition and of struggle against the coercion of a theoretical, unitary, form and scientific discourse. It is based on a reactivation of local knowledges. . . . If we were to characterise it in two terms, then 'archaeology' would be the appropriate methodology of this analysis of local discursivities, and 'genealogy' would be the tactics whereby, on the basis of the descriptions of these local discursivities, the subjected knowledges which were thus released would be brought into play" (Michel Foucault, "Two Lectures," *Power/Knowledge*, ed. Colin Gordon, trans. Alessandro Fontana and Pasquale Pasquino [New York: Pantheon, 1980], p. 85).

2. "The goal, which is Absolute Knowledge or Spirit knowing itself as Spirit, finds its pathway in the recollection of spiritual forms as they are in themselves and as they accomplish the organization of their spiritual kingdom" (G. W. F. Hegel, *Phenomenology of Mind*, trans. James Baillie [London: Allen & Unwin, 1931], p. 808).

3. See Rorty, *Philosophy and the Mirror of Nature*.

4. See chap. 1, note 62, for the categories of locality. For those who are suspicious of categories, I respond that even metaphysical categories are qualified, situated, finite; that they are so even when they claim

otherwise. That is the burden of my *Metaphysical Aporia and Philosophical Heresy*. A metaphysics that understands the finiteness of its own representativity and historicality must strive to find categories that express the finiteness of finiteness, the locality of locality, and the inexhaustibility of inexhaustibility. That has been the burden of my different treatments of locality, from ordinality to ergonality. See *Transition to an Ordinal Metaphysics*, *Inexhaustibility and Human Being*, and *Ring of Representation*.

5. I have, in my *Transition to an Ordinal Metaphysics*, expressed the relevant ontological categories as "order" and "constituent," following Justus Buchler's lead in his *Metaphysics of Natural Complexes*. Yet even the term "order" seems too restrictively unitary, not to carry the full force of entanglement, too suggestive of "ordering" and succession, and too passively a sphere of relationships rather than a domain of activity. Entanglement along with being follow Plato's principle in the *Sophist* that being is power. For all these reasons, I develop the theory here in a very different terminology. Again, see *Ring of Representation*.

6. We have seen how excessively grammar and the gift of language mark The Human over and against animals. See pp. 80–81. See also the discussions in *Ring of Representation* and *Injustice and Restitution*. See also the discussions on Nadia and Genie, chap. 2, note 46.

7. I have elsewhere and repeatedly developed an ethics based on a sense of inexhaustibility. I call it "charity." See *Locality and Practical Judgment* and *Injustice and Restitution*.

BIBLIOGRAPHY

Arendt, Hannah. *The Human Condition*. Chicago: The University of Chicago Press, 1958.

——. *The Life of the Mind*. New York: Harcourt Brace Jovanovich, 1978.

Aristotle. *The Basic Works of Aristotle*. Ed. Richard McKeon. New York: Random House, 1941.

Austin, John. *How to Do Things with Words*. Oxford: Clarendon, 1962.

Bakhtin, Mikhail M. "Discourse In the Novel." In *The Dialogic Imagination*. Ed. Michael Holquist. Trans. Caryl Emerson and Michael Holquist. Austin and London: University of Texas Press, 1981. Pp. 259–422.

Bernstein, Richard. *Beyond Objectivism and Relativism*. Philadelphia: University of Pennsylvania Press, 1983.

Buchler, Justus. *Metaphysics of Natural Complexes*. New York: Columbia University Press, 1966.

——. *Toward a General Theory of Human Judgment*. New York: Columbia University Press, 1951.

Chomsky, Noam. *Aspects of the Theory of Syntax*. Cambridge: The MIT Press, 1965.

——. *Cartesian Linguistics*. New York and London: Harper & Row, 1966.

——. *Reflections on Language*. London: Temple Smith, 1976.

——. *Syntactic Structures*. The Hague: Mouton, 1957.

——. *Topics In the Theory of Generative Grammar*. The Hague: Mouton, 1966.

Curtiss, Susan. *Genie: A Psycholinguistic Study of a Modern-Day "Wild Child."* New York: Academic Press, 1977.

Davidson, Donald. "What Metaphors Mean." *Critical Inquiry*, 5, No. 1 (Autumn 1978), 31–47.

Derrida, Jacques. "*Geschlecht* II: Heidegger's Hand." In *Deconstruction and Philosophy: The Texts of Jacques Derrida*. Ed. John Sallis. Chicago: The University of Chicago Press, 1987. Pp. 161–96.

——. *On Grammatology*. Trans. Gayatri Spivak. Baltimore: The Johns Hopkins University Press, 1974.

——. *Speech and Phenomena and Other Essays on Husserl's Theory of Signs*. Trans. David B. Allison. Evanston: Northwestern University Press, 1973.

——. *The Truth in Painting*. Trans. Geoff Bennington and Ian McLeod. Chicago: The University of Chicago Press, 1987.

Dewey, John. *Democracy in Education*. New York: Macmillan, 1916.

——. *Experience and Nature*. New York: Dover, 1929.

——. *Human Nature and Conduct*. New York: Holt, 1922.

——. *Logic: The Theory of Inquiry*. New York: Holt, 1938.

Edie, James M. *Speaking and Meaning*. Bloomington: Indiana University Press, 1976.

Feyerabend, Paul. *Against Method*. London: New Left Books, 1975.

Fodor, Jerry A. *Representations*. Cambridge: The MIT Press, 1981.

Foucault, Michel. *The Archaeology of Knowledge*. Trans. Alan M. Sheridan Smith. New York: Pantheon, 1972.

——. *Discipline and Punish*. Trans. Alan M. Sheridan Smith. New York: Vintage, 1979.

——. "The Discourse on Language." Trans. Rupert Swyer. Appendix to *The Archaeology of Knowledge*. Trans. Alan M. Sheridan Smith. New York: Pantheon, 1972.

——. *The History of Sexuality*. I. *An Introduction*. Trans. Robert Hurley. New York: Vintage, 1980.

——. *Language, Counter-Memory, Practice*. Ed. Donald F. Bouchard. Trans. Donald F. Bouchard and Sherry Simon. Ithaca: Cornell University Press, 1977.

——. *Madness and Civilization*: *A History of Insanity in the Age of Reason*. Trans. Richard Howard. New York: Pantheon, 1965.

——. *The Order of Things*: *An Archaeology of the Human Sciences*. New York: Random House, 1973.

——. "Two Lectures." In *Power/Knowledge*. Ed. Colin Gordon. Trans. Colin Gordon, Leo Marshall, John Mepham, and Kate Soper. New York: Pantheon, 1980. Pp. 78–108.

Gadamer, Hans-Georg. *Philosophical Hermeneutics*. Trans. David E. Linge. Berkeley and Los Angeles: University of California Press, 1976.

——. *Truth and Method*. New York: Seabury, 1975.

Goffman, Erving. *Forms of Talk*. Philadelphia: University of Pennsylvania Press, 1981.

——. *The Presentation of Self in Everyday Life*. Allen Lane: Penguin, 1969.

——. *Relations in Public: Microstudies of the Public Order*. Harmondsworth: Penguin, 1972.

Goodman, Nelson. *Languages of Art*: *An Approach to a Theory of Symbols*. 2nd ed. Indianapolis: Hackett, 1976.

——. "When is Art?" In *Ways of Worldmaking*. Indianapolis: Hackett, 1978, pp. 57–70.

Gould, Stephen Jay. *The Panda's Thumb*. New York: Norton, 1980.

Habermas, Jürgen. *Communication and the Evolution of Society*. Ed. Thomas McCarthy. Boston: Beacon, 1979.

Harré, Rom. *Personal Being: A Theory for Individual Psychology*. Cambridge: Harvard University Press, 1984.

——. *Social Being: A Theory for Social Psychology*. Totowa, N.J.: Rowman and Littlefield, 1980.

Harré, Rom, and Edward H. Madden. *Causal Powers*. Oxford: Blackwell, 1975.

Harris, Roy. *The Language Myth*. London: Duckworth, 1981.

Hegel, G. W. F. *Phenomenology of Mind*. Trans. James Baillie. London: Allen & Unwin, 1931.

Heidegger, Martin. *Basic Writings*. Ed. David Farrell Krell. New York: Harper & Row, 1977.

——. "The End of Philosophy and the Task of Thinking." In *On Time and Being*. Trans. J. Stambaugh. New York: Harper & Row, 1972.

——. *On the Way to Language*. Trans. Peter D. Hertz. New York: Harper & Row, 1971.

——. "The Origin of the Work of Art." In *Poetry, Language, Thought*. Trans. Albert Hofstadter. New York: Harper & Row, 1977. Pp. 238–317.

Hirsch, E. D. *Validity In Interpretation*. New Haven: Yale University Press, 1967.

Hobbes, Thomas. *Leviathan*. Indianapolis: Bobbs-Merrill, 1958.

Hockett, Charles Francis. *A Course In Modern Linguistics*. New York: Macmillan, 1958.

Husserl, Edmund. *Formal and Transcendental Logic*. Trans. Dorian Cairns. The Hague: Nijhoff, 1969.

Irigaray, Luce. *This Sex Which Is Not One*. Trans. Catherine Porter with Carolyn Burke. Ithaca, N.Y.: Cornell University Press, 1985.

——. *The Speculum of the Other Woman*. Trans. Gullian C. Gill. Ithaca, N.Y.: Cornell University Press, 1985.

James, William. *Essays in Radical Empiricism*. New York: Longmans, Green, 1912.

Kant, Immanuel. *Critique of Judgment*. Trans. J. H. Bernard. London and New York: Hafner, 1966.

——. *Critique of Practical Reason*. In *Kant's* Critique of Practical Reason *and Other Works on the Theory of Ethics*. Trans. T. K. Abbott. London: Longmans Green, 1954.

Konner, Melvin. *The Tangled Wing*. New York: Holt, Rinehart & Winston, 1982.

Kuhn, Thomas S. *The Structure of Scientific Revolutions*. Chicago: The University of Chicago Press, 1962.

——. *The Speculum of the Other Woman*. Trans. Gillian C. Gill. Ithaca: Cornell University Press, 1985.

Lakoff, George, and Mark Johnson. *Metaphors We Live By*. Chicago: The University of Chicago Press, 1980.

Language and Meaning: The Debate Between Jean Piaget and Noam Chomsky. Ed. Massimi Piatelli. Cambridge: Harvard University Press, 1980.

Levinas, Emmanuel. *Otherwise Than Being or Beyond Essence*. Trans. Alfonso Lingis. The Hague: Nijhoff, 1981.

Lyons, John. *Introduction to Theoretical Linguistics*. Cambridge: Cambridge University Press, 1968.

Lyotard, Jean-François. *The Differend: Phrases in Dispute*. Trans. Georges Van Den Abbeele. Minneapolis: University of Minnesota Press, 1988.

———. *The Postmodern Condition: A Report on Knowledge*. Trans. Geoff Bennington and Brian Massumi. Minneapolis: University of Minnesota Press, 1984.

———. "The Ontological Peculiarity of Works of Art." *Journal of Aesthetics and Art Criticism*, 36 (1977), 45–50.

Margolis, Joseph. *Persons and Minds*. Dordrecht, Holland: Reidel, 1978.

———. "The Ontological Peculiarity of Works of Art." *Journal of Aesthetics and Art Criticism*, 36 (1977), 45–50.

McNeill, David. *The Acquisition of Language: The Study of Developmental Psycholinguistics*. New York: Harper & Row, 1970.

Mead, George Herbert. *Mind, Self and Society*. Ed. Charles W. Morris. Chicago: The University of Chicago Press, 1934.

Merleau-Ponty, Maurice. *Consciousness and the Acquisition of Language*. Trans. Hugh Silverman. Evanston: Northwestern University Press, 1973.

———. *The Visible and the Invisible*. Trans. Alphonso Linguis. Evanston: Northwestern University Press, 1968.

Moskowitz, Breyne Arlene. "The Acquisition of Language." *Scientific American*, 239 (November 1978): 92–108.

Peirce, Charles Sanders. *Collected Papers of Charles Sanders Peirce*. 6 vols. Edd. C. Hartshorne and P. Weiss. Cambridge: Harvard University Press, 1931–1935.

———. "Logic as Semiotic: The Theory of Signs." In *Philosophical Writings of Peirce*. Ed. Justus Buchler. New York: Dover, 1955. Pp. 98–120.

———. "Pragmatism in Retrospect: A Last Formulation." In *Philosophical Writings of Peirce*. Ed. Justus Buchler. New York: Dover, 1955. Pp. 269–89.

Pettit, Philip. *The Concept of Structuralism*. Berkeley: University of California Press, 1977.

Plato. *The Collected Dialogues of Plato*. Edd. Edith Hamilton and Huntington Cairns. Bollingen Series 71. Princeton: Princeton University Press, 1969.

Polanyi, Michael. *Knowing and Being: Essays by Michael Polanyi*. Ed. Marjorie Grene. Chicago: The University of Chicago Press, 1969.

Putnam, Hilary. "Analyticity and Apriority: Beyond Wittgenstein and Quine." In *Studies in Metaphysics*, Edd. Peter A. French, Theodore E.

Vehling, et al. Midwest Studies in Philosophy 4. Minneapolis: University of Minnesota Press, 1979. Pp. 423–41.

——. *Realism and Reason*. Cambridge: Cambridge University Press, 1983.

Quine, Willard Von Orman. *Ontological Relativity and Other Essays*. New York: Columbia University Press, 1969.

Ricoeur, Paul. *The Conflict of Interpretations: Essays in Hermeneutics*. Ed. Don Inde. Evanston: Northwestern University Press, 1974.

Rorty, Richard. *Philosophy and the Mirror of Nature*. Princeton: Princeton University Press, 1979.

Ross, Stephen David. "Belonging to a Philosophic Discourse." *Philosophy and Rhetoric*, 19, No. 3 (1986), 166–77.

——. *Inexhaustibility and Human Being: An Essay on Locality*. New York: Fordham University Press, 1989.

——. *Injustice and Restitution: The Ordinance of Time*. Albany: State University of New York Press, 1993.

——. *Learning and Discovery*. London and New York: Gordon and Breach, 1981.

——. "The Limits of Sexuality." *Philosophy and Social Criticism*, 9, No. 3 (Spring 1984), 321–36.

——. *Metaphysical Aporia and Philosophical Heresy*. Albany: State University of New York Press, 1989.

——. "Metaphor, Inexhaustibility, and the Semasic Field." *New Literary History*, 18 (1986–1987), 517–33.

——. *Philosophical Mysteries*. Albany: State University of New York Press, 1981.

——. *The Ring of Representation*. Albany: State University of New York Press, 1992.

——. *A Theory of Art: Inexhaustibility by Contrast*. Albany: State University of New York Press, 1982.

——. *Transition to an Ordinal Metaphysics*. Albany: State University of New York Press, 1980.

——. "Translation and Similarity." In *Translation Spectrum: Essays in Theory and Practice*. Ed. Marilyn Gaddis Rose. Albany: State University of New York Press, 1981. Pp. 8–22.

——. "Translation as Transgression." *Translation Perspectives*, 5 (1990), 25–42.

——. "The Work of Art and its General Relations." *Journal of Aesthetics and Art Criticism*, 38, No. 4 (Summer 1980), 427–34.

Sacks, Oliver. *Awakenings, A Leg to Stand On, The Man Who Mistook his Wife for a Hat and Other Clinical Tales, Seeing Voices*. New York: Quality Paperback Book Club, 1990.

Sapir, Edward. *Selected Writings of Edward Sapir*. Ed. D. C. Mandelbaum. Berkeley: University of California Press, 1949.

de Saussure, Ferdinand. *Course In General Linguistics.* Trans. Wade Baskin. Edd. Charles Bally and Albert Sechehaye. New York: Philosophical Library, 1959.

Searle, John R. *Intentionality.* Cambridge: Cambridge University Press, 1983.

———. *Speech Acts: An Essay in the Philosophy of Language.* Cambridge: Cambridge University Press, 1969.

Selfe, Lorna. *Nadia: A Case Study of Extraordinary Drawing Ability in an Autistic Child.* New York and London: Harcourt Brace Jovanovich, 1977.

Skinner, B. F. *Verbal Behavior.* New York: Appleton-Century-Crofts, 1957.

Strawson, Peter. *Individuals.* London: Methuen, 1959.

Vygotsky. Lev S. *Mind in Society: The Development of Higher Psychological Processes.* Edd. Michael Cole et al. Cambridge: Harvard University Press, 1978.

———. *Thought and Language.* Edd. and trans. Eugenia Hoffman and Gertrude Vakar. Cambridge: The MIT Press, 1962.

Walzer, Michael. "The Politics of Michel Foucault." *Dissent* (Fall 1983), 490.

Whitehead, Alfred North. *Process and Reality.* Edd. D. R. Griffin and D. Sherburne. New York: Free Press, 1978.

Whorf, Benjamin Lee. *Language, Thought, and Reality.* Ed. J. B. Carroll. New York: Wiley, 1959.

Wittgenstein, Ludwig. *The Blue and Brown Books.* New York: Harper & Row, 1958.

———. *Philosophical Investigations.* Trans. G. E. M. Anscombe. Oxford: Blackwell, 1963.

———. *Tractatus Logico-Philosophicus.* Trans. D. F. Pears and B. F. McGuinness. London: Routledge & Kegan Paul, 1961.

INDEX